Annotated Book Lists *for* Every Teen Reader

The Best from the
Experts at YALSA-BK

by Julie Bartel and Pam Spencer Holley

for the Young Adult Library Services Association

Neal-Schuman Publishers, Inc.

New York   London

Published by Neal-Schuman Publishers, Inc.
100 William St., Suite 2004
New York, NY 10038

Printed and bound in the United States of America.

The paper used in this publication meets the minimum requirements of American National Standard for Information Sciences—Permanence of Paper for Printed Library Materials, ANSI Z39.48-1992.

Library of Congress Cataloging-in-Publication Data

Bartel, Julie.
    Annotated book lists for every teen reader : the best from the experts at YALSA-BK / Julie Bartel and Pam Spencer Holley for the Young Adult Library Services Association.
        p. cm.
    Includes bibliographical references and index.
    ISBN 978-1-55570-658-6 (alk. paper)
    1. Teenagers—Books and reading—United States. 2. Young adult literature—Bibliography. 3. Young adult literature—Stories, plots, etc. 4. Young adults' libraries—Book lists. 5. Best books—United States. I. Holley, Pam Spencer, 1944- II. Young Adult Library Services Association. III. Title.

Z1037.B279 2011
028.5'5—dc22
                                                                        2010033312

Contents

Preface

Librarians every day confront readers' advisory situations that go beyond a patron looking for a fantasy book or a biography of George Washington:

- What do you suggest for a nine-year-old girl who reads on a college level?
- What books might help a teen adjust to the idea of attending summer camp?
- Where are the best sources for finding suggestions for the 16-year-old who wants a romance novel written by a Latina?
- A teacher wants her students to read a book set in the state in which they were born—what titles are available?

Answers to these and hundreds of other situations can be found in the pages that follow. The lists in *Annotated Book Lists for Every Teen Readers: The Best from the Experts at YALSA-BK* are not only for readers' advisory work; they're also ideal for developing displays, creating bulletin boards, or just sparking ideas.

What Is YALSA-BK?

YALSA-BK is an electronic discussion list provided by the Young Adult Library Services Association (YALSA) division of the American Library Association (ALA). Founded in 1988, the purpose of "this open list for book discussion" is for "subscribers to discuss specific titles, as well as other issues concerning young adult reading and young adult literature." Open to anyone interested in young adult literature, whether a member of YALSA or not, the list offers subscribers a forum to discuss books they are currently reading, a place to offer suggestions of "good reads" to others on the list, and an opportunity to learn about nominations for YALSA and ALA's book awards. With more than 3,500 subscribers, YALSA-BK offers a wealth of information, including tips, titles, tricks, and advice generously shared by dedicated professionals, interested connoisseurs, and enthusiastic individuals.

The e-mail discussion list's archives contain scattered entries from 1988 to 1994, but these are too few in number to be really useful. The list's current form began taking shape in January 2000, where today's readers will find 13 pages of discussion during that month. Since 2000, those page numbers increase until there might be 40 or 50 pages of questions, answers, and comments for any one month. YALSA-BK's heaviest usage coincides with the start of the school year, from August through October, and then continues steadily throughout the year until there is a significant drop during summer vacation, after which the cycle begins again.

On a daily basis, there can be anywhere from 10 to 100 different messages asking for information on a fiction book for a twelfth-grade class studying the environment, or a comment about a recently read article, or a question about a review for a new title. In short, anything related to books, reading, and teens appears in the archive. The information in the archives is truly invaluable; the portion culled, updated, and organized for this book is the cream of the archive's crop.

How to Find YALSA-BK

Readers wishing to subscribe to the YALSA-BK discussion list can do so at the YALSA-BK website. To subscribe:

1. Go to lists.ala.org/wws/info/yalsa-bk.
2. Select "Subscribe" on the left-hand side.
3. Enter your e-mail address, and click the gray button.

Complete information on subscribing, unsubscribing, and receiving the digest mode of the list can be found at www.ala.org/ala/mgrps/divs/yalsa/electronicresourcesb/websitesmailing.cfm.

What's in This Book?

Annotated Book Lists for Every Teen Reader: The Best from the Experts at YALSA-BK represents the "best of the best." This book is the culmination of years of intensive reviewing, culling, and organizing the wealth of information found on the YALSA-BK list. The lists of books and resources in this book were evaluated and selected from the contributions of YALSA-BK's subscribers, the majority of whom are either young adult literature scholars or work in the field as school or public librarians, teachers, college professors, authors, or reviewers. The list topics and included titles were culled from the vast knowledge represented on YALSA-BK, and they represent a wide variety of opinions, suggestions, experiences, and communities.

The more than 1,100 titles included in *Annotated Book Lists for Every Teen Reader* are not absolute recommendations—reader mileage, as always, will vary—and librarians and other professionals will certainly want to exercise their own judgment when making use of these lists, utilizing their specialized knowledge of patrons and community to make informed recommendations.

Scope and Coverage

To compile the lists included in this book, the authors searched the archives of YALSA-BK from 2005 into 2010, which involved up to 40 to 50 pages of questions, answers, and comments for any one month. Spreadsheets were compiled by date and page number, and lists of possible topics were generated based on the subjects of messages. Similar topics were categorized into possible chapters, and, after extensive discussion and revision, 19 to 20 topics per chapter were selected based on frequency of the request, usefulness for both school and public libraries, or sometimes just the quirkiness and fun of a topic.

Then it was time to begin the hunt for titles, searching message to message (because subject lines don't always reflect the message content) to make sure there were sufficient titles generated to make a substantial list. Many topics that sounded promising turned into dead ends once the discussion thread was followed and had to be abandoned or morphed from one topic to another as members responded. Because each initial list depended on finding appropriate titles in the archives, chapters were often revised and fine tuned as work progressed. After titles were collected from the archives for each list, selections were made to limit lists to no more than 25, in most cases. To narrow down titles, a range of interpretations of the topic were selected; YA titles were given preference, although adult and children's titles were included where appropriate; and, with all other aspects being equal, newer titles were favored over older titles, hoping for wider availability.

Throughout the process, the authors relied on the collective wisdom of YALSA-BK to steer them toward useful topics and appropriate list titles, and the eclectic nature of the lists reflects the nature of YALSA-BK. As a result, although all lists should prove a helpful starting point, not all lists are meant to be strictly practical in the sense of responding to a common query. As with the list itself, the selection of topics ranges from the frequently requested, such as books about summer, to titles in which a bathroom plays a significant role.

Organization

As the authors mined the archives, the shape of the book changed over time, and the approach to organization evolved as well. After numerous discussions about the most helpful and appropriate way to present the material found in YALSA-BK, chapters in "Part I: The Lists" were organized into the following categories:

- Chapter 1, "The Right Title for the Right Reader." Chapter 1 is organized by reader, with lists for adults, avid readers, book haters, Latina and Latino teens, manga lovers, reluctant male readers, tweens, and so on. Depending on the reader's community, any or all of these lists would be useful when providing readers' advisory.

- Chapter 2, "Presentation Counts: Recommended Titles by Format." Chapter 2 focuses on the various formats available, from audiobooks for both high school and middle school readers to collections of poetry, plays, novels in verse, manga, paperback series, magazines, graphic novels, and so on.
- Chapter 3, "Places and Ideas: Recommended Books by Theme and Setting." Chapter 3 is arranged by theme and setting and ranges from books where bathrooms play a significant part to ones set in the Middle East, at summer camp, or in an institution. There are also titles about cookery, chocolate, winter and summer, the civil rights movement, and love.

"Part II: The Annotations" contains more than 1,100 alphabetically arranged annotations for the titles in the lists, written to be useful for librarians as they make decisions about whether they want to add a book to their collection or recommend it to their patrons. The annotations are fairly general and aren't necessarily intended to highlight a connection to a specific list (especially because many books appear on more than one list), but relevant details are included as appropriate.

CD-ROM

On the accompanying CD, the bibliographic information and annotations have been placed within the lists themselves. This value-added feature facilitates printing off annotated lists by topic, allowing easy creation of booklists for readers, bookmarks, bibliographies for teachers and parents, and collection development lists.

Purpose and Value

The lists included in this book certainly aren't meant to be definitive; they're a place to start. In her foreword to *Best Books for Young Adults* (ALA Editions, 2007), Betty Carter quotes Sally Estes, former Books for Youth editor of *Booklist*, who said, "the reason you make a list is so others will make their own lists." Take these lists and shape and mold them to the interests and needs of your teens; ask for their input to further sculpt the lists so that new titles are added and ones no longer read are discarded; dog-ear the pages, put notes in the margins, and share these lists and your lists with your teens and your peers.

Acknowledgments

With any writing project, it's helpful to have a mentor and an editor. We have been fortunate that Stevie Kuenn, Communications Specialist for YALSA, has assisted us and served as the intermediary between us and Neal-Schuman, freeing us to write while she took care of details. Our editor Sandy Wood has also been very helpful in noting the inconsistencies in the bibliographic citations that often occur when two people are working together on a book. We are grateful for their help.

Obviously this project never would have come to completion without the aid of our families. Julie would like to especially thank Ken and Halle for endless patience and support and Nora for being more understanding and good-natured than any one-year-old in history. Pam would like to thank Rick, who learned not to talk during the long hours she was at the computer but instead looked at the experience as a great opportunity to learn how to cook.

PART I

The Lists

Chapter 1

The Right Title for the Right Reader

Every day librarians meet a variety of readers, from book haters forced to read a book for an assignment to avid readers who are literally pulling books off the to-be-processed cart. YALSA-BK users asked for book titles that could be recommended to specific types of readers, from ethnicity to age or grade level or type of reader. These are some of the results we discovered. We denote nonfiction titles with NF.

1A. Adult Readers

YA literature is one of the best-selling areas of publishing, but the books are for adults too. Here are a few that will appeal to the teen in your adult patrons.

Alexie, Sherman. *The Absolutely True Diary of a Part-Time Indian*.
Anderson, M.T. *Feed*.
Bauer, Joan. *Rules of the Road*.
Bray, Libba. The Gemma Doyle Trilogy.
Cashore, Kristin. *Graceling*.
Dessen, Sarah. *The Truth about Forever*.
Farmer, Nancy. *The House of the Scorpion*.
Green, John. *Looking for Alaska*.
Hartinger, Brent. *Geography Club*.
Johnson, Maureen. *13 Little Blue Envelopes*.
Knox, Elizabeth. Dreamhunter Duet.
Lowry, Lois. *The Giver*.
Marchetta, Melina. *Jellicoe Road*.
Marillier, Juliet. *Wildwood Dancing*.
Myers, Walter Dean. *Monster*.
Portman, Frank. *King Dork*.
Pullman, Philip. His Dark Materials Trilogy.

Rosoff, Meg. *How I Live Now.*
Scott, Elizabeth. *Living Dead Girl.*
Stroud, Jonathan. The Bartimaeus Trilogy.
Takaya, Natsuki. Fruits Basket series.
Thomas, Rob. *Rats Saw God.*
Westerfeld, Scott. Uglies series.
Wooding, Chris. *The Haunting of Alaizabel Cray.*
Zusak, Marcus. *I Am the Messenger.*

1B. Avid Readers

A ninth-grade girl reads voraciously and likes spy books, thrillers, Meg Cabot, and *Twilight.* She, of course, has read through all of them. Her mom says, "no sex." What to read next? Give her this list.

Adlington, L.J. *The Diary of Pelly D.*
Bauer, Joan. *Squashed.*
Brennan, Herbie. *Faerie Wars.*
Cabot, Meg. *Haunted.* The Mediator series.
Carter, Ally. *Cross My Heart and Hope to Spy.*
Clark, Catherine. *Wurst Case Scenario.*
Du Maurier, Daphne. *Rebecca.*
Ewing, Lynne. *Goddess of the Night.* Daughters of the Moon, book 1.
Gaskin, Catherine. *A Falcon for a Queen.*
Higson, Charlie. *Hurricane Gold: A James Bond Adventure.*
Holt, Victoria. *The India Fan.*
Johnson, Maureen. *13 Little Blue Envelopes.*
Kidd, Sue Monk. *The Secret Life of Bees.*
King, Laurie R. *Beekeeper's Apprentice: Or, On the Segregation of the Queen.*
McKinley, Robin. *Beauty: A Retelling of the Story of Beauty and the Beast.*
Moriarty, Jaclyn. *Feeling Sorry for Celia.*
Peters, Elizabeth. *Crocodile on the Sandbank.*
Pratchett, Terry. *The Wee Free Men.*
Westerfeld, Scott. Uglies series.
Winspear, Jacqueline. *Maisie Dobbs.*

1C. Book Haters

A familiar situation: A young adult who professes a lifetime hatred of books to the librarian. He likes cars, the band Journey, the movie *300*, and the Discovery Channel. Here's a list of titles that could turn the tide.

Card, Orson Scott. *Ender's Game.*
Cohn, Rachel, and David Levithan. *Nick & Norah's Infinite Playlist.*
Gibbs, Chris. *Build Your Own Sports Car: On a Budget.* NF.
Gingerelli, Dain. *Hot Rod Roots: A Tribute to the Pioneers.* NF.
Horowitz, Anthony. *Stormbreaker.*
Hudson, Noel. *The Band Name Book.* NF.
Miller, Frank, and Lynn Varley. *300.*
Myers, Walter Dean. *Monster.*
————. *Sunrise over Fallujah.*
Packard, Mary, and the Discovery Channel. *Mythbusters: Don't Try This at Home.* NF.
Paulsen, Gary. *My Life in Dog Years.* NF.
Piven, Joshua, and David Borgenicht. *The Complete Worst-Case Scenario Survival Handbook.* NF.
Rahimzadeh, Auri, and Steve Wozniak. *Geek My Ride: Build the Ultimate Tech Rod.* NF.
Rottman, S.L. *Stetson.*
Shigeno, Shuichi. Initial D series.
Smedman, Lisa. *From Boneshakers to Choppers: The Rip-Roaring History of Motorcycles.* NF.
Strasser, Todd. *Boot Camp.*
————. *Slide or Die.* DriftX series, book 1.
Weaver, Will. *Saturday Night Dirt.*
Woodford, Chris, and Jon Woodcock. *Cool Stuff 2.0 and How It Works.* NF.

1D. Detention Home Girls

Collection development for youth in juvenile detention facilities can be particularly tricky; these titles aimed at girls offer stories about characters with whom they can relate.

Anderson, Laurie Halse. *Speak.*
Blume, Judy. *Forever.*
Brooks, Martha. *True Confessions of a Heartless Girl.*
Cohn, Rachel. *Gingerbread.*
Crutcher, Chris. *Whale Talk.*
Dessen, Sarah. *This Lullaby.*
Draper, Sharon. *Darkness Before Dawn.*
————. *Romiette and Julio.*
Farmer, Nancy. *A Girl Named Disaster.*
Ferris, Jean. *Bad.*

Flake, Sharon. *The Skin I'm In.*
———. *Who Am I Without Him? Short Stories about Girls & the Boys in Their Lives.*
Flinn, Alex. *Breathing Underwater.*
Franco, Betsy, ed. *Things I Have to Tell You: Poems and Writing by Teenage Girls.* NF.
Hartinger, Brent. *Last Chance Texaco.*
Hopkins, Ellen. *Crank.*
McCormick, Patricia. *Cut.*
McDonald, Janet. *Off-Color.*
Myers, Walter Dean. *What They Found: Love on 145th Street.*
Pearson, Mary E. *A Room on Lorelei Street.*
Voigt, Cynthia. *Bad Girls.*
Williams-Garcia, Rita. *Like Sisters on the Homefront.*
Wolff, Virginia Euwer. *Make Lemonade.*
Woodson, Jacqueline. *I Hadn't Meant to Tell You This.*
———. If You Come Softly.

1E. Gentlemanly Boys

Gentle reads offer stories of young people having adventures, with little to no sex, profanity, or violence, and are reminiscent of books from the early to mid-twentieth century. These clean reads will appeal to boys of all ages.

Anderson, M.T. *The Game of Sunken Places.*
Avi. *Crispin: The Cross of Lead.*
Balliett, Blue. *Chasing Vermeer.*
Bruchac, Joseph. *Code Talker: A Novel about the Navajo Marines of World War Two.*
Choldenko, Gennifer. *Al Capone Does My Shirts.*
Clements, Andrew. *Things Not Seen.*
Curtis, Christopher Paul. *Elijah of Buxton.*
Farmer, Nancy. *The House of the Scorpion.*
Haddix, Margaret Peterson. Shadow Children series.
Hiaasen, Carl. *Hoot.*
Jacques, Brian. Redwall series.
Juster, Norton. *The Phantom Tollbooth.*
Lowry, Lois. *The Giver.*
Lubar, David. *Dunk.*
Lupica, Mike. *Heat.*
Oppel, Kenneth. *Airborn.*

Paulsen, Gary. *Lawn Boy.*

Philbrick, Nathaniel. *The Revenge of the Whale: The True Story of the Whaleship Essex.* NF.

Riordan, Rick. Percy Jackson and the Olympians series.

Schmidt, Gary D. *The Wednesday Wars.*

Selznick, Brian. *The Invention of Hugo Cabret.*

Spinelli, Jerry. *Maniac Magee.*

Stewart, Trenton Lee. *The Mysterious Benedict Society.*

Weaver, Will. *Memory Boy.*

1F. Gifted Elementary Student Readers

A librarian requested help for a seven-year-old girl and a nine-year-old girl who were both reading well above their age levels, with the nine-year-old even taking community college classes. There is a wealth of titles available:

Balliett, Blue. *Chasing Vermeer.*

Collins, Suzanne. *Gregor the Overlander.*

DiCamillo, Kate. *The Tale of Despereaux: Being the Story of a Mouse, a Princess, Some Soup, and a Spool of Thread.*

Hale, Shannon. *The Goose Girl.*

Hunter, Erin. Warriors series.

Jacques, Brian. Redwall series.

Jones, Diana Wynne. *Howl's Moving Castle.*

Konigsburg, E.L. *The Outcasts of 19 Schuyler Place.*

———. *The View from Saturday.*

Lasky, Kathryn. Guardians of Ga'Hoole series.

Lord, Cynthia. *Rules.*

Lowry, Lois. *The Giver.*

McKay, Hilary. *Saffy's Angel.*

Montgomery, L.M. *Anne of Green Gables.*

Pratchett, Terry. *The Wee Free Men.*

Pullman, Philip. *The Ruby in the Smoke.*

Smith, Dodie. *I Capture the Castle.*

Stewart, Trenton Lee. *The Mysterious Benedict Society.*

Wrede, Patricia. *Dealing with Dragons.*

Wrede, Patricia, and Caroline Stevermer. *Sorcery and Cecelia, or, The Enchanted Chocolate Pot: Being the Correspondence of Two Young Ladies of Quality Regarding Various Magical Scandals in London and the Country.*

Yee, Lisa. *Millicent Min, Girl Genius.*

1G. Graphic Novel Lovers

Graphic novels are popular among teens, but sometimes teen readers may want a little more text. The following titles will appeal to the comics-loving teen at your library.

Barker, Clive. Books of Abarat series.
Castellucci, Cecil. *Boy Proof.*
Chabon, Michael. *The Amazing Adventures of Kavalier and Clay.*
———. *Summerland.*
Ehrenhaft, Daniel. *Drawing a Blank: Or, How I Tried to Solve a Mystery, End a Feud, and Land the Girl of My Dreams.*
Gaiman, Neil. *Coraline.*
———. *Stardust.*
Horowitz, Anthony. Alex Rider series.
Howe, Norma. Blue Avenger series.
Kinney, Jeff. Diary of a Wimpy Kid series.
Leavitt, Martine. *Heck Superhero.*
Lyga, Barry. *The Astonishing Adventures of Fanboy and Goth Girl.*
———. *Goth Girl Rising.*
Moore, Perry. *Hero.*
Myers, Walter Dean. *Autobiography of My Dead Brother.*
Sanderson, Brandon. *Alcatraz versus the Evil Librarians.*
Selznick, Brian. *The Invention of Hugo Cabret.*
Strasser, Todd. DriftX series.
Taylor, G.P., Tony Lee, and Dan Boultwood. *The Tizzle Sisters & Erik.*
Vizzini, Ned. *Teen Angst? Naaah . . . A Quasi-autobiography.*
Yancey, Rick. *The Extraordinary Adventures of Alfred Kropp.*

1H. Innocent Middle School Girls

These clean reads, which offer appealing stories with little or no sex, profanity, or violence, will delight middle school girls.

Abrahams, Peter. Echo Falls Mystery series.
Bauer, Joan. *Hope Was Here.*
Birdsall, Jeanne. *The Penderwicks: A Summer Tale of Four Sisters, Two Rabbits, and a Very Interesting Boy.*
Cabot, Meg. *All-American Girl.*
Ferris, Jean. *Once Upon a Marigold.*
Funke, Cornelia. *Inkheart.*
Hale, Shannon. *Princess Academy.*

Hale, Shannon, and Dean Hale. *Rapunzel's Revenge.*
Hanley, Victoria. *The Seer and the Sword.*
Horvath, Polly. *Everything on a Waffle.*
Kelly, Jacqueline. *The Evolution of Calpurnia Tate.*
Konigsburg, E.L. *The View from Saturday.*
Lord, Cynthia. *Rules.*
McKay, Hilary. *Saffy's Angel.*
McKinley, Robin. *Beauty: A Retelling of the Story of Beauty and the Beast.*
Moses, Sheila. *The Legend of Buddy Bush.*
Pattou, Edith. *East.*
Rallison, Janette. *All's Fair in Love, War, and High School.*
Schlitz, Laura Amy. *A Drowned Maiden's Hair: A Melodrama.*
Springer, Nancy. *The Case of the Missing Marquess: An Enola Holmes Mystery.*
Stead, Rebecca. *When You Reach Me.*
Tingle, Rebecca. *The Edge on the Sword.*
Westerfeld, Scott. Uglies series.
Wrede, Patricia, and Caroline Stevermer. *Sorcery and Cecelia, or, The Enchanted Chocolate Pot: Being the Correspondence of Two Young Ladies of Quality Regarding Various Magical Scandals in London and the Country.*
Yee, Lisa. *Millicent Min, Girl Genius.*

1I. Latina Teens

A patron requested books with a Hispanic or Hispanic American female protagonist.

Alegría, Malín. *Estrella's Quinceañera.*
———. *Sofi Mendoza's Guide to Getting Lost in Mexico.*
Alexander, Jill. *The Sweetheart of Prosper County.*
Alvarez, Julia. *Finding Miracles.*
———. *How the Garcia Girls Lost Their Accents.*
Bernardo, Anilú. *Fitting In.*
———. *Loves Me, Loves Me Not.*
Canales, Viola. *Tequila Worm.*
Chambers, Veronica. *Quinceañera Means Sweet Fifteen.*
Cofer, Judith Ortiz. *Call Me Maria.*
———. *The Meaning of Consuelo.*
Ewing, Lynne. *Party Girl.*
Gill, David Macinnis. *Soul Enchilada.*
Greene, Michelle Dominguez. *Chasing the Jaguar.*
Lachtman, Ofelia Dumas. *Summer of El Pintor.*
Osa, Nancy. *Cuba 15.*

Ostow, Micol. *Emily Goldberg Learns to Salsa.*
Parra, Kelly. *Graffiti Girl.*
Resau, Laura. *What the Moon Saw.*
Ryan, Pam Muñoz. *Becoming Naomi León.*
————. *Esperanza Rising.*
Sáenz, Benjamin Alire. *Sammy & Juliana in Hollywood.*
Sitomer, Alan Lawrence. *The Secret Story of Sonia Rodriguez.*
Triana, Gabby. *Cubanita.*
Valdes-Rodriguez, Alisa. *Haters.*

1J. Latino Teens

Titles for Hispanic boys were needed for summer reading programs, Accelerated Reader selections, or middle school reading assignments.

de la Peña, Matt. *Mexican Whiteboy.*
————. *We Were Here.*
Hernandez, David. *Suckerpunch.*
Herrera, Juan Felipe. *CrashBoomLove: A Novel in Verse.*
Hijuelos, Oscar. *Dark Dude.*
Hobbs, Will. *Crossing the Wire.*
Jaramillo, Ann. *La Línea.*
Jiménez, Francisco. *Breaking Through.*
Johnson, LouAnne. *Muchacho.*
Lupica, Mike. *Heat.*
Lynch, Janet Nichols. *Messed Up.*
Martinez, Manuel Luis. *Drift.*
Martinez, Victor. *Parrot in the Oven: Mi Vida.*
Peet, Mal. *Keeper.*
Pfeffer, Susan Beth. *The Dead and the Gone.*
Sáenz, Benjamin Alire. *He Forgot to Say Goodbye.*
————. *Last Night I Sang to the Monster.*
————. *Sammy & Juliana in Hollywood.*
Saldaña, René, Jr. *Finding Our Way.*
————. *The Jumping Tree.*
————. *The Whole Sky Full of Stars.*
Sitomer, Alan Lawrence. *Homeboyz.*
Soto, Gary. *The Afterlife.*
————. *Buried Onions.*
Stork, Francisco X. *Behind the Eyes.*
Voorhees, Coert. *The Brothers Torres.*

1K. Manga Lovers

Manga flies off the shelf with astonishing speed. For teens who have finished every manga title in your library but want to keep reading, start with this list of novels.

Asai, Carrie. Samurai Girl series.
Banks, L.G. *Sign of the Qin*.
Chen, Da. *Wandering Warrior*.
Dalkey, Kara. *Little Sister*.
Fukui, Isamu. *Truancy*.
Gaiman, Neil. *Sandman: The Dream Hunters*.
Gratz, Alan. *Samurai Shortstop*.
Hearn, Lian. Tales of the Otori series.
Hoobler, Dorothy, and Thomas Hoobler. Samurai Mysteries series.
Horowitz, Anthony. The Gatekeepers series.
Jones, Diana Wynne. *Howl's Moving Castle*.
Kikuchi, Hideyuki. Vampire Hunter D series.
Lockhart, E. *Fly on the Wall: How One Girl Saw Everything*.
Marks, Graham. *Missing in Tokyo*.
Miller, Kirsten. Kiki Strike series.
Ogiwara, Noriko. *Dragon Sword and Wind Child*.
Sonnenblick, Jordan. *Zen and the Art of Faking It*.
Soto, Gary. *Pacific Crossing*.
Stewart, Paul, and Chris Riddell. The Edge Chronicles.
Stone, Jeff. The Five Ancestors series.
Taylor, Laini. Faeries of Dreamdark series.
Uehashi, Nahoko. *Moribito: Guardian of the Spirit*.
Whitesel, Cheryl Aylward. *Blue Fingers: A Ninja's Tale*.
Yancey, Rick. *The Extraordinary Adventures of Alfred Kropp*.

1L. Offbeat Guys

A mid-twenties man requested YA titles that feature an "offbeat" kind of guy.

Alexie, Sherman. *The Absolutely True Diary of a Part-Time Indian*.
Anderson, M.T. *Burger Wuss*.
Auseon, Andrew. *Funny Little Monkey*.
Beaudoin, Sean. *Going Nowhere Faster*.
Cameron, Peter. *Someday This Pain Will Be Useful to You*.
Crutcher, Chris. *Deadline*.
Doyle, Larry. *I Love You, Beth Cooper*.

Going, K.L. *Saint Iggy.*
Green, John. *Paper Towns.*
Koja, Kathe. *Buddha Boy.*
Lubar, David. *Sleeping Freshmen Never Lie.*
Lyga, Barry. *The Astonishing Adventures of Fanboy and Goth Girl.*
Portman, Frank. *King Dork.*
Rosoff, Meg. *Just in Case.*
Stork, Francisco X. *Marcelo in the Real World.*
Tashjian, Janet. *The Gospel According to Larry.*
van de Ruit, John. *Spud.*
Vizzini, Ned. *Teen Angst? Naaah . . . A Quasi-autobiography.*
Wizner, Jake. *Spanking Shakespeare.*
Zusak, Markus. *Fighting Ruben Wolfe.*

1M. Picky Senior Girls

Knowing that tastes change rapidly, and are often influenced by peers, here's a list that will be of interest to some, though probably not all, "mature, picky" readers. Another source is the website for the Alex Award Winners at www.ala.org/yalsa/booklists/alex.

Brooks, Geraldine. *Year of Wonders: A Novel of the Plague.*
Dessen, Sarah. *That Summer.*
Donnelly, Jennifer. *A Northern Light.*
Fforde, Jasper. *The Eyre Affair.*
Frank, Hillary. *Better Than Running at Night.*
Frost, Helen. *The Braid.*
Goldberg, Myla. *Bee Season.*
Gruen, Sara. *Water for Elephants.*
Hale, Shannon. *Book of a Thousand Days.*
Irving, John. *A Prayer for Owen Meany.*
Jordan, Hillary. *Mudbound.*
Kingsolver, Barbara. *The Poisonwood Bible.*
Leavitt, Martine. *Keturah and Lord Death.*
Lutz, Lisa. *The Spellman Files.*
Marchetta, Melina. *Saving Francesca.*
McCaughrean, Geraldine. *Peter Pan in Scarlet.*
Packer, Ann. *The Dive from Clausen's Pier.*
Pearson, Mary E. *The Miles Between.*
Robbins, Alexandra. *The Overachievers.* NF.
Runyon, Brent. *The Burn Journals.* NF.

Sebold, Alice. *The Lovely Bones.*
Sherman, Delia. *Changeling.*
Vizzini, Ned. *It's Kind of a Funny Story.*
Vreeland, Susan. *Girl in Hyacinth Blue.*
Werlin, Nancy. *The Rules of Survival.*
Whitcomb, Laura. *A Certain Slant of Light.*

1N. Punk Readers

A librarian requested titles for an almost-16-year-old, punk girl who didn't like *Sisterhood of the Traveling Pants* because it was "too suburban/normal/boring." Try these books, with unconventional protagonists and stories.

Anderson, M.T. *Feed.*
Black, Holly. *Tithe: A Modern Faerie Tale.*
Block, Francesca Lia. *Weetzie Bat.*
Castellucci, Cecil. *Beige.*
———. *Boy Proof.*
de Lint, Charles. *The Blue Girl.*
Halpern, Julie. *Into the Wild Nerd Yonder.*
Hautman, Pete. *Sweetblood.*
Koertge, Ron. *Margaux with an X.*
Korman, Gordon. *Born to Rock.*
Krovatin, Christopher. *Heavy Metal and You.*
Lane, Dakota. *The Orpheus Obsession.*
Lloyd, Saci. *Carbon Diaries 2015.*
Lockhart, E. *The Disreputable History of Frankie Landau-Banks.*
Lyga, Barry. *Goth Girl Rising.*
Nelson, Blake. *Girl.*
Plath, Sylvia. *The Bell Jar.*
Siana, Jolene. *Go Ask Ogre: Letters from a Deathrock Cutter.* NF.
Tabb, George. *Playing Right Field: A Jew Grows in Greenwich.* NF.
Westerfeld, Scott. Midnighters series.

1O. Reluctant Male Readers

You know the type: a boy who can read, but would rather not. Make him a repeat customer at the library by suggesting these exciting, adventurous, boy-centric titles.

Booth, Coe. *Tyrell.*
Butcher, A.J. Spy High series.

Colfer, Eoin. Artemis Fowl series.
Collins, Suzanne. *The Hunger Games*.
Curtis, Christopher Paul. *Bud, Not Buddy*.
Dashner, James. *The Maze Runner*.
de la Peña, Matt. *Ball Don't Lie*.
Green, John. *An Abundance of Katherines*.
Grimes, Nikki. *Bronx Masquerade*.
Horowitz, Anthony. Alex Rider series.
Jenkins, A.M. *Repossessed*.
Korman, Gordon. *Son of the Mob*.
Lubar, David. *Hidden Talents*.
McNamee, Graham. *Acceleration*.
Myers, Walter Dean. *Monster*.
Porter, Connie Rose. *Imani All Mine*.
Portman, Frank. *King Dork*.
Riordan, Rick. Percy Jackson and the Olympians series.
Sachar, Louis. *Holes*.
Shan, Darren. Cirque du Freak series.
Shusterman, Neal. *Unwind*.
Thomas, Rob. *Rats Saw God*.
Trueman, Terry. *Stuck in Neutral*.
Volponi, Paul. *Black and White*.
Westerfeld, Scott. *Peeps: A Novel*.

1P. Striving Readers

Books were needed for high school students reading on the elementary level from grades 1 to 6. We suggest combining a print book with its matching audiobook might help these students become more comfortable with reading.

YALSA-BKers suggested The Orca Soundings series, which contains titles on contemporary topics that are written for teens who read below grade level. This series was the most frequently mentioned suggestion to any request for high interest, easy reading books. More information is available at us.orcabook.com/client/client_pages/Orca_Soundings_Info.cfm.

Bertrand, Diane Gonzales. *Trino's Time*.
Creech, Sharon. *Love That Dog*.
Ewing, Lynne. *Drive-By*.
Fields, Terri. *After the Death of Anna Gonzales*.
Franco, Betsy, ed. *You Hear Me? Poems and Writing by Teenage Boys*. NF.

Gallo, Donald R., ed. *No Easy Answers: Short Stories about Teenagers Making Tough Choices.*

Gantos, Jack. *Hole in My Life.* NF.

Goobie, Beth. *Sticks and Stones.*

Grimes, Nikki. *Bronx Masquerade.*

Kyi, Tanya Lloyd. *Truth.*

Larson, Kirby. *Hattie Big Sky.*

Paulsen, Gary. *The Schernoff Discoveries.*

Rodriguez, Art. *East Side Dreams.* NF.

Rylant, Cynthia. *I Had Seen Castles.*

Sachar, Louis. *Holes.*

Schraff, Anne. *Lost and Found.* Bluford High series, book 1.

Scieszka, Jon. *Knucklehead: Tall Tales and Almost True Stories about Growing Up Scieszka.* NF.

Tillage, Leon. *Leon's Story.* NF.

White, Robb. *Deathwatch.*

Zindel, Paul. *Doom Stone.*

————. *Reef of Death.*

1Q. Troubled Teen Boys

Teens often identify with books that tell stories that mirror their own lives. At-risk teen boys can find a variety of titles that help them understand the particular brand of trouble they find themselves in—and how they can grow after living through it.

Brooks, Kevin. *Martyn Pig.*

Chbosky, Stephen. *The Perks of Being a Wallflower.*

Cormier, Robert. *The Rag and Bone Shop.*

Crutcher, Chris. *Whale Talk.*

Curtis, Christopher Paul. *Bucking the Sarge.*

Draper, Sharon. *Tears of a Tiger.*

Flinn, Alex. *Breathing Underwater.*

Gantos, Jack. *Hole in My Life.* NF.

Hartinger, Brent. *Last Chance Texaco.*

Hinton, S.E. *The Outsiders.*

Johnson, Angela. *The First Part Last.*

Klass, David. *Home of the Braves.*

Lubar, David. *Hidden Talents.*

Mikaelsen, Ben. *Touching Spirit Bear.*

Myers, Walter Dean. *Bad Boy: A Memoir.* NF.

————. *Monster.*

————. *Shooter.*
Paulsen, Gary. *Hatchet.*
————. *How Angel Peterson Got His Name: And Other Outrageous Tales about Extreme Sports.* NF.
Rapp, Adam. *33 Snowfish.*
Rottman, S.L. *Head Above Water.*
Soto, Gary. *The Afterlife.*
————. *Buried Onions.*
Trueman, Terry. *Inside Out.*
Weill, Sabrina Solin. *We're Not Monsters: Teens Speak Out about Teens in Trouble.* NF.

1R. Tweens

A new group of readers, identified as "tweens," are in grades 3 to 6 or are ages 8 to 12. This group is not quite old enough for YA materials but has outgrown most of the children's section.

Anderson, M.T. *Jasper Dash and the Flame-Pits of Delaware.*
Berlin, Eric. *The Potato Chip Puzzles: The Puzzling World of Winston Breen.*
Broach, Elise. *Shakespeare's Secret.*
Cabot, Meg. *Moving Day.* Allie Finkle's Rules for Girls series, book 1.
Flake, Sharon. *The Broken Bike Boy and the Queen of 33rd Street.*
Hale, Bruce. *The Chameleon Wore Chartreuse: From the Tattered Casebook of Chet Gecko, Private Eye.*
Hobbs, Will. *Go Big or Go Home.*
Holm, Jennifer L., and Matthew Holm. Babymouse series.
Hulme, John, and Michael Wexler. *The Glitch in Sleep.* Seems Trilogy, book 1.
Kinney, Jeff. Diary of a Wimpy Kid series.
Klise, Kate. *Regarding the Fountain: A Tale, in Letters, of Liars and Leaks.*
Korman, Gordon. *No More Dead Dogs.*
Lane, Dakota. *The Orpheus Obsession.*
Law, Ingrid. *Savvy.*
Nix, Garth. *Mister Monday.* Keys to the Kingdom series, book 1.
Reeve, Philip. *Larklight: A Rousing Tale of Dauntless Pluck in the Farthest Reaches of Space.*
Rex, Adam. *The True Meaning of Smekday.*
Riordan, Rick. *The Maze of Bones.* The 39 Clues series, book 1.
Sachar, Louis. *There's a Boy in the Girls' Bathroom.*
Trueman, Terry. *Hurricane.*
Varrato, Tony. *Fakie.*

1S. Urban Teens: Beyond Street Lit

The following titles, while not street lit per se, will appeal to the edgier sensibilities of urban teens and fans of the more graphic urban fiction genre.

Black, Holly. *Tithe: A Modern Faerie Tale.*
Cameron, Peter. *Someday This Pain Will Be Useful to You.*
Cohn, Rachel, and David Levithan. *Nick & Norah's Infinite Playlist.*
Curtis, Christopher Paul. *Bucking the Sarge.*
Davidson, Dana. *Jason & Kyra.*
———. *Played.*
Divine, L. Drama High series.
Draper, Sharon. *Romiette and Julio.*
Flake, Sharon. *Bang!*
Flinn, Alex. *Beastly.*
———. *Breaking Point.*
Giles, Gail. *Shattering Glass.*
———. *What Happened to Cass McBride?*
Going, K.L. *Saint Iggy.*
Johnson, Angela. *The First Part Last.*
McDonald, Janet. *Brother Hood.*
———. *Harlem Hustle.*
Myers, Walter Dean. *Bad Boy: A Memoir.* NF.
———. *The Beast.*
———. *Monster.*
Nelson, Blake. *Paranoid Park.*
Pagliarulio, Antonio. *A Different Kind of Heat.*
Porter, Connie Rose. *Imani All Mine.*
Rapp, Adam. *33 Snowfish.*
Tyree, Omar. *Flyy Girl.*
Woodson, Jacqueline. *After Tupac & D Foster.*
Wright, Bil. *When the Black Girl Sings.*

Chapter 2

Presentation Counts: Recommended Titles by Format

Reading material is now packaged or presented in many different formats, so a teen reader might become a listener or understand all the acronyms used in e-mail or curl up with a picture book. This chapter includes lists of paperback series; graphic novels and manga; books written in letter, journal, e-mail, blog, and instant messaging (IM) formats; collections of poetry; and novels in verse. Take a look at the many different venues available for reading and listening.

2A. Audiobooks for High School Listeners

Encourage older teens to read with their ears.

Alexie, Sherman. *The Absolutely True Diary of a Part-Time Indian*.
Anderson, Laurie Halse. *Speak*.
Anderson, M.T. *Feed*.
Bray, Libba. *A Great and Terrible Beauty*.
Chabon, Michael. *Summerland*.
Dessen, Sarah. *Just Listen*.
Fforde, Jasper. *The Eyre Affair*.
Gaiman, Neil. *Anansi Boys*.
Going, K.L. *Fat Kid Rules the World*.
Green, John. *Paper Towns*.
Haddon, Mark. *The Curious Incident of the Dog in the Night-Time*.
Haig, Matthew. *The Dead Father's Club*.
Horowitz, Anthony. *Snakehead*.
Lee, Harper. *To Kill a Mockingbird*.
Levithan, David. *Boy Meets Boy*.
Lubar, David. *Sleeping Freshmen Never Lie*.

Meyer, L.A. *Bloody Jack: Being an Account of the Curious Adventures of Mary "Jacky" Faber, Ship's Boy.*

Murdock, Catherine Gilbert. *Dairy Queen.*

Oates, Joyce Carol. *Big Mouth & Ugly Girl.*

Pearson, Mary E. *The Miles Between.*

Pratchett, Terry. *Nation.*

————. *The Wee Free Men.*

Rees, Celia. *Pirates: The True and Remarkable Adventures of Minerva Sharpe and Nancy Kington, Female Pirates.*

Rosoff, Meg. *How I Live Now.*

Verne, Jules. *Around the World in 80 Days.*

Zusak, Markus. *The Book Thief.*

2B. Audiobooks for Middle School Listeners

Encourage younger teens and tweens to read with their ears with these titles.

Brashares, Ann. *The Sisterhood of the Traveling Pants.*

Choldenko, Gennifer. *Al Capone Does My Shirts.*

Colfer, Eoin. *Artemis Fowl.*

Curtis, Christopher Paul. *Elijah of Buxton.*

DiCamillo, Kate. *The Tale of Despereaux: Being the Story of a Mouse, a Princess, Some Soup, and a Spool of Thread.*

Fünke, Cornelia. *The Thief Lord.*

Gaiman, Neil. *The Graveyard Book.*

Hale, Shannon. *The Goose Girl.*

Helgerson, Joseph. *Crows and Cards.*

Heneghan, James. *The Grave.*

Hiaasen, Carl. *Flush.*

Higson, Charlie. *SilverFin.*

Howe, James. *Misfits.*

Martin, Ann M. *Everything for a Dog.*

Montgomery, L.M. *Anne of Green Gables.*

Nimmo, Jenny. *Midnight for Charlie Bone.*

Oppel, Kenneth. *Airborn.*

Patterson, James. *The Angel Experiment.*

Peck, Richard. *The Teacher's Funeral: A Comedy in Three Parts.*

Pierce, Tamora. *Terrier.*

Pullman, Philip. *Count Karlstein.*

Riordan, Rick. *The Lightning Thief.*

Rowling, J.K. *Harry Potter and the Sorcerer's Stone.*

Sage, Angie. *Magyk.*

Schmidt, Gary D. *Lizzie Bright and the Buckminster Boy.*
Stroud, Jonathan. *The Amulet of Samarkand.* The Bartimaeus Trilogy, book 1.

2C. Blogs, E-mails, and IMs in Fiction

The epistolary novel (see 2F) moves into the digital age with these books, which tell engaging stories and feature e-mails, blogs, and IM conversations.

Amato, Mary. *The Naked Mole-Rat Letters.*
Baratz-Logsted, Lauren. *Secrets of My Suburban Life.*
Bradley, Alex. *24 Girls in 7 Days.*
Carman, Patrick. *Skeleton Creek.*
Dellasega, Cheryl. *sistrsic92 (Meg).*
D'Lacey, Chris, and Linda Newbery. *From E to You.*
Draper, Sharon. *Romiette & Julio.*
Flinn, Alex. *Beastly.*
Goldschmidt, Judy. *The Secret Blog of Raisin Rodriguez.*
Halpin, Brendan. *Donorboy.*
Holm, Jennifer L. *Middle School Is Worse Than Meatloaf.*
Hooper, Mary. *Amy.*
Jaffe, Michele. *Bad Kitty.*
Lundgren, Mary Beth. *Love, Sarah.*
Maxwell, Katie. *The Year My Life Went Down the Loo.*
Moriarty, Jaclyn. *The Murder of Bindy Mackenzie.*
Myracle, Lauren. *l8r, g8r.*
Norris, Shana. *Something to Blog About.*
Peterson, P.J., and Ivy Ruckman. *Rob&Sara.com.*
Rosen, Michael. *ChaseR: A Novel in E-mails.*
Schindler, Nina. *An Order of Amelie, Hold the Fries.*
Sloan, Brian. *Tale of Two Summers.*
Spooner, M. *Entr@pment: A High School Comedy in Chat.*
Strasser, Todd. *Wish You Were Dead.*
Sutherland, Tui. *This Must Be Love.*
Vega, Denise. *Access Denied (and Other Eighth Grade Error Messages).*
Wittlinger, Ellen. *Heart on My Sleeve.*

2D. Classic Manga

Show teens the titles that helped this format achieve its white-hot status.

Akamatsu, Ken. Love Hina series.
Arakawa, Hiromu. Fullmetal Alchemist series.

Chmakova, Svetlana. Dramacon series.
CLAMP. Tsubasa: RESERVoir CHRoNiCLE series.
Fujishima, Kosuke. Oh My Goddess! series.
Higuri, You. Cantarella series.
Hotta, Yumi. Hikaru No Go series.
Ikumi, Mia, et al. Tokyo Mew Mew series.
Kishimoto, Masashi. Naruto series.
Kubo, Tite. Bleach series.
Miyazaki, Hayao. Nausicaa of the Valley of the Wind series.
Ohba, Tsugumi. Death Note series.
Sadamoto, Yoshiyuki. Neon Genesis Evangelion series.
Seino, Shizuru. Girl Got Game series.
Shigeno, Shuichi. Initial D series.
Soryo, Fuyumi. Mars series.
Takahashi, Kazuki. Yu-Gi-Oh! series.
Takahashi, Rumiko. Ranma ½ series.
Takaya, Natsuki. Fruits Basket series.
Toriyama, Akira. Dragon Ball Z series.
Tsuda, Masami. Kare Kano: His and Her Circumstances series.
Watase, Yuu. Ceres: Celestial Legend series.
Watsuki, Nobuhiro. Rurouni Kenshin series.
Yazawa, Ai. Paradise Kiss series.
Yoshinaga, Fumi. Antique Bakery series.

2E. Core Graphic Novels

Without duplicating too many of the titles on our other graphic novel lists, here are 25 titles that would make an excellent start for a new graphic novel collection.

Abel, Jessica, and Gabriel Soria. *Life Sucks.*
Bendis, Brian Michael. *House of M.*
Bendis, Brian Michael, and Michael Avon Oeming. *Powers: Who Killed Retro Girl?*
Black, Holly. The Good Neighbors series.
Clugston-Majors, Chynna. Blue Monday series.
Crilley, Mark. Akiko series.
Gaiman, Neil. The Sandman series.
Hale, Shannon, and Dean Hale. *Rapunzel's Revenge.*
Hernandez, Gilbert. *Sloth.*
Jemas, Bill, and Brian Michael Bendis. *Ultimate Spider-Man: Power and Responsibility.*
Kibuishi, Kazu, ed. Flight series.

Medley, Linda. *Castle Waiting*.

Meltzer, Brad. *Identity Crisis*.

Millar, Mark. *Ultimate X-Men: The Tomorrow People*.

Miller, Frank. *Batman: The Dark Knight Returns*.

Moore, Alan. *Watchmen*.

Peterson, David. *Mouse Guard: Fall 1152*.

Sakai, Stan. Usagi Yojimbo series.

Schrag, Ariel, ed. *Stuck in the Middle: 17 Comics from an Unpleasant Age*.

Smith, Jeff. *Bone: The Complete Cartoon Epic in One Volume*.

Talbot, Bryan. *The Tale of One Bad Rat*.

Thompson, Craig. *Good-Bye Chunky Rice*.

Vaughn, Brian K. Runaways series.

Way, Gerard. Umbrella Academy series.

Willingham, Bill. Fables series.

2F. Diaries and Epistolary Novels

Like the titles in 2C, these books use diaries, letters, and other epistolary forms to tell their stories.

Adlington, L.J. *The Diary of Pelly D.*

Alexie, Sherman. *The Absolutely True Diary of a Part-Time Indian*.

Avi. *Nothing but the Truth*.

Cabot, Meg. The Princess Diaries series.

Cary, Kate. *Bloodline*.

Cushman, Karen. *Catherine, Called Birdy*.

Flinn, Alex. *Breathing Underwater*.

Garfinkle, D.L. *Storky: How I Lost My Nickname and Won the Girl*.

Grimes, Nikki. *Jazmin's Notebook*.

Hale, Shannon. *Book of a Thousand Days*.

Juby, Susan. Alice series.

Koertge, Ron. *Shakespeare Bats Cleanup*.

Lee, Tanith. The Claidi Journals series.

Lubar, David. *Sleeping Freshmen Never Lie*.

McCafferty, Megan. Jessica Darling series.

Moriarty, Jaclyn. *The Year of Secret Assignments*.

Myers, Walter Dean. *The Journal of Joshua Loper, A Black Cowboy*. My Name Is America series.

Pfeffer, Susan Beth. *Life as We Knew It*.

Rees, Celia. *Witch Child*.

Rennison, Louise. Confessions of Georgia Nicolson series.

Wrede, Patricia C., and Caroline Stevermer. *Sorcery and Cecelia, or, The Enchanted Chocolate Pot: Being the Correspondence of Two Young Ladies of Quality Regarding Various Magical Scandals in London and the Country.*
Yee, Lisa. *Millicent Min, Girl Genius.*
Yolen, Jane. *Briar Rose.*

2G. Fictionalized Biographies

These fictionalized biographies feature authors interpreting the lives of inspiring real people for teen audiences.

Barakat, Ibtisam. *Tasting the Sky: A Palestinian Childhood.*
Bennett, Veronica. *Cassandra's Sister.*
Bruchac, Joseph. *Jim Thorpe: Original All-American.*
Engle, Margarita. *The Poet Slave of Cuba: A Biography of Juan Francisco Manzano.* NF.
Hausman, Gerald, and Loretta Hausman. *Escape from Botany Bay.*
Hautzig, Esther. *The Endless Steppe: Growing Up in Siberia.*
Hemphill, Stephanie. *Your Own, Sylvia: A Verse Portrait of Sylvia Plath.*
Janson, Hanna. *Over a Thousand Hills I Walk with You.*
Latham, Jean Lee. *Carry On, Mr. Bowditch.*
Lenski, Lois. *Indian Captive: The Story of Mary Jemison.*
Libby, Alisa. *The King's Rose.*
Meyer, Carolyn. *Marie, Dancing.*
———. *Where the Broken Heart Still Beats: The Story of Cynthia Ann Parker.*
Miller, Sarah. *Miss Spitfire: Reaching Helen Keller.*
Ottaviani, Jim. *Bone Sharps, Cowboys, and Thunder Lizards: A Tale of Edward Drinker Cope, Othniel Charles Marsh, and the Gilded Age of Paleontology.*
Rabin, Staton. *Betsy and the Emperor.*
Rinaldi, Ann. *Hang a Thousand Trees with Ribbons: The Story of Phillis Wheatley.*
———. *Taking Liberty.*

2H. Graphic Novels in the Classroom

Graphic novels aren't all about superheroes—many cover serious topics and can be a helpful tool in the classroom.

Abadzis, Nick. *Laika.*
Eisner, Will. *Fagin the Jew.*
Hennessey, Jonathan. *The United States Constitution: A Graphic Adaptation.* NF.

Hinds, Gareth. *Beowulf.*

Keller, Michael. *Charles Darwin's* On the Origin of Species: *A Graphic Adaptation.* NF.

Kiyama, Henry. *The Four Immigrants Manga: A Japanese Experience in San Francisco, 1904–1924.* NF.

Lat. *Kampung Boy.*

————. *Town Boy.*

Lutes, Jason. *Berlin: City of Stones: Book One.*

————. *Berlin Book Two: City of Smoke.*

Medley, Linda. *Castle Waiting.*

Morales, Robert. *Truth: Red, White & Black.*

Nakazawa, Keiji. Barefoot Gen series.

Porcellino, John. *Thoreau at Walden.* NF.

Shanower, Eric. Age of Bronze series.

Siegel, Siena Cherson. *To Dance: A Ballerina's Graphic Novel.* NF.

Small, David. *Stitches: A Memoir.* NF.

Spiegelman, Art. *In the Shadow of No Towers.* NF.

————. *Maus I: A Survivor's Tale: My Father Bleeds History.*

————. *Maus II: A Survivor's Tale: And Here My Troubles Began.*

Stassen, J.P. *Deogratias: A Tale of Rwanda.*

Sturm, James. *Satchel Paige: Striking Out Jim Crow.* NF.

Tezuka, Osamu. Buddha series.

Vaughan, Brian K. *Pride of Baghdad.*

Ware, Chris. *Jimmy Corrigan: The Smartest Kid on Earth.*

Yang, Gene Luen. *American Born Chinese.*

2I. Historical Novels in Verse

These novels use poetry and other forms of verse to make historical fiction come alive.

Bryant, Jen. *Kaleidoscope Eyes.*

————. *Ringside, 1925: Views from the Scopes Trial.*

Burg, Ann E. *All the Broken Pieces.*

Carvell, Marlene. *Sweetgrass Basket.*

Cormier, Robert. *Frenchtown Summer.*

Frost, Helen. *The Braid.*

————. *Crossing Stones.*

Hemphill, Stephanie. *Your Own, Sylvia: A Verse Portrait of Sylvia Plath.*

Herrick, Steven. *Cold Skin.*

Hesse, Karen. *Aleutian Sparrow.*

————. *Out of the Dust.*

————. *Witness.*
Janeczko, Paul. *Worlds Afire: The Hartford Circus Fire of 1944.*
LeZotte, Ann Clare. *T4: A Novel in Verse.*
Sandell, Lisa Ann. *Song of the Sparrow.*
Wolf, Allan. *New Found Land: Lewis and Clark's Voyage of Discovery.*

2J. Must-Have Anthologies

Anthologies aimed at teens can offer guidance and solace or simply a short, entertaining story from many teens' favorite authors. These titles top the list.

Bauer, Marion Dane, ed. *Am I Blue? Coming Out from the Silence.*
Black, Holly, and Cecil Castellucci, eds. *Geektastic: Stories from the Nerd Herd.*
Blume, Judy, ed. *Places I Never Meant to Be: Original Stories by Censored Writers.*
Bray, Libba, et al. *Vacations from Hell.*
Bruchac, Joseph, et al. *Sports Shorts.*
Busby, Cylin, ed. *First Kiss (Then Tell): A Collection of True Lip-Locked Moments.*
Cabot, Meg, et al. *Prom Nights from Hell.*
Gallo, Donald R., ed. *No Easy Answers: Short Stories about Teenagers Making Tough Choices.*
————, ed. *On the Fringe: Stories.*
Howe, James, ed. *13: Thirteen Stories That Capture the Agony and Ecstasy of Being Thirteen.*
————, ed. *The Color of Absence: 12 Stories about Loss and Hope.*
Marr, Melissa, et al. *Love Is Hell.*
Mazer, Anne, ed. *America Street: A Multicultural Anthology of Stories.*
November, Sharyn, ed. *Firebirds: An Anthology of Original Fantasy and Science Fiction.*
————, ed. *Firebirds Rising: An Anthology of Original Fantasy and Science Fiction.*
————, ed. *Firebirds Soaring: An Anthology of Original Speculative Fiction.*
Noyes, Deborah, ed. *Gothic! Ten Original Dark Tales.*
Scieszka, Jon, ed. *Guys Write for Guys Read: Boys' Favorite Authors Write about Being Boys.*
Singer, Marilyn, ed. *Face Relations: Eleven Stories about Seeing Beyond Color.*
Windling, Terri, and Ellen Datlow, eds. *The Coyote Road: Trickster Tales.*
————, eds. *The Faery Reel: Tales from the Twilight Realm.*
————, eds. *The Green Man: Tales from the Mythic Forest.*

2K. Nonfiction Graphic Novels

Graphic novels can tell nonfiction stories, too. These titles will make a great addition to your nonfiction collection.

Anderson, Ho Che. *King: A Comics Biography of Martin Luther King, Jr.* NF.

B., David. *Epileptic.* NF.

Barry, Lynda. *One Hundred Demons.* NF.

Briggs, Raymond. *Ethel & Ernest: A True Story.* NF.

Delisle, Guy. *The Burma Chronicles.* NF.

————. *Pyongyang: A Journey in North Korea.* NF.

Geary, Rick. *The Beast of Chicago.* NF.

————. *The Borden Tragedy: A Memoir of the Infamous Double Murder at Fall River, Mass., 1892.* NF.

Gonick, Larry. Cartoon History of the Universe series. NF.

Hosler, Jay. *Clan Apis.* NF.

Jacobson, Sid, and Ernie Colon. *The 9/11 Report: A Graphic Adaptation.* NF.

Katin, Miriam. *We Are on Our Own.* NF.

Krueger, Jim. *Testament.* NF.

Kubert, Joe. *Fax from Sarajevo: A Story of Survival.* NF.

Ottaviani, Jim. *Dignifying Science: Stories about Women Scientists.* NF.

————. *T-Minus: The Race to the Moon.* NF.

Sacco, Joe. *Safe Area Gorazde: The War in Eastern Bosnia 1992–1995.* NF.

Satrapi, Marjane. *Persepolis: The Story of a Childhood.* NF.

————. *Persepolis 2: The Story of a Return.* NF.

Schultz, Mark. *The Stuff of Life: A Graphic Guide to Genetics and DNA.* NF.

Thompson, Craig. *Blankets.* NF.

Vining, James. *First in Space.* NF.

Winick, Judd. *Pedro and Me: Friendship, Loss, and What I Learned.* NF.

2L. Novels with Script or Screenplay Format

Teens who like movies may enjoy these books, which feature lots of dialogue or are written like a script.

Almond, David. *Two Plays.*

Avi. *Nothing but the Truth.*

Fleischman, Paul. *Mind's Eye.*

————. *Seek.*

————. *Zap: A Play.*

Korman, Gordon. *Son of the Mob: Hollywood Hustle.*

Lester, Julius. *Day of Tears.*

Myers, Walter Dean. *Monster.*
Nelson, Theresa. *Ruby Electric.*
Schlitz, Laura Amy. *Good Masters! Sweet Ladies! Voices from a Medieval Village.*
Soto, Gary. *Novio Boy: A Play.*

2M. Paperback Series

For the avid readers at your library, encourage them to try these popular series, all available in paperback.

Asai, Carrie. Samurai Girl series.
Bird, Isobel. Circle of Three series.
Brian, Kate. Private series.
Bryant, Bonnie. Pine Hollow series.
Cabot, Meg. 1-800-Where-R-You? series.
———. The Mediator series.
———. The Princess Diaries series.
Cast, P.C., and Kristin Cast. House of Night series.
Halo series.
Harrison, Lisi. The Clique series.
Hopkins, Cathy. Mates, Dates, and . . . series.
———. Truth or Dare series.
Kimani Tru series.
Lane, Amy. Little Goddess series.
Langan, Paul, series editor. Bluford series.
Mead, Richelle. Vampire Academy series.
Metz, Melinda. Roswell High series.
Muchamore, Robert. CHERUB series.
Pascal, Francine. Fearless series.
Petrucha, Stefan, and Thomas Pendleton. Wicked Dead series.
Stolarz, Laurie Faria. Blue Is for Nightmares series.
Tiernan, Cate. Balefire series.
———. Sweep series.
von Ziegesar, Cecily. Gossip Girl series.

2N. Picture Books for Teens

Picture books aren't just for little kids! These books appeal to older audiences or may be a good way to encourage reluctant readers.

Bang, Molly. *Nobody Particular: One Woman's Fight to Save the Bays.* NF.
Birch, David. *The King's Chessboard.*

Bryan, Ashley. *Beautiful Blackbird.*
Bunting, Eve. *Terrible Things: An Allegory of the Holocaust.*
Decker, Timothy. *Run Far, Run Fast.*
Gaiman, Neil. *The Wolves in the Walls.*
Gerstein, Mordicai. *The Man Who Walked between the Towers.* NF.
Innocenti, Roberto. *Rose Blanche.*
Krull, Kathleen. *Harvesting Hope: The Story of Cesar Chavez.* NF.
Martin, Jacqueline Briggs. *Snowflake Bentley.* NF.
Morrison, Toni, and Slade Morrison. *The Big Box.*
Munsch, Robert N. *The Paper Bag Princess.*
Myers, Walter Dean. *Patrol: An American Soldier in Vietnam.*
Raven, Nicky. *Beowulf: A Tale of Blood, Heat, and Ashes.*
Rohmann, Eric. *Time Flies.*
Scieszka, Jon. *Math Curse.*
Sís. Peter. *A Small Tall Tale from the Far Far North.*
———. *The Wall: Growing Up Behind the Iron Curtain.* NF.
Stockton, Frank R. *The Bee-Man of Orn.*
Tan, Shaun. *The Lost Thing.*
———. *The Red Tree.*
Tsuchiya, Yukio. *Faithful Elephants: A True Story of Animals, People, and War.*
Wild, Margaret. *Woolvs in the Sitee.*
Winter, Jeanette. *The Librarian of Basra: A True Story from Iraq.* NF.
Woodson, Jacqueline. *Show Way.*

2O. Poetry Anthologies for High School Readers

Poetry-loving teens can get their verse fix with these anthologies.

Adoff, Arnold, ed. *I Am the Darker Brother: An Anthology of Modern Poems by African Americans.* NF.
Appelt, Kathi. *Poems from the Homeroom: A Writer's Place to Start.* NF.
Ashanti. *Foolish/Unfoolish: Reflections on Love.* NF.
Astley, Neil, ed. *Staying Alive: Real Poems for Unreal Times.* NF.
Carlson, Lori, ed. *Red Hot Salsa: Bilingual Poems on Being Young and Latino in the United States.* NF.
Franco, Betsy, ed. *Falling Hard: 100 Love Poems by Teenagers.* NF.
Giovanni, Nikki. *The Selected Poems of Nikki Giovanni.* NF.
Keillor, Garrison, ed. *Good Poems for Hard Times.* NF.
Nye, Naomi Shihab. *19 Varieties of Gazelle: Poems of the Middle East.* NF.
———, ed. *This Same Sky: A Collection of Poems from Around the World.* NF.
Paint Me Like I Am: Teen Poems from Writers Corps. NF.

Pinsky, Robert, ed. *Essential Pleasures: A New Anthology of Poems to Read Aloud*. NF.

Pinsky, Robert, and Maggie Dietz, eds. *Americans' Favorite Poems: The Favorite Poem Project Anthology*. NF.

———, eds. *Poems to Read: A New Favorite Poem Project Anthology*. NF.

Soto, Gary. *Neighborhood Odes*. NF.

Tom, Karen, ed. *Angst! Teen Verses from the Edge*. NF.

Watson, Esther Pearl, and Mark Todd, eds. *The Pain Tree: And Other Teenage Angst-Ridden Poetry*. NF.

2P. Poetry Anthologies for Middle School Readers

These poetry anthologies are appropriate for younger teens.

Adoff, Arnold. *The Basket Counts*. NF.

Carlson, Lori, ed. *Cool Salsa: Bilingual Poems on Growing Up Latino in the United States*. NF.

Clinton, Catherine, ed. *A Poem of Her Own: Voices of American Women Yesterday and Today*. NF.

Dahl, Roald. *Vile Verses*. NF.

Fitch, Sheree. *If I Had a Million Onions*. NF.

George, Kristine O'Connell. *Swimming Upstream: Middle School Poems*. NF.

Ghigna, Charles. *A Fury of Motion: Poems for Boys*. NF.

Giovanni, Nikki, ed. *Hip Hop Speaks to Children: A Celebration of Poetry with a Beat*. NF.

Grandits, John. *Blue Lipstick*. NF.

———. *Technically, It's Not My Fault: Concrete Poems*. NF.

Hughes, Langston. *The Dream Keeper and Other Poems*. NF.

Janeczko, Paul B., selector. *A Kick in the Head: An Everyday Guide to Poetic Forms*. NF.

Kennedy, X.J. *Exploding Gravy: Poems to Make You Laugh*. NF.

Liu, Siyu, and Orel Protopopescu. *A Thousand Peaks: Poems from China*. NF.

Myers, Walter Dean. *Jazz*. NF.

Nye, Naomi Shihab. *A Maze Me: Poems for Girls*. NF.

Rex, Adam. *Frankenstein Makes a Sandwich*. NF.

Shakur, Tupac Amaru. *The Rose That Grew from Concrete*. NF.

Shields, Carol Diggery. *Brain Juice: Science, Fresh Squeezed!* NF.

Siebert, Diane. *Tour America: A Journey through Poems and Art*. NF.

Smith, Charles R., Jr. *Hoop Queens*. NF.

2Q. Teen Issue Novels in Verse

In a relatable verse format, these titles tackle difficult issues that teens face every day.

Drug-, Food-, or Sex-Related Abuses

Chaltas, Thalia. *Because I Am Furniture.*
Friedman, Robin. *Nothing.*
Hopkins, Ellen. *Burned.*
————. *Crank.*
————. *Glass.*
————. *Tricks.*
McCormick, Patricia. *Sold.*
Myers, Walter Dean. *Amiri & Odette: A Love Story.*

Loss of a Parent or Sibling

Adoff, Jaime. *Jimi & Me.*
Bryant, Jen. *Pieces of Georgia.*
Carvell, Marlene. *Who Will Tell My Brother?*
Grimes, Nikki. *What Is Goodbye?*
Herrick, Steven. *By the River.*
Holt, Kimberly Willis. *Keeper of the Night.*
Schroeder, Lisa. *Far from You.*
Sones, Sonya. *One of Those Hideous Books Where the Mother Dies.*
Williams, Julie. *Escaping Tornado Season.*
Yeomans, Ellen. *Rubber Houses.*

Suicide

Adoff, Jaime. *The Death of Jayson Porter.*
Fields, Terri. *After the Death of Anna Gonzales.*
Fullerton, Alma. *Walking on Glass.*
Hemphill, Stephanie. *Things Left Unsaid: A Novel in Poems.*
Hopkins, Ellen. *Impulse.*

2R. Two or More Voices in Novels

Two (or more) protagonists are better than one! Teens may enjoy these titles featuring multiple narrators and voices.

Avi, and Rachel Vail. *Never Mind! A Twin Novel.*
Barkley, Brad, and Heather Hepler. *Scrambled Eggs at Midnight.*
Brashares, Ann. The Sisterhood of the Traveling Pants series.

Cohn, Rachel, and David Levithan. *Nick & Norah's Infinite Playlist.*
de Lint, Charles. *The Blue Girl.*
Fleischman, Paul. *Whirligig.*
Flinn, Alex. *Fade to Black.*
Frost, Helen. *The Braid.*
Giles, Gail. *What Happened to Cass McBride?*
Hearn, Judith. *The Minister's Daughter.*
Jenkins, A.M. *Beating Heart: A Ghost Story.*
Johnson, Kathleen Jeffrie. *A Fast and Brutal Wing.*
Jones, Patrick. *Things Change.*
Konigsburg, E.L. *The View from Saturday.*
Mass, Wendy. *Leap Day.*
Moriarty, Jaclyn. *The Year of Secret Assignments.*
Stone, Tanya Lee. *A Bad Boy Can Be Good for a Girl.*
Strasser, Todd. *Give a Boy a Gun.*
Stroud, Jonathan. The Bartimaeus Trilogy.
van Draanen, Wendelin. *Flipped.*
Volponi, Paul. *Black and White.*
Westerfeld, Scott. *The Last Days.*
Wrede, Patricia, and Caroline Stevermer. *Sorcery and Cecelia, or, The Enchanted Chocolate Pot: Being the Correspondence of Two Young Ladies of Quality Regarding Various Magical Scandals in London and the Country.*
Yolen, Jane, and Bruce Coville. *Armageddon Summer.*
Zeises, Lara M. *Anyone but You: A Novel in Two Voices.*

Chapter 3

Places and Ideas: Recommended Books by Theme and Setting

Where and when does all the action in these books occur and what are they about? This chapter highlights books that take place in summer or winter, at summer camp, or even in bathrooms; books that feature cooking, chocolate, or bugs; books about big issues such as civil rights or the environment; titles about being quiet or enduring heartache; and even some curriculum-related titles about math and science.

3A. Bathrooms

It's surprising how many significant events happen in the bathrooms of YA literature.

Anderson, Laurie Halse. *Speak*.
Bennett, Cherie. *Life in the Fat Lane*.
Card, Orson Scott. *Ender's Game*.
Chappell, Crissa-Jean. *Total Constant Order*.
Cohn, Rachel, and David Levithan. *Nick & Norah's Infinite Playlist*.
Collins, Suzanne. *The Hunger Games*.
Crutcher, Chris. *Staying Fat for Sarah Byrnes*.
Doctorow, Cory. *Little Brother*.
Draper, Sharon. *November Blue*.
Flake, Sharon. *The Skin I'm In*.
Fredericks, Mariah. *The True Meaning of Cleavage*.
Jones, Patrick. *Chasing Tail Lights*.
Limb, Sue. *Girl, 15, Charming but Insane*.
Lockhart, E. *The Boyfriend List*.
———. *Fly on the Wall: How One Girl Saw Everything*.
MacHale, D.J. *The Merchant of Venice*. Pendragon series, book 1.

Mackler, Carolyn. *The Earth, My Butt, and Other Big, Round Things*.
Powell, Randy. *The Whistling Toilets*.
Rowling, J.K. Harry Potter series.
Ruditis, Paul. *Rainbow Party*.
Shusterman, Neal. *Unwind*.
Soto, Gary. *The Afterlife*.
Stone, Tanya Lee. *A Bad Boy Can Be Good for a Girl*.
Taylor, Brooke. *Undone*.
Wittlinger, Ellen. *Parrotfish*.

3B. Chocolate

Chocolate can be a calorie-filled treat, a necessity of life, or a synonym for something deliciously forbidden, as these books reveal.

Allenbaugh, Kay. *Chocolate for a Teen's Dream: Heartwarming Stories about Making Your Wishes Come True*. NF.
Almond, Steve. *Candyfreak: A Journey through the Chocolate Underbelly of America*. NF.
Brody, Lola. *Chocolate American Style*. NF.
Burleigh, Robert. *Chocolate: Riches from the Rain Forest*. NF.
Carle, Megan, and Jill Carle. *Teens Cook Dessert*. NF.
Cormier, Robert. *The Chocolate War*.
D'Antonio, Michael. *Hershey: Milton S. Hershey's Extraordinary Life of Wealth, Empire, and Utopian Dreams*. NF.
Davidson, Diane Mott. *Dying for Chocolate*.
Dionne, Erin. *Models Don't Eat Chocolate Cookies*.
Donovan, Jennifer. *The Big Book of Chocolate: 365 Decadent and Irresistible Treats*. NF.
Esquivel, Laura. *Like Water for Chocolate: A Novel in Monthly Installments with Recipes, Romances, and Home Remedies*.
Harris, Joanne. *Chocolat*.
Hopkins, Cathy. *Mates, Dates, and Chocolate Cheats*.
Klause, Annette Curtis. *Blood and Chocolate*.
Lewis, Thomas H. *Chilies to Chocolate: Food the Americas Gave the World*. NF.
Lopez, Ruth. *Chocolate: The Nature of Indulgence*. NF.
Mills, Kevin, and Nancy Mills. *Chocolate on the Brain: Foolproof Recipes for Unrepentant Chocoholics*. NF.
Rosenblum, Mort. *Chocolate: A Bittersweet Saga of Dark and Light*. NF.
Rozin, Elisabeth. *Blue Corn and Chocolate*. NF.

Saulsbury, Camilla V. *Enlightened Chocolate: More Than 200 Decadently Light, Lowfat, and Inspired Recipes Using Dark Chocolate and Unsweetened Cocoa Powder*. NF.

Springer, Nancy. *Somebody*.

Temple, Lou Jane. *Death Is Semisweet*.

Wrede, Patricia, and Carolyn Stevermer. *Sorcery and Cecelia, or, The Enchanted Chocolate Pot: Being the Correspondence of Two Young Ladies of Quality Regarding Various Magical Scandals in London and the Country*.

3C. The Civil Rights Movement

These nonfiction and historical fiction titles will help teens understand the tumult of the American civil rights movement.

Armistead, John. *The Return of Gabriel*.

Boyd, Herb. *We Shall Overcome: The History of the Civil Rights Movement as It Happened*. NF.

Bridges, Ruby. *Through My Eyes*. NF.

Crowe, Chris. *Getting Away with Murder: The True Story of the Emmett Till Case*. NF.

———. *Mississippi Trial, 1955*.

Curtis, Christopher Paul. *The Watsons Go to Birmingham—1963*.

Draper, Sharon. *Fire from the Rock*.

Fradin, Dennis Brindell, and Judith Bloom Fradin. *Fight On! Mary Church Terrell's Battle for Integration*. NF.

———. *The Power of One: Daisy Bates and the Little Rock Nine*. NF.

Freedman, Russell. *The Voice That Challenged a Nation: Marian Anderson and the Struggle for Equal Rights*. NF.

Haines, Carolyn. *My Mother's Witness: The Peggy Morgan Story*. NF.

Houston, Julian. *New Boy*.

Levine, Ellen S. *Freedom's Children: Young Civil Rights Activists Tell Their Own Stories*. NF.

McWhorter, Diane. *A Dream of Freedom: The Civil Rights Movement from 1954 to 1968*. NF.

Miller, Calvin Craig. *No Easy Answers: Bayard Rustin and the Civil Rights Movement*. NF.

Murphy, Rita. *Black Angels*.

Nelson, Marilyn. *A Wreath for Emmett Till*. NF.

Rembert, Winfred. *Don't Hold Me Back: My Life and Art*. NF.

Rodman, Mary Ann. *Yankee Girl*.

Sharenow, Robert. *My Mother the Cheerleader*.

Taylor, Mildred. *Roll of Thunder, Hear My Cry*.
Thomas, Joyce Carol. *Linda Brown, You Are Not Alone: The* Brown v. Board of Education *Decision*. NF.
Tocher, Timothy. *Chief Sunrise, John McGraw, and Me*.
Wormser, Richard. *The Rise and Fall of Jim Crow*. NF.

3D. Consequences and Fate

Actions have consequences but sometimes, fate can intervene. See how consequences and fate tie together in these titles for teens.

Brooks, Bruce. *Asylum for Nightface*.
Brooks, Kevin. *Lucas*.
Caletti, Deb. *Honey, Baby, Sweetheart*.
Crutcher, Chris. *Whale Talk*.
Dessen, Sarah. *Someone Like You*.
Flinn, Alex. *Nothing to Lose*.
Giles, Gail. *Shattering Glass*.
Hartinger, Brent. *Grand & Humble*.
Hautman, Pete. *Godless*.
Lowry, Lois. *The Giver*.
Lynch, Chris. *Freewill*.
Martel, Yann. *Life of Pi*.
McNamee, Graham. *Acceleration*.
Myers, Walter Dean. *Autobiography of My Dead Brother*.
———. *Monster*.
Nelson, Blake. *New Rules of High School*.
Qualey, Marsha. *Just Like That*.
Rowling, J.K. *Harry Potter and the Deathly Hallows*.
Spinelli, Jerry. *Stargirl*.
Voigt, Cynthia. *Izzy, Willy-Nilly*.
Westerfeld, Scott. *Peeps: A Novel*.
Wittlinger, Ellen. *Sandpiper*.

3E. Cookery

Get in the kitchen (or read about one!) with this list of titles.

Ando, Natsumi, and Miyuki Kobayashi. *Kitchen Princess*.
Bauer, Joan. *Hope Was Here*.
Bradley, Alex. *Hot Lunch*.

Buford, Bill. *Heat: An Amateur's Adventures as Kitchen Slave, Line Cook, Pasta-Maker, and Apprentice to a Dante-Quoting Butcher in Tuscany.* NF.

Carle, Megan, and Jill Carle. *Teens Cook: How to Cook What You Want to Eat.* NF.

Creech, Sharon. *Granny Torrelli Makes Soup.*

Davis, Tanita S. *A la Carte.*

Dessen, Sarah. *The Truth about Forever.*

Elliot, Jessie. *Girls Dinner Club.*

Ferber, Brenda. *Julia's Kitchen.*

Forde, Catherine. *Fat Boy Swim.*

Horvath, Polly. *Everything on a Waffle.*

Juby, Susan. *Getting the Girl: A Guide to Private Investigation, Surveillance, and Cookery.*

Muldrow, Diane. *Stirring It Up.*

O'Keefe, Susan Heyboer. *Death by Eggplant.*

Powell, Julie. *Julie & Julia: 365 Days, 524 Recipes, 1 Tiny Apartment Kitchen.* NF.

Saijyo, Shinji. Iron Wok Jan series.

Shaw, Tucker. *Flavor of the Week.*

Smith, Cynthia Leitich. *Tantalize.*

Smith, Sherri L. *Hot, Sour, Salty, Sweet.*

Whytock, Cherry. *My Cup Runneth Over: The Life of Angelica Cookson Potts.*

Yoo, Paula. *Good Enough.*

Yoshinaga, Fumi. Antique Bakery series.

Zemser, Amy Bronwen. *Dear Julia.*

3F. The Environment

Contemplate our planet with these fiction and nonfiction titles.

Bastedo, Jamie. *On Thin Ice.*

Bertagna, Julie. *Zenith.*

Burns, Loree Griffin. *Tracking Trash: Flotsam, Jetsam, and the Science of Ocean Motion.* NF.

Collard, Sneed B., III. *Flash Point.*

Cowan, Jennifer. *Earthgirl.*

Evans, Kate. *Weird Weather: Everything You Didn't Want to Know about Climate Change, but Probably Should Find Out.* NF.

Gore, Al. *An Inconvenient Truth: The Crisis of Global Warming.* NF.

Greenwald, Lisa. *My Life in Pink and Green.*

Henry, April. *Torched.*

Hiaasen, Carl. *Flush*.
Hobbs, Will. *Jackie's Wild Seattle*.
Klass, David. *Whirlwind*.
McKay, Kim, and Jenny Bonnie. *True Green: 100 Everyday Ways You Can Contribute to a Healthier Planet*. NF.
Myers, Anna. *Flying Blind*.
MySpace Community and Jeca Taudte. *MySpace/Our Planet: Change Is Possible*. NF.
Nelson, Blake. *Destroy All Cars*.
Sivertsen, Linda, and Tosh Sivertsen. *Generation Green: The Ultimate Teen Guide to Living an Eco-Friendly Life*. NF.
Smith, Roland. *Jaguar*.
Tanaka, Shelley. *Climate Change*. NF.
Todd, Pamela. *The Blind Faith Hotel*.
Weisman, Alan. *The World Without Us*. NF.
Williams, Dar. *Lights, Camera, Amalee*.

3G. Horses

Once upon a time, horse stories figured prominently in young adult literature, with insights into humanity, class differences, and the bonds that can form between people and pets. These titles bring the horse story back, with a modern update.

Adler, C.S. *One Unhappy Horse*.
Amateau, Gigi. *Chancey of the Maury River*.
Farley, Steven. *The Black Stallion and the Shape-Shifter*.
Francis, Dick. *Under Orders*.
Ghent, Natale. *No Small Thing*.
Grant, K.M. *Blood Red Horse*.
Harlow, Joan Hiatt. *Midnight Rider*.
Hoffman, Mary. *Stravaganza: City of Stars*.
Juby, Susan. *Another Kind of Cowboy*.
Lester, Alison. *The Snow Pony*.
Luper, Eric. *Bug Boy*.
McCaffrey, Anne. *Black Horses for the King*.
Morpurgo, Michael. *War Horse*.
Peck, Robert Newton. *Horse Thief*.
Peterson, Shelley. *Sundancer*.
Peyton, K.M. *Blind Beauty*.
Roberts, Katherine. *I Am the Great Horse*.
Rottman, S.L. *Hero*.

Savage, Deborah. *Under a Different Sky.*
Volponi, Paul. *Homestretch.*
Wedekind, Annie. *A Horse of Her Own.*
Welch, Sheila Kelly. *A Horse for All Seasons: Collected Stories.*
Whitney, Kim Ablon. *The Perfect Distance.*
Wilson, Diane Lee. *Firehorse.*
———. *I Rode a Horse of Milk White Jade.*

3H. Insects

Creepy crawlies, insects, and other bugs abound in these titles.

Carter, Dean Vincent. *The Hand of the Devil.*
Collins, Suzanne. *Gregor the Overlander.*
Cousins, Steven. *Frankenbug.*
Fleischman, Paul, and Eric Beddows. *Joyful Noise: Poems for Two Voices.* NF.
George, Jean Craighead. *Fire Bug Connection: An Ecological Mystery.*
Glausiusz, Josie. *Buzz: The Intimate Bond between Humans and Insects.* NF.
Hawdon, Robin. *A Rustle in the Grass.*
Hölldobler, Bert, and Edward O. Wilson. *Journey to the Ants: A Story of Scientific Exploration.* NF.
Hosler, Jay. *Clan Apis.* NF.
Hubbell, Sue. *Broadsides from the Other Orders: A Book of Bugs.* NF.
James, Mary. *Shoebag.*
Kidd, Sue Monk. *The Secret Life of Bees.*
Klass, David. *California Blue.*
Menzel, Peter, and Faith D'Alusio. *Man Eating Bugs: The Art and Science of Eating Insects.* NF.
Ramos-Elodury, Julita. *Creepy Crawly Cuisine: The Gourmet Guide to Edible Insects.* NF.
Savage, Candace. *Bees: Nature's Little Wonders.* NF.
Voake, Steve. *The Dreamwalker's Child.*
Werber, Bernard. *Empire of the Ants.*
Zollman, Pam. *Don't Bug Me.*

3I. Institutions

These books take place in institutions like juvenile detention centers; residential treatment centers for substance abuse, sexual abusers and survivors, and physical abusers and victims; hospital wards; psych wards; psychiatric institutions; and prisons.

Dessen, Sarah. *Dreamland*.
Doyle, Malachy. *Georgie*.
Ferris, Jean. *Bad*.
Frank, E.R. *America*.
Hartinger, Brent. *Last Chance Texaco*.
Hobbs, Will. *The Maze*.
Marsden, John. *Checkers*.
————. *Letters from the Inside*.
McCormick, Patricia. *Cut*.
Mowry, Jess. *Babylon Boyz*.
Myers, Walter Dean. *Monster*.
Porter, Connie Rose. *Imani All Mine*.
Rapp, Adam. *The Buffalo Tree*.
————. *Under the Wolf, Under the Dog*.
Rodriguez, Luis J. *Always Running: La Vida Loca, Gang Days in L.A.* NF.
Runyon, Brent. *The Burn Journals*. NF.
Sachar, Louis. *Holes*.
Shaw, Susan. *Black-Eyed Suzie*.
Sones, Sonya. *Stop Pretending: What Happened When My Big Sister Went Crazy*.
Souljah, Sister. *Coldest Winter Ever*.
Toten, Teresa. *The Game*.
Tyree, Omar. *Flyy Girl*.
Vona, Abigail. *Bad Girl: Confessions of a Teenage Delinquent*. NF.
Weill, Sabrina Solin. *We're Not Monsters: Teens Speak Out about Teens in Trouble*. NF.
Wilson, Dawn. *Saint Jude*.

3J. Love Hurts

Books for the fabulously unromantic and cynical.

Anderson, Laurie Halse. *Prom*.
————. *Twisted*.
Anderson, M.T. *Burger Wuss*.
Bauer, Joan. *Thwonk*.
Brooks, Martha. *True Confessions of a Heartless Girl*.
Garfinkle, D.L. *Storky: How I Lost My Nickname and Won the Girl*.
Graham, Rosemary. *Thou Shalt Not Dump the Skater Dude and Other Commandments I Have Broken*.
Green, John. *Paper Towns*.

Hantman, Clea. *30 Days to Getting Over the Dork You Used to Call Your Boyfriend: A Heartbreak Handbook*. NF.

Kantor, Melissa. *The Breakup Bible*.

Levithan, David. *Marly's Ghost*.

Lockhart, E. *The Boyfriend List*.

———. *The Disreputable History of Frankie Landau-Banks*.

Lynch, Chris. *Inexcusable*.

McCaughrean, Geraldine. *Cyrano*.

McNeal, Tom, and Laura McNeal. *Crushed*.

More, J. *The Anti-Valentine's Handbook*. NF.

Naylor, Phyllis Reynolds. *Alice Alone*.

Nilsson, Pers. *Heart's Delight*.

O'Connell, Tyne. *Dumping Princes*.

Peters, Julie Anne. *Rage: A Love Story*.

Rabb, Margo. *Cures for Heartbreak*.

Thomas, Rob. *Rats Saw God*.

Wittlinger, Ellen. *Hard Love*.

Zarr, Sara. *Story of a Girl*.

3K. Luck

Feelin' lucky, kid? Relate to these books: some feature St. Patrick's Day, some are set in Ireland, and some simply focus on "luck" in general.

Brian, Kate. *Lucky T*.

Carlson, Melody. *Notes from a Spinning Planet—Ireland*.

Cassidy, Cathy. *Scarlett*.

Colfer, Eoin. *Artemis Fowl*.

———. *Wish List*.

Collins, Yvonne. *Introducing Vivian Leigh Reid: Daughter of the Diva*.

Dowd, Siobhan. *Bog Child*.

———. *A Pure Swift Cry*.

Duane, Diane. *A Wizard Abroad*.

Giff, Patricia Riley. *Maggie's Door*.

Heneghan, James. *The Grave*.

Jones, Diana Wynne. *The Game*.

Luper, Eric. *Big Slick*.

McKinty, Adrian. *The Lighthouse Land*.

Melling, O. R. *The Hunter's Moon*.

Napoli, Donna Jo. *Hush: An Irish Princess' Tale*.

Ostow, Micol. *Gettin' Lucky*.

Rowling, J. K. *Harry Potter and the Half-Blood Prince.*
Snell, Gordon. *Thicker Than Water: Coming of Age Stories by Irish and Irish American Authors.*
Thesman, Jean. *A Sea So Far.*
Thompson, Kate. *Creature of the Night.*
————. *The New Policeman.*
Wilson, Diane Lee. *I Rode a Horse of Milk White Jade.*
Wood, Maryrose. *Why I Let My Hair Grow Out.*

3L. Mathematics

Math: a work of art? These fiction titles argue yes.

Abbott, Edwin. *Flatland: A Romance of Many Dimensions.*
Balliett, Blue. *Chasing Vermeer.*
Beil, Michael D. *The Red Blazer Girls: The Ring of Rocamadour.*
Bradshaw, Gillian. *The Sand-Reckoner.*
Bruce, Colin. *Conned Again, Watson! Cautionary Tales of Logic, Math and Probability.*
Carey, Benedict. *The Unknowns.*
Enzensberger, Hans Magnus. *The Number Devil: A Mathematical Adventure.*
Fienberg, Anna. *Number 8.*
Green, John. *An Abundance of Katherines.*
Griffin, Adele. *Hannah, Divided.*
Haddon, Mark. *The Curious Incident of the Dog in the Night-Time.*
Halpin, Brendan. *Forever Changes.*
Jinks, Catherine. *Evil Genius.*
Johnson, Varian. *My Life as a Rhombus.*
Lalwani, Nikita. *Gifted.*
Lewis, Richard. *Monster's Proof.*
Lichtman, Wendy. *Do the Math: Secrets, Lies, and Algebra.*
Luper, Eric. *Big Slick.*
Moranville, Sharelle Byars. *A Higher Geometry.*
Papademetriou, Lisa. *Drop.*
Pearsall, Shelley. *All of the Above.*
Sleator, William. *The Last Universe.*
Spiller, Robert. *The Witch of Agnesi.*
Stewart, Ian. *Flatterland: Like Flatland, Only More So.*
Yoo, Paula. *Good Enough.*

3M. The Middle East

Help teens understand some of the conflicts and cultures of the Middle East with the titles in this list.

Ellis, Deborah. *The Breadwinner.*
————. *Parvana's Journey.*
Fletcher, Susan. *Shadow Spinner.*
Hosseini, Khaled. *The Kite Runner.*
Jolin, Paula. *In the Name of God.*
Laird, Elizabeth. *Kiss the Dust.*
Latifa. *My Forbidden Face: Growing Up Under the Taliban: A Young Woman's Story.* NF.
Levitin, Sonia. *The Singing Mountain.*
Markandaya, Kamala. *Nectar in a Sieve.*
McCormick, Patricia. *Sold.*
Mortenson, Greg, and David Oliver Relin. *Three Cups of Tea: One Man's Mission to Fight Terrorism and Build Nations—One School at a Time.* NF.
Napoli, Donna Jo. *Song of the Magdalene.*
Nye, Naomi Shihab. *19 Varieties of Gazelle: Poems of the Middle East.* NF.
Orlev, Uri. *The Lady with the Hat.*
Sandell, Lisa Ann. *The Weight of the Sky.*
Satrapi, Marjane. *Persepolis: The Story of a Childhood.* NF.
————. *Persepolis 2: The Story of a Return.* NF.
Sayres, Meghan Nuttall. *Anahita's Woven Riddle.*
Staples, Suzanne Fisher. *Haveli.*
————. *Shabanu, Daughter of the Wind.*
————. *Under the Persimmon Tree.*
Vaughan, Brian K. *Pride of Baghdad.*

3N. Science

Whether the science is cloning, evolution, endangered species, or environmentalism, the impact of science on our lives is far-reaching, as these fiction titles show.

Anderson, Laurie Halse. *Catalyst.*
Brande, Robin. *Evolution, Me & Other Freaks of Nature.*
Bryant, Jen. *Ringside, 1925: Views from the Scopes Trial.*
Collard, Sneed B., III. *Flash Point.*
Cooney, Caroline B. *Code Orange.*
Dickinson, Peter. *Eva.*

Doctorow, Cory. *Little Brother.*
Farmer, Nancy. *The House of the Scorpion.*
Haddix, Margaret Peterson. *Double Identity.*
Halam, Ann. *Dr. Franklin's Island.*
Haworth-Attard, Barbara. *Theories of Relativity.*
Hesse, Karen. *The Music of Dolphins.*
Hiaasen, Carl. *Hoot.*
Hobbs, Will. *Go Big or Go Home.*
Hogan, James. *Bug Park.*
Klages, Ellen. *The Green Glass Sea.*
Klass, David. *California Blue.*
————. *Firestorm.*
Koja, Kathe. *Kissing the Bee.*
Kostick, Conor. *Epic.*
Malloy, Brian. *Twelve Long Months.*
Maynard, Joyce. *The Cloud Chamber.*
Patterson, James. *Maximum Ride: The Angel Experiment.*
Pearson, Mary E. *The Adoration of Jenna Fox.*
Pfeffer, Susan Beth. *Life as We Knew It.*
Werlin, Nancy. *Double Helix.*
Wood, Don. *Into the Volcano.*

3O. Silence

Silence speaks volumes.

Anderson, Laurie Halse. *Speak.*
Atkins, Catherine. *Alt Ed.*
Connor, Leslie. *Waiting for Normal.*
Couloumbis, Audrey. *Getting Near to Baby.*
Crutcher, Chris. *The Sledding Hill.*
————. *Staying Fat for Sarah Byrnes.*
Cushman, Karen. *The Loud Silence of Francine Green.*
Dessen, Sarah. *Just Listen.*
Duey, Kathleen. *Skin Hunger.*
Easton, Kelly. *Aftershock.*
Ellis, Ann Dee. *This Is What I Did.*
Frank, E.R. *America.*
Frank, Hillary. *I Can't Tell You.*
Giles, Gail. *What Happened to Cass McBride?*
Hayden, Torey. *Ghost Girl: The True Story of a Child in Peril and the Teacher Who Saved Her.* NF.

Johnson, Kathleen Jeffrie. *Target.*
Koja, Kathe. *Buddha Boy.*
Konigsburg, E.L. *Silent to the Bone.*
Marsden, John. *So Much to Tell You.*
McCormick, Patricia. *Cut.*
McNamee, Graham. *Hate You.*
Nelson, R.A. *Breathe My Name.*
Scott, Elizabeth. *Living Dead Girl.*
Werlin, Nancy. *The Rules of Survival.*
Woodson, Jacqueline. *Hush.*
————. *I Hadn't Meant to Tell You This.*

3P. State Books

Explore the 50 states and the District of Columbia through fiction.

ALABAMA	Green, John. *Looking for Alaska.*
ALASKA	Smelcer, John E. *The Trap.*
ARIZONA	Spinelli, Jerry. *Stargirl.*
ARKANSAS	Draper, Sharon. *Fire from the Rock.*
CALIFORNIA	Ryan, Pam Muñoz. *Esperanza Rising.*
COLORADO	Avi. *The Secret School.*
CONNECTICUT	Acampora, Paul. *Defining Dulcie.*
DELAWARE	Zeises, Lara. *Bringing Up the Bones.*
FLORIDA	Cirrone, Dorian. *Dancing in Red Shoes Will Kill You.*
GEORGIA	Anderson, Jodi Lynn. *Peaches.*
HAWAII	Salisbury, Graham. *Night of the Howling Dogs.*
IDAHO	Crutcher, Chris. *Deadline.*
ILLINOIS	Leitch, Will. *Catch.*
INDIANA	Peck, Richard. *Here Lies the Librarian.*
IOWA	Bradley, Alex. *24 Girls in 7 Days.*
KANSAS	Peters, Julie Anne. *Far from Xanadu.*
KENTUCKY	White, Ruth. *Tadpole.*
LOUISIANA	Holt, Kimberly Willis. *Part of Me: Stories of a Louisiana Family.*
MAINE	Schmidt, Gary D. *Lizzie Bright and the Buckminster Boy.*
MARYLAND	Cummings, Priscilla. *Red Kayak.*
MASSACHUSETTS	Anderson, M.T. *The Astonishing Life of Octavian Nothing, Traitor to the Nation, Volume I: The Pox Party.*
MICHIGAN	Curtis, Christopher Paul. *Bucking the Sarge.*

MINNESOTA	Hautman, Pete. *Godless*.
MISSISSIPPI	Crowe, Chris. *Getting Away with Murder: The True Story of the Emmett Till Case*. NF.
MISSOURI	Myrick, Leland. *Missouri Boy*.
MONTANA	Larson, Kirby. *Hattie Big Sky*.
NEBRASKA	Gray, Dianne E. *Together Apart*.
NEVADA	Hopkins, Ellen. *Burned*.
NEW HAMPSHIRE	Schmidt, Gary D. *First Boy*.
NEW JERSEY	Lubar, David. *Dunk*.
NEW MEXICO	Sáenz, Benjamin Alire. *Sammy & Juliana in Hollywood*.
NEW YORK	Cohn, Rachel, and David Levithan. *Nick & Norah's Infinite Playlist*.
NORTH CAROLINA	Johnson, Harriet McBryde. *Accidents of Nature*.
NORTH DAKOTA	Schultz, Jan Neubert. *Battle Cry*.
OHIO	Creech, Sharon. *Absolutely Normal Chaos*.
OKLAHOMA	Westerfeld, Scott. Midnighters series.
OREGON	Nelson, Blake. *Paranoid Park*.
PENNSYLVANIA	Pfeffer, Susan Beth. *Life as We Knew It*.
RHODE ISLAND	McLarty, Ron. *Traveler*.
SOUTH CAROLINA	Matthews, Kezi. *John Riley's Daughter*.
SOUTH DAKOTA	Meyers, Kent. *The Work of Wolves*.
TENNESSEE	Green, John. *An Abundance of Katherines*.
TEXAS	Smith, Cynthia Leitich. *Tantalize*.
UTAH	Zarr, Sara. *Sweethearts*.
VERMONT	Hesse, Karen. *Witness*.
VIRGINIA	Elliott, L.M. *Give Me Liberty*.
WASHINGTON	Meyer, Stephenie. The Twilight Saga.
WASHINGTON, DC	Cohn, Rachel. *You Know Where to Find Me*.
WEST VIRGINIA	Rylant, Cynthia. *A Blue-Eyed Daisy*.
WISCONSIN	Murdock, Catherine Gilbert. *Dairy Queen*.
WYOMING	Yep, Laurence. *The Traitor: Golden Mountain Chronicles: 1885*.

3Q. Summer Camp

Experience summer camp all over again with these titles.

Belton, Sandra. *Ernestine and Amanda: Summer Camp, Ready or Not!*
Brown, Todd D. *Entries from a Hot Pink Notebook*.
Childs, Tera Lynn. *Goddess Boot Camp*.

Cole, Brock. *The Goats*.
Friesen, Gayle. *The Isabel Factor*.
Hartinger, Brent. *The Order of the Poison Oak*.
Headley, Justina Chen. *Nothing but the Truth (and a Few White Lies)*.
Herman, John. *Deep Waters*.
Howell, Simmone. *Everything Beautiful*.
Johnson, Harriet McBryde. *Accidents of Nature*.
Larson, Hope. *Chiggers*.
Lehmann-Haupt, Christopher. *The Mad Cook of Pymatuning*.
Lockhart, E. *Dramarama*.
Lupica, Mike. *Summer Ball*.
Lynch, Chris. *Slot Machine*.
Mlynowski, Sarah. *Spells & Sleeping Bags*.
Murphy, Pat. *The Wild Girls*.
Naylor, Phyllis Reynolds. *Patiently Alice*.
Nixon, Joan Lowery. *Nightmare*.
Paley, Sasha. *Huge*.
Riordan, Rick. *The Lightning Thief*.
Ryan, Sara. *Empress of the World*.
Sloan, Brian. *Tale of Two Summers*.
Vail, Rachel. *Daring to Be Abigail*.
Wedekind, Annie. *A Horse of Her Own*.
Williams, Kathryn. *The Lost Summer*.

3R. Summertime

It's always summer in this list of tales.

Barkley, Brad, and Heather Hepler. *Scrambled Eggs at Midnight*.
Birdsall, Jeanne. *The Penderwicks: A Summer Tale of Four Sisters, Two Rabbits, and a Very Interesting Boy*.
Boylan, James Finney. *Getting In*.
Brashares, Ann. *The Sisterhood of the Traveling Pants*.
Calame, Don. *Swim the Fly*.
Dessen, Sarah. *That Summer*.
Elkeles, Simone. *How to Ruin a Summer Vacation*.
Graham, Rosemary. *My Not-So-Terrible Time at the Hippie Hotel*.
Griffin, Adele. *My Almost Epic Summer*.
Hartinger, Brent. *Project Sweet Life*.
Herbsman, Cheryl Renee. *Breathing*.
Kantor, Melissa. *Girlfriend Material*.

Melling, O.R. *The Hunter's Moon.*
Murdock, Catherine Gilbert. *Dairy Queen.*
Myers, Walter Dean. *Harlem Summer.*
Naylor, Phyllis Reynolds. *Intensely Alice.*
Perez, Marlene. *Dead Is So Last Year.*
Resau, Laura. *What the Moon Saw.*
Smith, Charles R., Jr. *Chameleon.*
Wittlinger, Ellen. *Zigzag.*
Zindel, Paul. *The Amazing and Death-Defying Diary of Eugene Dingman.*

3S. Teen Immigrants

Today's teens are the most diverse generation yet; help immigrant teens adjust to their new surroundings or encourage others to gain understanding of the immigrant experience with this list of titles.

Alvarez, Julia. *How the Garcia Girls Lost Their Accents.*
Asgedom, Mawi. *Of Beetles and Angels: A Boy's Remarkable Journey from a Refugee Camp to Harvard.* NF.
Auch, Mary Jane. *Ashes of Roses.*
Budhos, Marina. *Ask Me No Questions.*
Cofer, Judith Ortiz. *Call Me Maria.*
Dau, John Bul. *God Grew Tired of Us: A Memoir.* NF.
de la Cruz, Melissa. *Fresh Off the Boat.*
Deng, Benson, Alephonsian Deng, Benjamin Ajak, and Judy Bernstein. *They Poured Fire on Us from the Sky: The True Story of Three Lost Boys from Sudan.* NF.
Dumas, Firoozeh. *Funny in Farsi: A Memoir of Growing Up Iranian in America.* NF.
Guilbault, Rose Castillo. *Farmworker's Daughter: Growing Up Mexican.* NF.
Hart, Elva Treviño. *Barefoot Heart: Stories of a Migrant Child.* NF.
Hesse, Karen. *Letters from Rifka.*
Hobbs, Will. *Crossing the Wire.*
Jaramillo, Ann. *La Línea.*
Jiménez, Francisco. *The Circuit: Stories from the Life of a Migrant Child.* NF.
Mead, Alice. *Swimming to America.*
Murphy, Jim. *Pick and Shovel Poet: The Journeys of Pascal D'Angelo.* NF.
Na, An. *A Step from Heaven.*
Naidoo, Beverley. *The Other Side of Truth.*
Napoli, Donna Jo. *King of Mulberry Street.*
Ryan, Pam Muñoz. *Esperanza Rising.*

Sheth, Kashmira. *Blue Jasmine*.
Testa, Maria. *Something about America*.
Warren, Andrea. *Escape from Saigon: How a Vietnam War Orphan Became an American Boy*. NF.
Zephaniah, Benjamin. *Refugee Boy*.

3T. Wintertime

Brr! If you feel a little chilly, it's from the wintry setting in this list of books.

Brenna, Duff. *Too Cool*.
Crutcher, Chris. *The Sledding Hill*.
Durbin, William. *Wintering*.
Fisher, Catherine. *Snow-Walker*.
Gray, Dianne E. *Together Apart*.
Hill, Stuart. *The Cry of the Icemark*.
Hobbs, Will. *Far North*.
Hokenson, Terry. *The Winter Road*.
Holt, Simon. *The Devouring*.
Libbrecht, Kenneth, and Patricia Rasmussen. *The Snowflake: Winter's Secret Beauty*. NF.
London, Jack. *The Call of the Wild*.
Mazer, Harry. *Snowbound*.
Mourlevat, Jean-Claude. *Winter's End*.
Mowat, Farley. *Lost in the Barrens*.
Murphy, Jim. *Blizzard! The Storm That Changed America*. NF.
Napoli, Donna Jo. *Stones in Water*.
Naylor, Phyllis Reynolds. *Blizzard's Wake*.
Paulsen, Gary. *Brian's Winter*.
———. *Winterdance: The Fine Madness of Running the Iditarod*. NF.
Pratchett, Terry. *Wintersmith*.
Qualey, Marsha. *Just Like That*.
Reiss, Kathryn. *Blackthorn Winter*.
Rottman, S.L. *Slalom*.
Smelcer, John E. *The Great Death*.
———. *The Trap*.
Taylor, Theodore. *Ice Drift*.

PART II

The Annotations

A

ABADZIS, NICK. 2007. *Laika*. Roaring Brook.
Fact and fiction blend together in this graphic retelling of the story of Laika, the stray dog that became the first living being launched into outer space, and the Soviet scientists who sent her there.
(2H. Graphic Novels in the Classroom)

ABBOTT, EDWIN. 1884. *Flatland: A Romance of Many Dimensions*. Seeley & Co.
A. Square's two-dimensional world of polygons, triangles, and circles is turned upside down by the appearance of a three-dimensional sphere in this satire on the Victorian era's rigidity.
(3L. Mathematics)

ABEL, JESSICA, AND GABRIEL SORIA. 2007. *Life Sucks*. Illustrated by Warren Pleece. Roaring Brook.
Vampire and convenience store clerk Dave prefers to get his blood from a bank, not people, but when vampire surfer Wes uses Dave's resulting weakness to go after his girl, Dave has to make some hard choices to keep her safe.
(2E. Core Graphic Novels)

ABRAHAMS, PETER. 2005– . Echo Falls Mystery series. HarperCollins.
Thirteen-year-old Sherlock Holmes fan and budding actress Ingrid finds herself at the center of more than one local mystery and must use her considerable wits and powers of observation to reveal the truth.
(1H. Innocent Middle School Girls)

ACAMPORA, PAUL. 2006. *Defining Dulcie*. Dial.
Because it's impossible for Dulcie to grieve for her father in their new home in California, she drives herself back to Connecticut where familiar places help her remember her dad and she begins to heal.
(3P. State Books)

ADLER, C.S. 2001. *One Unhappy Horse*. Clarion.
When money is tight and Jen's horse Dove needs an expensive operation to cure his lameness, only a chance friendship with elderly Mattie provides the funds for surgery, while also giving Mattie a new interest in life.
(3G. Horses)

ADLINGTON, L.J. 2005. *The Diary of Pelly D*. Greenwillow.
On the colonized planet Home from Home, Tony V is clearing rubble when he finds a diary, written by Pelly D, which describes a wealthy lifestyle until her family's gene traits are classified as undesirable, leaving Tony fearful of her fate.
(1B. Avid Readers; 2F. Diaries and Epistolary Novels)

ADOFF, ARNOLD, ED. 1997. *I Am the Darker Brother: An Anthology of Modern Poems by African Americans.* Illustrated by Benny Andrews. Aladdin. NF.
> Updated since the original 1968 edition, 21 new writers, including ten women, contribute to this mix of classic and contemporary works that are often left out of anthologies.
> (2O. Poetry Anthologies for High School Readers)

————. 2000. *The Basket Counts.* Illustrated by Mike Weaver. Simon & Schuster. NF.
> Basketball, as played in pick-up games on neighborhood courts with netless baskets, is highlighted in the free verse and concrete poetry of Adoff and extended through the action illustrations of Mike Weaver.
> (2P. Poetry Anthologies for Middle School Readers)

ADOFF, JAIME. 2005. *Jimi & Me.* Jump at the Sun/Hyperion.
> After his wealthy record producer father is murdered, Keith and his mother move to Ohio where during the day he evades the bullies at his school and at night loses himself in playing Jimi Hendrix songs on his guitar.
> (2Q. Teen Issue Novels in Verse)

————. 2008. *The Death of Jayson Porter.* Jump at the Sun/Hyperion.
> Jayson's grim life includes an abusive mother; a crack addict for a father; wealthy, scornful classmates; and a home in the projects, all of which make him want to jump over the railing outside his apartment.
> (2Q. Teen Issue Novels in Verse)

AKAMATSU, KEN. 2002–2003. Love Hina series. Tokyopop.
> Keitaro is kicked out of the house when he fails his university entrance exam for the second time, so when his grandmother offers him the caretaker position at Hinata Lodge he jumps at the opportunity, even though it means being the only guy around.
> (2D. Classic Manga)

ALEGRÍA, MALIN. 2006. *Estrella's Quinceañera.* Simon & Schuster.
> Now attending a prestigious private school, Estrella worries that her quinceañera will be a cheesy, gaudy affair, until she takes control and plans the party she wants.
> (1I. Latina Teens)

————. 2007. *Sofi Mendoza's Guide to Getting Lost in Mexico.* Simon & Schuster.
> Stopped at the Mexican border when trying to return to her California home, teen Sofi learns her green card is a fake and moves in with her Mexican aunt, where she begins to appreciate her culture.
> (1I. Latina Teens)

ALEXANDER, JILL S. 2009. *The Sweetheart of Prosper County*. Feiwel and Friends.
Since Austin's dad died, her mother has been overly protective and it's only her good friend Maribel who's able to raise her spirits, especially when she invites Austin to join her loud, happy family at her quinceañera.
(1I. Latina Teens)

ALEXIE, SHERMAN. 2007. *The Absolutely True Diary of a Part-Time Indian*. Little, Brown.
When a teacher encourages him to leave the rez and attend an all-white high school, Junior enrolls and discovers that he doesn't know the rules by which the white kids play and now is considered a turncoat by his tribe in this semi-autobiographical work.
(1A. Adult Readers; 1L. Offbeat Guys; 2F. Diaries and Epistolary Novels)

—————. 2008. *The Absolutely True Diary of a Part-Time Indian*. Read by Sherman Alexie. Recorded Books. Unabridged, 5 hours.
Alexie's lilting narration and perfect pacing capture the struggles of Junior as he adapts to the white world beyond his reservation.
(2A. Audiobooks for High School Listeners)

ALLENBAUGH, KAY. 2003. *Chocolate for a Teen's Dream: Heartwarming Stories about Making Your Wishes Come True*. Simon & Schuster. NF.
The rich sweetness of chocolate is epitomized here in 50 true stories for young women that illustrate the richness and sweetness of life and the importance of not letting disappointment or failure hold you back.
(3B. Chocolate)

ALMOND, DAVID. 2005. *Two Plays*. Random House.
A dramatization of Almond's *Skellig*, the story of a young boy caring for what might be an angel, is accompanied by his novel, *Wild Girl, Wild Boy*, in which a grieving Elaine conjures up a Wild Boy to help her deal with her father's death.
(2L. Novels with Script or Screenplay Format)

ALMOND, STEVE. 2004. *Candyfreak: A Journey through the Chocolate Underbelly of America*. Algonquin. NF.
Having eaten at least one piece of candy every day of his life, Almond describes the products of the three major candy manufacturers, Mars, Hershey, and Nestle, as well as those of the small regional candy manufacturers that help fuel his sweet tooth.
(3B. Chocolate)

ALVAREZ, JULIA. 1991. *How the Garcia Girls Lost Their Accents.* Algonquin.
Through a series of flashbacks, the four Garcia sisters tell of their difficulties adjusting to life in America, especially when they return each summer to the Dominican Republic and visit their wealthy grandparents.
(1I. Latina Teens; 3S. Teen Immigrants)

————. 2004. *Finding Miracles.* Knopf.
Milly Kaufman has never felt totally at ease being adopted and living in Vermont when she's from Central America until Pablo Bolivar joins her class and she travels with Pablo and his family back to what may be her birth place.
(1I. Latina Teens)

AMATEAU, GIGI. 2008. *Chancey of the Maury River.* Candlewick.
Claire works with an abandoned albino Appaloosa to return him to his former prowess as a jumper, but poor eyesight affords Chancey the opportunity to become a therapy horse for cancer patients.
(3G. Horses)

AMATO, MARY. 2005. *The Naked Mole-Rat Letters.* Holiday House.
Frankie tries to discourage Ayanna from sending her widowed father more e-mails, but Ayanna turns the tables and e-mails Frankie instead, helping her through her grief over her mother's death.
(2C. Blogs, E-mails, and IMs in Fiction)

ANDERSON, HO CHE. 2005. *King: A Comics Biography of Martin Luther King, Jr.* Fantagraphics. NF.
The life and death of Martin Luther King Jr., are chronicled in this graphic recounting of King's early life, college years, and leadership of the civil rights movement.
(2K. Nonfiction Graphic Novels)

ANDERSON, JODI LYNN. 2006. *Peaches.* HarperCollins.
Shy Birdie, her wealthy cousin Leeda, and rebellious Murphy spend the summer before their last year in high school picking peaches at Darlington Orchard where they also form bonds of friendship.
(3P. State Books)

ANDERSON, LAURIE HALSE. 1999. *Speak.* Farrar, Straus and Giroux.
Though Melinda longs to explain why she called 911 the night of a pre-school party, she can't bring herself to speak until her ex-best friend dates the boy Melinda calls "the beast."
(1D. Detention Home Girls; 3A. Bathrooms; 3O. Silence)

―――. 2000. *Speak*. Read by Mandy Siegfried. Listening Library. Unabridged, 5 hours.

Narrator Siegfried's youthful-sounding voice is spot on for revealing Melinda's thoughts after being sexually attacked, as she combines the sounds of healing with the vibrant teen world of high school life.

(2A. Audiobooks for High School Listeners)

―――. 2002. *Catalyst*. Viking.

Determined to study chemistry at MIT, her deceased mother's alma mater, Kate applies and is devastated when she's not accepted, but she has a bigger problem when a fellow student's home burns and Teri and her brother move in with Kate's family.

(3N. Science)

―――. 2005. *Prom*. Penguin Putnam.

Even though she doesn't care one whit about prom, Ashley finds herself helping her best friend Nat save the event after their math teacher runs off with the funds.

(3J. Love Hurts)

―――. 2007. *Twisted*. Penguin Putnam.

A summer spent in court-ordered physical labor transforms Tyler from high school nobody to high school hottie, but the attention of the girl of his dreams turns out to be more of a problem than a dream come true.

(3J. Love Hurts)

ANDERSON, M.T. 1999. *Burger Wuss*. Candlewick.

Dumped by his girlfriend, Anthony takes a job flipping burgers to exact revenge against her new boyfriend Turner by setting him up for the theft of the Burger Queen's "condiment troll" in a laugh-a-minute tale.

(1L. Offbeat Guys; 3J. Love Hurts)

―――. 2002. *Feed*. Candlewick.

All of Earth's inhabitants are obsessed with consumerism because of the computer feeds in their brains, except for home-schooled Violet, whose feed is damaged so badly she's told to expect total shutdown.

(1A. Adult Readers; 1N. Punk Readers)

―――. 2003. *Feed*. Read by David Aaron Baker and others. Listening Library. Unabridged, 5 hours.

The constant chatter of the feed, with its inane staccato pitch, is voiced by a full cast and matches the speech patterns of most teens, with the exception of Violet's slower tempo and more thoughtful speech, which is well articulated by narrator Baker.

(2A. Audiobooks for High School Listeners)

————. 2004. *The Game of Sunken Places.* Scholastic.
Friends Gregory and Brian are sucked into a mysterious board game while visiting
Gregory's enigmatic Uncle Max, and they must not only find a way to win but also
discover exactly who their opponent is and what they are playing for.
(1E. Gentlemanly Boys)

————. 2006. *The Astonishing Life of Octavian Nothing, Traitor to the Nation, Volume I: The Pox Party.* Candlewick.
Raised by members of the Novanglian College of Lucidity, young, black Octavian
slowly realizes he's a glorified slave who, though educated, is also a lab experiment, and when his mother dies following a smallpox inoculation, he flees.
(3P. State Books)

————. 2009. *Jasper Dash and the Flame-Pits of Delaware.* Illustrated by Kurt
Cyrus. Simon & Schuster.
Jasper Dash receives a telepathic cry for help in the midst of the Stare-Eyes Championship, so he, Katie, and Lily track their cry to a monastery in jungle-torn Delaware where they find their old teachers are being held hostage.
(1R. Tweens)

ANDO, NATSUMI, AND MIYUKI KOBAYASHI. 2007. *Kitchen Princess.* Del Rey.
After her parents die, a young boy gives Najika a special gift of an unusual silver
spoon that she takes to the Seika Academy where she studies to become a chef and
hopes to meet her unknown hero.
(3E. Cookery)

APPELT, KATHI. 2002. *Poems from the Homeroom: A Writer's Place to Start.* Holt. NF.
Each poem in this work is accompanied by a page that explains where the idea for
the poem originated and any special techniques used in its creation.
(2O. Poetry Anthologies for High School Readers)

ARAKAWA, HIROMU. 2005– . Fullmetal Alchemist series. VIZ Media.
Brothers Edward and Alphonse Elric are powerful government agents in a world
where alchemy is real and not everyone who wields its power is benevolent.
(2D. Classic Manga)

ARMISTEAD, JOHN. 2002. *The Return of Gabriel.* Milkweed Editions.
When civil rights workers come to Cooper's segregated Mississippi town, racial tensions threaten his friendship with Jubal and his relationship with his own family.
(3C. The Civil Rights Movement)

ASAI, CARRIE. 2003–2004. Samurai Girl series. Simon & Schuster.
Adopted by the wealthy Kogo family after she survives the plane crash that killed her parents, Heaven is horrified when a ninja crashes her (forced) wedding and kills her brother, so vowing revenge, she leaves home to learn the ways of the samurai.
(1K. Manga Lovers; 2M. Paperback Series)

ASGEDOM, MAWI. 2002. *Of Beetles and Angels: A Boy's Remarkable Journey from a Refugee Camp to Harvard.* Little, Brown/Megan Tingley. NF.
Mawi, his parents, and his siblings flee Ethiopia, spend three years in a Sudanese refugee camp, and eventually arrive in Chicago where they adjust to life in a lily-white suburb and his formerly professional father feels like a "beetle."
(3S. Teen Immigrants)

ASHANTI. 2002. *Foolish/Unfoolish: Reflections on Love.* Hyperion. NF.
Hip-hop artist Ashanti wrote love poems during her teen years and here shares them, along with the story behind each poem, in a work where photos of her as a child are sprinkled throughout.
(2O. Poetry Anthologies for High School Readers)

ASTLEY, NEIL, ED. 2003. *Staying Alive: Real Poems for Unreal Times.* Hyperion. NF.
Five hundred modern poems, arranged thematically with an introductory essay for each of the 12 sections, offer an intriguing collection with noted poets arranged beside lesser-known ones.
(2O. Poetry Anthologies for High School Readers)

ATKINS, CATHERINE. 2003. *Alt Ed.* Penguin Putnam.
Outcasts Susan and Brendan are forced to attend an afterschool class for students facing expulsion after an act of vandalism, and during the following weeks they learn a great deal about the other members of the group and about themselves.
(3O. SILENCE)

AUCH, MARY JANE. 2002. *Ashes of Roses.* Holt.
Sixteen-year-old Rose Nolan is finally settling down to life in America, despite being left on her own to care for her young sister, and when her friend Gussie gets her a job at the Triangle Shirtwaist Factory she thinks all her troubles are over.
(3S. Teen Immigrants)

AUSEON, ANDREW. 2005. *Funny Little Monkey.* Harcourt.
Midget-sized Arty has been angry with his 6'2" brother Kurt ever since he began taking shots for his growth hormone deficiency, but when he sets his brother up to take a fall for stealing their high school's mascot, Arty realizes he's gone too far.
(1L. Offbeat Guys)

Avɪ. 1991. *Nothing but the Truth.* Scholastic.
  When Philip Malloy defies school policy and hums along during the national anthem in an attempt to get kicked out of his English class, he finds himself at the center of a national crisis.
  (2F. Diaries and Epistolary Novels; 2L. Novels with Script or Screenplay Format)

————. 2001. *The Secret School.* Houghton Mifflin.
  When their teacher leaves unexpectedly, 14-year-old Ida Bidson agrees to teach the other students rather than close the school, even though it means keeping it all a secret.
  (3P. State Books)

————. 2002. *Crispin: The Cross of Lead.* Hyperion.
  Forced to run from his home after being unfairly accused of murder, Crispin finds a solid traveling companion in Bear, a juggler who helps Crispin search for the truth about his name and family.
  (1E. Gentlemanly Boys)

Avɪ, ᴀɴᴅ Rᴀᴄʜᴇʟ Vᴀɪʟ. 2004. *Never Mind! A Twin Novel.* HarperCollins.
  Twins Meg and Edward go to different schools, have nothing in common, and don't get along, so it's no surprise when Meg finds herself the victim of an elaborate hoax (engineered by Edward) designed to curb her desire for popularity at any cost.
  (2R. Two or More Voices in Novels)

B

B., Dᴀᴠɪᴅ. 2005. *Epileptic.* Random House. NF.
  David B.'s childhood was defined by his parents' obsession with finding a cure for his brother's epilepsy, but the other interests he shared with his family, such as art and military history, also play a part in the cartoonist's memoir.
  (2K. Nonfiction Graphic Novels)

Bᴀʟʟɪᴇᴛᴛ, Bʟᴜᴇ. 2004. *Chasing Vermeer.* Scholastic.
  Attending the University of Chicago Lab School, Petra and Calder search for a missing Vermeer painting, receiving clues through dreams, secret codes, and math tools called "pentominoes."
  (1E. Gentlemanly Boys; 1F. Gifted Elementary Student Readers; 3L. Mathematics)

Bᴀɴɢ, Mᴏʟʟʏ. 2000. *Nobody Particular: One Woman's Fight to Save the Bays.* Holt. NF.
  Diane Wilson, a "nobody" from East Texas, goes from commercial shrimper to environmental activist when she turns her life upside down to fight against the chemical plants destroying her bays.
  (2N. Picture Books for Teens)

BANKS, L.G. 2004. *Sign of the Qin*. Hyperion.
Raised by Monkey after his mother is forced to flee the Emperor's palace, Prince Zong bears a magical birthmark indicating he has a central role to play in the coming battle between the King of Heaven and the King of Hell.
(1K. Manga Lovers)

BARAKAT, IBTISAM. 2007. *Tasting the Sky: A Palestinian Childhood*. Farrar, Straus and Giroux.
Barakat recalls her life before, during, and after the Six Day War, when, at three years old, she was temporarily separated from her family as they fled across the Palestinian border to Jordan.
(2G. Fictionalized Biographies)

BARATZ-LOGSTED, LAUREN. 2008. *Secrets of My Suburban Life*. Simon & Schuster/Simon Pulse.
After IMing her friends in Manhattan to tell them how miserable she is in the suburbs and how mean the "Queen Bee" at her school is, Ren finds "Queen Bee" talking to a guy in a sex chat room and tries to halt what could be a tragic meeting.
(2C. Blogs, E-mails, and IMs in Fiction)

BARKER, CLIVE. 2002– . Books of Abarat series. HarperCollins.
Candy Quakenbush, formerly of Chickentown, Minnesota, finds herself on the run from the Lord of Midnight, who plans to bring a Permanent Midnight to the islands of Abarat.
(1G. Graphic Novel Lovers)

BARKLEY, BRAD, AND HEATHER HEPLER. 2006. *Scrambled Eggs at Midnight*. Dutton.
Tired of accompanying her mother as she peddles jewelry at Renaissance faires, Cal meets Eliot, whose born-again father runs a Christian weight loss camp in town, and Cal hopes to stay long enough to develop a relationship with Eliot.
(2R. Two or More Voices in Novels; 3R. Summertime)

Barry, Lynda. 2002. *One Hundred Demons*. Sasquatch Books. NF.
Barry's "autobifictionalographic" work features 100 demons that take the form of objects, events, and milestones from her early life.
(2K. Nonfiction Graphic Novels)

BASTEDO, JAMIE. 2006. *On Thin Ice*. Red Deer.
Moving to the Arctic town of Nanurtalik, Ashley dreams of a bear–man shaman, a polar bear mangles a classmate, and townsfolk worry that the warming weather will lead to the appearance of more polar bears.
(3F. The Environment)

BAUER, JOAN. 1992. *Squashed.* Delacorte.
> In small town Rock River, teen Ellie Morgan is determined to win the prize for largest pumpkin and lavishes her energy on 611-pound-pumpkin Max in this first novel by Bauer.
> (1B. Avid Readers)

————. 1995. *Thwonk.* Random House.
> When the stuffed cupid she almost runs over comes to life, high school photographer A.J. gets her heart's desire—the devoted attention of hunky Peter—but quickly learns that wishes don't always turn out the way you imagine.
> (3J. Love Hurts)

————. 1998. *Rules of the Road.* Putnam.
> Just as her alcoholic father reappears in her life, Jenna Boller has the chance to chauffeur her 73-year-old boss, owner of Gladstone shoes, to a stockholder's meeting in Texas where Mrs. Gladstone hopes to forestall her son's attempt at a takeover.
> (1A. Adult Readers)

————. 2000. *Hope Was Here.* Putnam.
> Hope feels at home in the small Wisconsin diner where her aunt is now the cook and wishes they could finally settle down and stay in one place.
> (1H. Innocent Middle School Girls; 3E. Cookery)

BAUER, MARION DANE, ED. 1994. *Am I Blue? Coming Out from the Silence.* HarperCollins.
> This anthology of gay and lesbian–themed fiction features well-known writers, including M.E. Kerr, Nancy Garden, William Sleator, Jane Yolen, and Bruce Coville.
> (2J. Must-Have Anthologies)

BEAUDOIN, SEAN. 2007. *Going Nowhere Faster.* Little, Brown.
> With his 165 IQ not helping him attain greatness, Stan works at a video store, tries to ignore his hippie vegan parents, and writes film treatments, but it takes being the prime suspect in a burglary at the video store to wake Stan up and help him get a grip on his life.
> (1L. Offbeat Guys)

BEIL, MICHAEL D. 2009. *The Red Blazer Girls: The Ring of Rocamadour.* Knopf.
> Aided by math clues and word puzzles, four girls set off on a scavenger hunt to solve a 20-year-old mystery involving a wish-granting ring.
> (3L. Mathematics)

BELTON, SANDRA. 1997. *Ernestine and Amanda: Summer Camp, Ready or Not!* Simon & Schuster.

Best friends Ernestine and Amanda head off to camp, with Ernestine at an all-black camp and Amanda attending a predominantly white one, though the two will be reunited in the fall when they enroll at the same school.

(3Q. Summer Camp)

BENDIS, BRIAN MICHAEL. 2006. *House of M.* Illustrated by Olivier Coipel. Marvel.

Former Avenger Wanda Maximoff, the Scarlet Witch, is losing control of her ability to alter reality, and the Avengers and the X-Men must somehow come together despite an altered timeline to set things right.

(2E. Core Graphic Novels)

BENDIS, BRIAN MICHAEL, AND MICHAEL AVON OEMING. 2000. *Powers: Who Killed Retro Girl?* Image Comics.

Homicide detective Christian Walker teams up with rookie Deena Pilgrim to investigate the death of one of the world's most popular superheroes, Retro Girl, a search that takes them from dirty alleys to the pristine tower homes of heroes.

(2E. Core Graphic Novels)

BENNETT, CHERIE. 1998. *Life in the Fat Lane.* Random House.

Lara is pretty, thin, smart, and popular, but once she starts gaining weight due to the onset of Axell-Crowne Syndrome she finds herself ridiculed and ostracized.

(3A. Bathrooms)

BENNETT, VERONICA. 2007. *Cassandra's Sister.* Candlewick.

Jane, called Jenny, and her older sister Cassandra are best friends and confidantes, sharing all the details of their country life, but when a sophisticated cousin arrives their cozy world expands in unexpected ways, propelling Jenny into a life of writing.

(2G. Fictionalized Biographies)

BERLIN, ERIC. 2009. *The Potato Chip Puzzles: The Puzzling World of Winston Breen.* Putnam.

Winston Breen and his friends, encouraged by their math teacher Mr. Garvey, take part in a puzzle competition sponsored by a potato chip company that offers a $50,000 award, but a competitor from a rival school will do anything to stop them.

(1R. Tweens)

BERNARDO, ANILÚ. 1996. *Fitting In.* Piñata.

This series of five stories features Cuban American girls who try hard to fit into American life, but they are often embarrassed by their family members or subjected to harassment. Spanish edition available.

(1I. Latina Teens)

————. 1999. *Loves Me, Loves Me Not*. Piñata.
Cuban American Maggie loses her crush on the grandson of the elderly woman she helps when she realizes that good-looking Zach is mean to his grandmother and dismissive of minorities.
(1I. Latina Teens)

BERTAGNA, JULIE. 2009. *Zenith*. Walker.
Global warming leaves land flooded and unsuitable for homes, forcing Mara and her boatload of refugees to sail for Greenland where some of them manage to settle around a glacial lake in a sequel to *Exodus* (Walker Books for Young Readers, 2008).
(3F. The Environment)

BERTRAND, DIANE GONZALES. 2001. *Trino's Time*. Arte Público.
Still living in the trailer park and dealing with guilt following the death of a friend in an attempted robbery, Trino goes to work when his mother loses her job and finally befriends classmates at school, which helps his self-confidence.
(1P. Striving Readers)

BIRCH, DAVID. 1988. *The King's Chessboard*. Illustrated by Devis Grebu. Penguin Putnam.
In a palace in ancient India a king grants the reluctant request of a wiseman—a grain of rice doubled for each square on the chessboard—but when it becomes clear he has miscalculated the worth of such a request the king is forced to rescind his offer.
(2N. Picture Books for Teens)

BIRD, ISOBEL. 2001–2002. Circle of Three series. HarperTeen.
Meeting in high school, three teens from different social backgrounds discover they've each checked out the same spellbook from the library, which leads them to study Wicca.
(2M. Paperback Series)

BIRDSALL, JEANNE. 2005. *The Penderwicks: A Summer Tale of Four Sisters, Two Rabbits, and a Very Interesting Boy*. Knopf.
The Penderwicks vacation at a cottage on the grounds of Arundel mansion in the Berkshire Mountains where the four daughters, often accompanied by their dog Hound, meet and play with Jeffrey Tifton, son of the snooty owner of Arundel.
(1H. Innocent Middle School Girls; 3R. Summertime)

BLACK, HOLLY. 2002. *Tithe: A Modern Faerie Tale*. Simon & Schuster.
In this first book of a series, Kaye learns she's a changeling and that the "imaginary" fairies she remembers from her childhood want her to serve as the sacrificial "tithe" so they can be free for seven years and only the knight Roiben seems able to help.
(1N. Punk Readers; 1S. Urban Teens: Beyond Street Lit)

————. 2008– . The Good Neighbors series. Illustrated by Ted Naifeh. Scholastic.
Rue Silver begins to notice strange creatures in her small town and successfully ig-
nores them until the day her mother's faerie family shows up to claim her as their
own.
(2E. Core Graphic Novels)

BLACK, HOLLY, AND CECIL CASTELLUCCI, EDS. 2009. *Geektastic: Stories from the Nerd
Herd.* Hachette.
This anthology features an impressive array of authors, including John Green,
Libba Bray, Scott Westerfeld, M.T. Anderson, and Kelly Link, riffing on the ups
and downs of life as a geek.
(2J. Must-Have Anthologies)

BLOCK, FRANCESCA LIA. 1989. *Weetzie Bat.* Harper & Row.
Weetzie Bat finds happiness when she locates "My Secret Agent Lover Man" and
the two settle down in wedded bliss.
(1N. Punk Readers)

BLUME, JUDY. 1975. *Forever.* Simon & Schuster.
After meeting at a party, Katherine and Michael discover that true love isn't exactly
what they were expecting.
(1D. Detention Home Girls)

————, ED. 1999. *Places I Never Meant to Be: Original Stories by Censored Writers.*
Simon & Schuster.
Editor Judy Blume, a target of censors for decades, presents fellow targets Jacque-
line Woodson, Chris Lynch, Katherine Paterson, Julius Lester, Walter Dean Myers,
Susan Beth Pfeffer, and Paul Zindel.
(2J. Must-Have Anthologies)

BOOTH, COE. 2006. *Tyrell.* Scholastic.
Tyrell's life in the South Bronx is anything but ideal as he struggles to keep his little brother safe, to raise money doing something other than selling drugs, and to
stay faithful to his girlfriend Novisha.
(1O. Reluctant Male Readers)

BOYD, HERB. 2004. *We Shall Overcome: The History of the Civil Rights Movement as
It Happened.* Sourcebooks. NF.
Using the voices of the participants themselves accompanied by photographs and
recordings, Boyd examines the struggle for civil rights, from the murder of
Emmett Till through the assassination of Dr. Martin Luther King Jr.
(3C. The Civil Rights Movement)

BOYLAN, JAMES FINNEY. 1998. *Getting In.* Warner.
A summer tour of the New England colleges finds three adults and four teens traveling in a Winnebago as they visit Yale, miss Harvard because of traffic, and discover that the worst student of the four is the only one to enter the school of his choice.
(3R. Summertime)

BRADLEY, ALEX. 2005. *24 Girls in 7 Days.* Dutton.
When his girlfriend ditches him just before the prom, Jack's friends place a personal ad to find a date for him, and now Jack must speed date 24 girls in just seven days to decide on a prom date.
(2C. Blogs, E-mails, and IMs in Fiction; 3P. State Books)

————. 2007. *Hot Lunch.* Penguin.
Paired for an English assignment, Molly and Cassie act out their dislike for one another in the cafeteria and as punishment must prepare lunches for their classmates until the student body grades the meals as satisfactory.
(3E. Cookery)

BRADSHAW, GILLIAN. 2000. *The Sand-Reckoner.* Forge.
Returning home to Syracuse, Greece, when his father is dying, Archimedes finds his city at war with the Roman army and volunteers his mathematical and engineering skills to design bigger and better catapults for the king.
(3L. Mathematics)

BRANDE, ROBIN. 2007. *Evolution, Me & Other Freaks of Nature.* Knopf.
After Mena's Fundamentalist church tries to reform a possibly gay student, she writes him a letter of apology, which sets her former friends against her and comes to a head when her biology class studies the chapter on evolution.
(3N. Science)

BRASHARES, ANN. 2001. *The Sisterhood of the Traveling Pants.* Delacorte.
Four friends prepare to spend the summer apart as camps, trips, and jobs separate them, but they remain united by a special pair of pants that each wears before sending on to the next friend.
(3R. Summertime)

————. 2001. *The Sisterhood of the Traveling Pants.* Read by Angela Goethals. Listening Library. Unabridged, 6 hours, 30 minutes.
Narrator Goethals relays the dismay of four teen friends as they prepare to spend their first summer apart, united only by a pair of jeans, as she gives each of the girls a distinctive voice as they relate their vacation adventures.
(2B. Audiobooks for Middle School Listeners)

————. 2001–2007. The Sisterhood of the Traveling Pants series. Random House.
Four childhood friends—Lena, Carmen, Libby, and Bridget—share everything
with each other, including a magical pair of jeans that fits all of them despite their
differences.
(2R. Two or More Voices in Novels)

Bray, Libba. 2003–2007. The Gemma Doyle Trilogy. Random House.
Gemma Doyle chafes at the restrictions Victorian society places on her and her
friends, especially when she learns the truth about the Order, a secret society her
mother was part of, and accepts the power that seems to be her birthright.
(1A. Adult Readers)

————. 2004. *A Great and Terrible Beauty*. Read by Josephine Bailey. Listening Library. Unabridged, 12 hours.
Taking place in the nineteenth century at Spence Academy for Girls, Bailey's voicing of the various characters helps listeners distinguish among Gemma, a teen
who discovers her ability to see the future; the stiffly elitist headmistress; and
stuffy-nosed student Ann.
(2A. Audiobooks for High School Listeners)

Bray, Libba, et al. 2009. *Vacations from Hell*. HarperCollins.
Vacations across the globe are the focus of supernatural stories from authors
Libba Bray, Cassandra Clare, Claudia Gray, Maureen Johnson, and Sarah
Mlynowski.
(2J. Must-Have Anthologies)

Brenna, Duff. 1998. *Too Cool*. Doubleday.
Stealing a car to escape from reform school, Elbert Earl Evans, aka Triple E, picks
up his girlfriend Jeanne and evades the police by driving into a Colorado blizzard;
stuck on a mountain road, Triple E has lots of time to think about how he ended
up in that car.
(3T. Wintertime)

Brennan, Herbie. 2003. *Faerie Wars*. Bloomsbury.
To escape a crisis in his family, Henry Atherton does chores for old Mr. Fogarty, a
retired physicist and armed robber, and together the two pool their wits and unlock a portal to send lost fairy Prince Pyrgus to safety in an alternate world.
(1B. Avid Readers)

BRIAN, KATE. 2005. *Lucky T.* Simon & Schuster.
Carrie Fitzgerald's luck changed after her lucky T-shirt was inadvertently donated to an orphanage in India, and the only solution she can think of is to go and get it back. (3K. Luck)

————. 2006– . Private series. Simon Pulse.
Reed Brennan, a new student at the posh Easton Academy, meets the Billings Girls when she is attracted to senior Thomas Pearson, who has connections to the influential clique. (2M. Paperback Series)

BRIDGES, RUBY. 1999. *Through My Eyes.* Scholastic. NF.
Ruby Bridges was the first black child to attend a public elementary school in New Orleans, an experience she recounts here in her own words. (3C. The Civil Rights Movement)

BRIGGS, RAYMOND. 1999. *Ethel & Ernest: A True Story.* Random House. NF.
Ethel and Ernest, the author's parents, met, courted, married, and raised a family against a backdrop of progress and political turmoil. (2K. Nonfiction Graphic Novels)

BROACH, ELISE. 2005. *Shakespeare's Secret.* Holt.
Hero's next-door neighbor Mrs. Roth tells her about a diamond, once part of an heirloom necklace, that is rumored to have been lost in her home, leading Hero to embark on a stealthy search. (1R. Tweens)

BRODY, LOLA. 2004. *Chocolate American Style.* Clarkson Potter. NF.
Chocolate chip muffins, chocolate-covered potato chips, chocolate cream pie, and chocolate chili cake are a few of the recipes in this collection, which includes tips for working with different types of chocolate. (3B. Chocolate)

BROOKS, BRUCE. 1996. *Asylum for Nightface.* HarperCollins.
Fourteen-year-old Zimmerman, devout Christian, is shocked when his worldly parents return from vacation as converts themselves, followers of the charismatic Pastor John, a man who has definite plans for Zimmerman. (3D. Consequences and Fate)

BROOKS, GERALDINE. 2001. *Year of Wonders: A Novel of the Plague.* Viking.
In the mid-1600s, the English village of Eyam walls itself off after plague strikes and initially the villagers cooperate, but, as the deaths mount, cries about witches are heard and the village healer is a target of blame. (1M. Picky Senior Girls)

BROOKS, KEVIN. 2002. *Martyn Pig*. Scholastic.
Few people know that Martyn's father has died, except for his friend Alex and her boyfriend Dean, who help Martyn hide his father, but when Martyn receives a small inheritance, Alex tries to blackmail him.
(1Q. Troubled Teen Boys)

————. 2003. *Lucas*. Scholastic.
Lucas is a drifter who lives off the land and seems utterly alone, and while Caitlin finds him intriguing and somehow comforting, the other islanders regard him with suspicion that turns, inevitably, to violence.
(3D. Consequences and Fate)

BROOKS, MARTHA. 2004. *True Confessions of a Heartless Girl*. HarperCollins.
Troubled Noreen arrives in a stolen truck and wreaks havoc on the weary inhabitants of a small Canadian town.
(1D. Detention Home Girls; 3J. Love Hurts)

BROWN, TODD D. 1995. *Entries from a Hot Pink Notebook*. Washington Square.
After being "outed" when caught kissing another boy in a supply closet, Ben's parents send him to camp to get over his crush, but he instead uses the time to think about who he really is.
(3Q. Summer Camp)

BRUCE, COLIN. 2001. *Conned Again, Watson! Cautionary Tales of Logic, Math and Probability*. Perseus.
This collection of 12 stories follows Sherlock Holmes and Dr. Watson as they avoid common sense and rely on the use of mathematics, including probability, statistics, and logic, to solve mysteries.
(3L. Mathematics)

BRUCHAC, JOSEPH. 2005. *Code Talker: A Novel about the Navajo Marines of World War Two*. Dial.
Ned Begay, a Navajo who hated the time he spent in the Navajo mission school, relates the irony of the Navajos being recruited by the U.S. Army during World War II to create a code, using their language, that proves unbreakable by the Japanese.
(1E. Gentlemanly Boys)

————. 2006. *Jim Thorpe: Original All-American*. Penguin Putnam.
Using documentary sources, this first-person narrative tells the story of Jim Thorpe, extraordinary amateur athlete, from his early years on an Oklahoma reservation to his Olympic performance and beyond.
(2G. Fictionalized Biographies)

BRUCHAC, JOSEPH, ET AL. 2005. *Sports Shorts*. Darby Creek Publishing.
Athletic endeavors both successful and embarrassing are explored by authors including Joseph Bruchac, David Lubar, Dorian Cirrone, Marilyn Singer, Terry Trueman, Alexandra Siy, and Jamie McEwan.
(2J. Must-Have Anthologies)

BRYAN, ASHLEY. 2003. *Beautiful Blackbird*. Simon & Schuster.
Though Blackbird repeatedly tells his friends that it's what's on the inside that counts, he's also more than willing to share his beautiful black markings with the birds around him.
(2N. Picture Books for Teens)

BRYANT, BONNIE. 1998–2001. Pine Hollow series. Bantam.
Carole, Stevie, and Lisa, who are featured in The Saddle Club series, are now in high school but continue to ride horseback, study dressage, and compete against their rival, wealthy Veronica.
(2M. Paperback Series)

BRYANT, JEN. 2006. *Pieces of Georgia*. Knopf.
Still grieving over her mother's death six years ago, Georgia's father withdraws and Georgia's poor grades put her on the "at risk" list, but her counselor allows her to write to her mom in a journal instead of attending weekly counseling sessions.
(2Q. Teen Issue Novels in Verse)

———. 2008. *Ringside, 1925: Views from the Scopes Trial*. Knopf.
Written in verse, students, merchants, a reporter, and attorneys Clarence Darrow and William Jennings Bryant each offer a point of view on the famous court trial about the teaching of human evolution, which was then illegal in Tennessee.
(2I. Historical Novels in Verse; 3N. Science)

———. 2009. *Kaleidoscope Eyes*. Knopf.
While cleaning out her deceased grandfather's attic, Lyza finds an envelope addressed to her that's filled with maps and clues that she and two friends use in the summer of 1968 to search for the legendary treasure of Captain Kidd.
(2I. Historical Novels in Verse)

BUDHOS, MARINA. 2006. *Ask Me No Questions*. Atheneum.
Following the 9/11 attacks, immigration officials plan to deport Nadira and her family because their visas have expired; suddenly, the solution to their troubles must come from Nadira, who's always lived in the shadow of her older, smarter sister.
(3S. Teen Immigrants)

BUFORD, BILL. 2006. *Heat: An Amateur's Adventures as Kitchen Slave, Line Cook, Pasta-Maker, and Apprentice to a Dante-Quoting Butcher in Tuscany.* Knopf. NF.
    After a stint working with a New York chef, journalist Buford wants a different experience and travels to Italy where he apprentices to a pasta maker and a butcher and savors the frenetic kitchen activity and the chef's crude and often outrageous behavior.
(3E. Cookery)

BUNTING, EVE. 1989. *Terrible Things: An Allegory of the Holocaust.* Illustrated by Steven Gammell. Jewish Publication Society.
    When the Terrible Things arrive in the forest looking for every creature with feathers, the other animals quickly agree that they're all better off without birds, but then the Terrible Things turn their attention to the next group.
(2N. Picture Books for Teens)

BURG, ANN E. 2009. *All the Broken Pieces.* Scholastic.
    Airlifted out of Vietnam, war refugee Matt Pin is adopted by an American couple, but he is haunted by images and memories of the war until a support group of Vietnam veterans helps him deal with his past.
(2I. Historical Novels in Verse)

BURLEIGH, ROBERT. 2002. *Chocolate: Riches from the Rain Forest.* Abrams. NF.
    This richly illustrated book reviews the history of chocolate as a food, from its use by the Mayans and the Aztecs to the exclusive British chocolate shops and the mass-produced product of today.
(3B. Chocolate)

BURNS, LOREE GRIFFIN. 2007. *Tracking Trash: Flotsam, Jetsam, and the Science of Ocean Motion.* Houghton Mifflin. NF.
    A Pacific Ocean cargo spill of Nike sneakers washes up on the coast of Washington, and two oceanographers use a combination of computer modeling and beachcomber observations to predict landfall of floating objects, most of which are harmful to sea life.
(3F. The Environment)

BUSBY, CYLIN, ED. 2008. *First Kiss (Then Tell): A Collection of True Lip-Locked Moments.* Bloomsbury.
    This book contains true stories of first kisses by authors including Deb Caletti, Cecil Castelluci, Nikki Grimes, Shannon Hale, David Levithan, and Justin Larbalestier.
(2J. Must-Have Anthologies)

BUTCHER, A.J. 2003–2005. Spy High series. Hachette.
   The six members of Bond Team are students at Spy High, a training school for the best secret agents, but before they can save the world they have to learn to work as a team.
(1O. Reluctant Male Readers)

C

CABOT, MEG. 2000–2009. The Princess Diaries series. HarperCollins.
   Mia Thermopolis is a typical teenager, worried about algebra, her boyfriend, sex, and college, but it turns out she's also the princess of Genovia, a role that brings with it more worries, surprises, and triumphs than Mia ever imagined.
(2F. Diaries and Epistolary Novels; 2M. Paperback Series)

————. 2001–2006. 1-800-Where-R-You? series. Simon Pulse.
   After being struck by lightning, 16-year-old Jessica Mastriani's psychic power allows her to locate missing children by dreaming about them. Originally published under Cabot's pseudonym Jenny Carroll.
(2M. Paperback Series)

————. 2002. *All-American Girl.* HarperCollins.
   After accidentally saving the life of the President of the United States, Samantha finds herself at the center of a media whirlwind, an instant celebrity with White House dinner invitations and a date with the president's son.
(1H. Innocent Middle School Girls)

————. 2004–2005. The Mediator series. HarperCollins.
   Suze Simon is able to see ghosts, even falling in love with one from the nineteenth century, although her primary task is to help them move away from an earthly presence into the afterlife.
(2M. Paperback Series).

————. 2005. *Haunted.* The Mediator series, book 5. HarperCollins.
   Susannah has always helped ghosts move along to their next stop, but another mediator, Paul Slater, doesn't feel as kindly about the ghosts, so between the two of them they may be able to nudge along a handsome ghost who seeks revenge against his brother.
(1B. Avid Readers)

————. 2008. *Moving Day*. Allie Finkle's Rules for Girls series, book 1. Scholastic.
Allie lives by rules that she writes in her notebook, adding a new rule anytime it's appropriate, but she is unhappy when she finds her parents are breaking the rule about not moving.
(1R. Tweens)

CABOT, MEG, ET AL. 2007. *Prom Nights from Hell*. HarperCollins.
Scary supernatural tales about the teen rite of passage, offered by authors Meg Cabot, Kim Harrison, Michele Jaffe, Stephenie Meyer, and Lauren Myracle.
(2J. Must-Have Anthologies)

CALAME, DON. 2009. *Swim the Fly*. Candlewick.
After Matt, Sean, and Coop set the unrealistic and totally idiotic summer goal of seeing a naked girl, Matt chooses the even more idiotic goal of swimming the 100-yard butterfly to impress a girl when he can barely tread water.
(3R. Summertime)

CALETTI, DEB. 2004. *Honey, Baby, Sweetheart*. Simon & Schuster.
Troubled that her daughter Ruby is involved with a wealthy, reckless young man, Mrs. McQueen enlists Ruby's help with her book group, the Casserole Queens, who are feisty senior citizens.
(3D. Consequences and Fate)

CAMERON, PETER. 2007. *Someday This Pain Will Be Useful to You*. Farrar, Straus and Giroux.
Peter is unhappy, he doesn't like his peers, wishes he were living in the Midwest instead of New York, tries to find out if he's gay, and only gradually reveals why he's miserable and dislikes people so much.
(1L. Offbeat Guys; 1S. Urban Teens: Beyond Street Lit)

CANALES, VIOLA. 2005. *The Tequila Worm*. Random/Wendy Lamb.
Growing up in her Texas barrio, Sofia thrives on the stories she hears and wants to prove her bravery by eating a worm from the tequila bottle, but when offered a chance to attend boarding school in Austin, she realizes that accepting the offer will take real courage.
(1I. Latina Teens)

CARD, ORSON SCOTT. 1992. *Ender's Game*. Tor.
This classic science fiction tale, given to all non-lovers of science fiction, features young Ender Wiggins, whose prowess at Battle School against the alien Buggers is called into action sooner than he expected.
(1C. Book Haters; 3A. Bathrooms)

CAREY, BENEDICT. 2009. *The Unknowns.* Abrams.
Their math tutor Mrs. Clark is missing and Diaphanta and Tamir search for her, relying on math puzzle clues she's left behind that helps them to draw a map, which leads to secret underground workstations close to a nuclear energy plant. (3L. Mathematics)

CARLE, MEGAN, AND JILL CARLE. 2004. *Teens Cook: How to Cook What You Want to Eat.* Ten Speed. NF.
Translating their unique food tastes to cookbook format, the Carle teens provide a range of recipes from American comfort to ethnic, add tips for cooking, and describe their colossal cooking mistakes, which should empower all teens to try to cook. (3E. Cookery)

———. 2006. *Teens Cook Dessert.* Ten Speed Press. NF.
Intended for novice cooks, this book offers tips for success, stories about the recipes, and both new and family recipes, such as Peach Clafouti, Chocolate Eclairs, Fresh Berry Pie, and other delicious-sounding desserts. (3B. Chocolate)

CARLSON, LORI, ED. 1994. *Cool Salsa: Bilingual Poems on Growing Up Latino in the United States.* Introduction by Oscar Hijuelos. Holt. NF.
Translations and a mix of Spanish and English create the feel of Latino culture with its dolares (dollars) and dolores (pains) of the teen who must merge two cultures yet still have a sense of belonging in a new country. (2P. Poetry Anthologies for Middle School Readers)

———, ED. 2005. *Red Hot Salsa: Bilingual Poems on Being Young and Latino in the United States.* Holt. NF.
In addition to works by such poets as Gary Soto, Luis J. Rodriguez, and Gina Valdes, this book also includes several poems written by New York Public School students that reveal thoughts on family life, language, and identity. (2O. Poetry Anthologies for High School Readers)

CARLSON, MELODY. 2006. *Notes from a Spinning Planet—Ireland.* Random House.
Traveling the Irish countryside with her aunt's godson Ryan, Maddie comes to question what exactly she wants out of life while at the same time helping Ryan piece together the truth about the IRA bombing that killed his father. (3K. Luck)

CARMAN, PATRICK. 2009. *Skeleton Creek.* Scholastic.
Web videos accompany this book in which Ryan tells about his broken leg, Sarah continues to track down clues about ghost sightings in an old mine, and their parents forbid both of them to conduct any more investigations. (2C. Blogs, E-mails, and IMs in Fiction)

CARTER, ALLY. 2007. *Cross My Heart and Hope to Spy.* Hyperion.
Cammie's in training at Gallagher Academy to be a spy, and when boys from the counterpart school, Ethan Frome Academy, come on campus as guests, there's a security breach and Cammie's blamed.
(1B. Avid Readers)

CARTER, DEAN VINCENT. 2006. *The Hand of the Devil.* Delacorte.
Searching for the story of the gigantic mosquito that's able to extract a human body's worth of blood, journalist Ashley Reeves becomes trapped on the island that harbors the mosquito and the mad scientist and serial killer Dr. Mather.
(3H. Insects)

CARVELL, MARLENE. 2002. *Who Will Tell My Brother?* Hyperion.
Continuing the crusade begun by his deceased older brother, part Mohawk Evan asks school authorities to discontinue using the Indian as a school mascot and is met with indifference, threats, and the killing of his dog.
(2Q. Teen Issue Novels in Verse)

————. 2005. *Sweetgrass Basket.* Dutton.
After their mother dies, sisters Mattie and Sarah are sent to the Carlisle Indian School where they struggle to retain their language and remnants of their former lives despite being forbidden to display any signs of their native culture.
(2I. Historical Novels in Verse)

CARY, KATE. 2005. *Bloodline.* Razorbill.
John Shaw, sent home to recover from his World War I war wound, is visited by his commander, Capt. Harker, who falls in love with and becomes engaged to John's sister Lily, but too late John realizes that Harker's battlefield bloodlust may be of the vampiric type.
(2F. Diaries and Epistolary Novels)

CASHORE, KRISTIN. 2008. *Graceling.* Harcourt.
Though her uncle King Rando chooses her to be his henchwoman, Graceling Katsu hates her special talent of killing and maiming and atones for it by establishing a secret council that fights against corruption.
(1A. Adult Readers)

CASSIDY, CATHY. 2006. *Scarlett.* Penguin Putnam.
Scarlett has been kicked out of five schools since her parents' divorce two year ago, and when she's sent from London to rural Ireland to live with her father's new

family it only adds to her anger, but her new stepsister and a mysterious gypsy boy help her adjust.
(3K. Luck)

CAST, P.C., AND KRISTIN CAST. 2007– . House of Night series. St. Martin's Press.
Marked by a vampire, Zoey Redbird is sent to the House of Night boarding school to achieve full vampirism but discovers her special powers make her different from her classmates.
(2M. Paperback Series)

CASTELLUCCI, CECIL. 2005. *Boy Proof.* Candlewick.
Victoria Jurgen answers only to her chosen name of "Egg" and stays aloof from others as she strives to be the eccentric class valedictorian, but new student Max sees past her façade and slowly lures her out of her self-imposed security.
(1G. Graphic Novel Lovers; 1N. Punk Readers)

———. 2007. *Beige.* Candlewick.
Skeptical of spending time with her drummer father and his punk rock band Suck while her mother studies artifacts in Peru, unmusical Katy understands why a young punker calls her "beige" for being so boring.
(1N. Punk Readers)

CHABON, MICHAEL. 2000. *The Amazing Adventures of Kavalier and Clay.* Random House.
After Joseph escapes from the Nazis and makes his way to New York, he teams up with his cousin Sammy to create the Escapist, a comic book superhero.
(1G. Graphic Novel Lovers)

———. 2002. *Summerland.* Hyperion.
New to rainy Clam Island, Washington, Ethan's youth baseball career is sidetracked when an evil being from an alternate world kidnaps his father, forcing Ethan and his teammates to play the game of their lives.
(1G. Graphic Novel Lovers)

———. 2002. *Summerland.* Read by Michael Chabon. HighBridge. Unabridged, 15 hours.
Author and narrator Chabon brings energy to his tale of baseball and alternate worlds, especially in the various characters he portrays whose voices range from gravelly to sad, endearing, and wicked.
(2A. Audiobooks for High School Listeners)

CHALTAS, THALIA. 2009. *Because I Am Furniture.* Viking.
Anke feels as invisible as the family furniture because she's ignored by her father, who beats her brother and rapes her sister, until the day she forces him to look at her after he tried to rape a member of her volleyball team.
(2Q. Teen Issue Novels in Verse).

CHAMBERS, VERONICA. 2001. *Quinceañera Means Sweet Fifteen.* Hyperion.
Marisol returns after spending a year visiting her grandmother in Panama to find her mother can't afford her quinceañera party and her best friend Magdalena has changed.
(1I. Latina Teens)

CHAPPELL, CRISSA-JEAN. 2007. *Total Constant Order.* HarperCollins.
Numbers have always ruled Fin's life, but when she's diagnosed with OCD and given medication to help her cope she finds herself feeling more messed up than ever.
(3A. Bathrooms)

CHBOSKY, STEPHEN. 1999. *The Perks of Being a Wallflower.* Simon & Schuster.
Charlie's letters to an unknown recipient describe his troubled freshman year as he makes friends, lives through an agonizing crush, and deals with the depression that threatens to overwhelm him after the suicide of a friend.
(1Q. Troubled Teen Boys)

CHEN, DA. 2003. *Wandering Warrior.* Random House.
Using the kung fu techniques taught to him by his protector, Atami, Luka defies the Mogo warriors who have invaded his Chinese homeland, rescues his master from a Mogo prison, and fights Clob, a truly monstrous monster.
(1K. Manga Lovers)

CHILDS, TERA LYNN. 2009, ©2008. *Goddess Boot Camp.* Dutton.
Descendent of the Greek goddess Nike, Phoebe is sent to Goddess Boot Camp to learn to control her powers but is unhappy to discover she's older than the other campers and her hateful stepsister is one of the counselors.
(3Q. Summer Camp)

CHMAKOVA, SVETLANA. 2005–2007. Dramacon series. Tokyopop.
Chris is excited to attend her first anime convention and to sell her manga in the artists' alley, but when she meets an unusual cosplayer named Matt, her convention experience takes an unexpected turn.
(2D. Classic Manga)

CHOLDENKO, GENNIFER. 2004. *Al Capone Does My Shirts.* Putnam.
When his father lands a job as an electrician at the prison in 1935, Moose's entire family moves to Alcatraz Island where he watches over his autistic older sister, whose odd behavior sometimes lands him in embarrassing situations.
(1E. Gentlemanly Boys)

————. 2004. *Al Capone Does My Shirts.* Read by Johnny Heller. Recorded Books. Unabridged, 5 hours, 45 minutes.
Living on Alcatraz with his autistic sister alternately frustrates and angers Moose, moods that are conveyed by Heller's narration as he provides distinct voices for both major and minor characters.
(2B. Audiobooks for Middle School Listeners)

CIRRONE, DORIAN. 2006. *Dancing in Red Shoes Will Kill You.* HarperCollins.
Sisters Kayla and Paterson both attend an arts high school where each runs into trouble, Kayla when her extra large breasts prevent her from getting a part she wishes to dance in a ballet and Paterson when her senior art project is deemed obscene.
(3P. State Books)

CLAMP. 2004. Tsubasa: RESERVoir CHRoNiCLE series. Random House.
Princess Sakura is about to confess her love to Syaoran as he works on an archaeological dig, but when a mystical symbol they uncover steals her memories and scatters them across worlds Syaoran sets off on a quest to find them and save Sakura.
(2D. Classic Manga)

CLARK, CATHERINE. 2001. *Wurst Case Scenario.* HarperCollins.
Courtney wonders whether the financial support she receives is worth attending a college in rural Wisconsin when she's a vegan and everyone else eats meat and potatoes and her roommate's up with the chickens while Courtney's still snoozing.
(1B. Avid Readers)

CLEMENTS, ANDREW. 2001. *Things Not Seen.* Penguin Putnam.
Alicia, a blind 15-year-old girl whom Bobby meets at the library, becomes his only friend after he wakes up one morning to find he's invisible.
(1E. Gentlemanly Boys)

CLINTON, CATHERINE, ED. 2003. *A Poem of Her Own: Voices of American Women Yesterday and Today.* Illustrated by Stephen Alcorn. Abrams. NF.
From Anne Bradstreet's 1678 poem "The Author to Her Book" to contemporary works by Julia Alvarez and Naomi Shihab Nye, the voices of 25 women offer poems of their lives that in turn parallel the story of America.
(2P. Poetry Anthologies for Middle School Readers)

CLUGSTON-MAJORS, CHYNNA. 2000–2004. Blue Monday series. Oni Press.
Bleu has to deal with parents who don't understand, boys with no sense of appropriate humor, and a substitute teacher who somehow can't see that she is his perfect match.
(2E. Core Graphic Novels)

COFER, JUDITH ORTIZ. 2003. *The Meaning of Consuelo.* Farrar, Straus and Giroux.
Puerto Rican Consuelo tries to figure out her place in a family where her father looks to the future, her mother lives in the past, and her younger sister shows signs of mental illness.
(1I. Latina Teens)

―――. 2006. *Call Me Maria.* Scholastic.
Born in Puerto Rico where her mother remains, but living in the barrio in New York City with her father who's the super of their apartment building, Maria tries to fit into the American lifestyle of her new home.
(1I. Latina Teens; 3S. Teen Immigrants)

COHN, RACHEL. 2002. *Gingerbread.* Simon & Schuster.
Considered out of control after being expelled from boarding school, Cyd Charisse is sent to live with her biological father in New York City, where her missteps help her learn what family is all about.
(1D. Detention Home Girls)

―――. 2008. *You Know Where to Find Me.* Simon & Schuster.
Having always coveted her cousin Laura's perfect life, until Laura commits suicide, Miles, shocked by Laura's death, turns to drugs, but after overdosing and almost dying herself, she's forced to confront her problems and accept help.
(3P. State Books)

COHN, RACHEL, AND DAVID LEVITHAN. 2006. *Nick & Norah's Infinite Playlist.* Knopf.
Nick, straight bassist in a queer-punk band, and Norah, who's been raised on music, meet one night at a New York club and pretend to be a couple for a five-minute scene, but the five minutes continues on through morning as each takes a chance on a new romance.
(1C. Book Haters; 1S. Urban Teens: Beyond Street Lit; 2R. Two or More Voices in Novels; 3A. Bathrooms; 3P. State Books)

COLE, BROCK. 1990. *The Goats.* Farrar, Straus and Giroux.
Immediately pegged as misfits, Howie and Laura's camp experience becomes a nightmare when they are stripped and abandoned on an isolated island, a cruel act

that helps them muster their strength, leave the island, and vow to never again be victims.
(3Q. Summer Camp)

COLFER, EOIN. 2001. *Artemis Fowl.* Hyperion.
Attempting to restore some of his criminal family's fortunes, Artemis kidnaps Holly for her fairy gold, but because she's a member of the Lower Elements Police, dwarfs, trolls, satyrs, and other fairies soon search for her.
(3K. Luck)

————. 2001– . Artemis Fowl series. Hyperion.
Artemis Fowl is a genius with unlimited wealth and no conscience to speak of, but his kidnapping of fairy Captain Holly Short sets off a chain of events that will change everything.
(1O. Reluctant Male Readers)

————. 2003. *Wish List.*
When a gas tank explodes, killing Meg and her partners in crime Belch and the pit bull Raptor, only Meg is judged to have some good in her, so she's returned to Earth to help terminally ill Lowrie attain what's on his wish list, including revenge on a bully.
(3K. Luck)

————. 2004. *Artemis Fowl.* Read by Nathaniel Parker. Listening Library. Unabridged, 6 hours.
Artemis makes a poor decision in his choice of a kidnapping victim, but narrator Parker brings humor to this fast-paced fantasy with his British and Irish accents that maintain the book's fast pace.
(2B. Audiobooks for Middle School Listeners)

COLLARD, SNEED B., III. 2006. *Flash Point.* Peachtree.
Ironically Luther and new student Alex, who have both spoken out about the proper management of forests, now face an encroaching forest fire that threatens to destroy the birds of prey they tend for the local vet.
(3F. The Environment; 3N. Science)

COLLINS, SUZANNE. 2003. *Gregor the Overlander.* Scholastic.
When his two-year-old sister Boots falls down an air duct, Gregor follows, and they land in an underground world of giant talking cockroaches, spiders, behemoth rats, and huge bats that are used to transport humans.
(1F. Gifted Elementary Student Readers; 3H. Insects)

————. 2008. *The Hunger Games*. Scholastic.
Katniss volunteers to represent her district in the 74th Hunger Games, a gladiator-type competition that brings honor to the districts but forces teens to train and make alliances while they strive to permanently eliminate one another in the arena.
(1O. Reluctant Male Readers; 3A. Bathrooms)

COLLINS, YVONNE. 2005. *Introducing Vivian Leigh Reid: Daughter of the Diva*. St. Martin's.
Leigh is sent to Ireland to repair her relationship with her movie star mother, but what she finds is a bit part, a broken heart, new love, and a tattoo.
(3K. Luck)

CONNOR, LESLIE. 2008. *Waiting for Normal*. HarperCollins/Katherine Tegen.
Staying with her mother after "the littles" are removed to live upstate with her stepfather, Addie gains more and more backbone as her mother's neglect increases.
(3O. Silence)

COONEY, CAROLINE B. 2005. *Code Orange*. Delacorte.
Procrastinating on his biology project about infectious diseases, Mitty finds an envelope in an old textbook and inadvertently exposes himself to smallpox scabs from 1902, which makes him a prime candidate for kidnapping by a bioterrorist group who wants the virus.
(3N. Science)

CORMIER, ROBERT. 1974. *The Chocolate War*. Knopf.
When freshman Jerry Renault balks at selling boxes of chocolate as a school fundraiser, he little realizes the ramifications of being a nonconformist in a school run by a group of bullies called the Vigils.
(3B. Chocolate)

————. 1999. *Frenchtown Summer*. Delacorte.
Twelve-year-old Eugene observes everything and everybody around him in Frenchtown and then tells about the woman who ponders suicide, the priest who oversees confessions, the back alleys of his town, and the mystery surrounding his Uncle Med.
(2I. Historical Novels in Verse)

————. 2001. *The Rag and Bone Shop*. Random House.
In an effort to extract an admission of guilt, professional interrogator Trent presses 12-year-old Jason to confess to the horrific murder of a little girl, even though it's clear that Jason is innocent.
(1Q. Troubled Teen Boys)

COULOUMBIS, AUDREY. 1999. *Getting Near to Baby*. Penguin Putnam.
Willa Jo Dean and silent Little Sister spend the day on the roof of Aunt Patty's house, where they've been sent following the accidental death of Baby.
(3O. Silence)

COUSINS, STEVEN. 2000. *Frankenbug*. Holiday House.
Adam Cricklestein wants revenge against another student, so he combines various bug parts to create the monster insect Frankenbug, brings it to life with lightning bugs, and sends it out to attack.
(3H. Insects)

COWAN, JENNIFER. 2009. *Earthgirl*. Groundwood.
A woman tosses trash out her car window and a friend of Sabine's captures her environmentally correct reaction and posts it on YouTube, inspiring Sabine to transform from blogger to eco-warrior.
(3F. The Environment)

CREECH, SHARON. 1997. *Absolutely Normal Chaos*. HarperCollins.
Required to keep a journal over the summer, Mary Lou tells of her quiet cousin Carl Ray who stays with them, gets a job, and then is left a small inheritance, all of which puzzles her, but not for long as she and her best friend Beth Ann are busy discovering boys.
(3P. State Books)

———. 2001. *Love That Dog*. HarperCollins.
Jack resists his teacher's writing assignment, but after reading some poetry and being introduced to Walter Dean Myers's poem "Love That Boy," Jack writes his own poem and then invites author Myers to visit his class.
(1P. Striving Readers)

———. 2003. *Granny Torrelli Makes Soup*. HarperCollins.
When Rosie makes soup with her Granny Torrelli, they talk about her blind best friend Bailey, and Rosie begins to understand how Bailey's blindness is changing him and what she can do to remain friends with him.
(3E. Cookery)

CRILLEY, MARK. 1995–2002. Akiko series. Sirius Entertainment.
Ten-year-old Akiko is unprepared when she's whisked away to the Planet Smoo one night at the request of the King, who has chosen her to help rescue Prince Froptoppit.
(2E. Core Graphic Novels)

CROWE, CHRIS. 2002. *Mississippi Trial, 1955*. Penguin Putnam.
Hiram, returning home to visit his aging grandfather, meets young Emmett Till and renews his childhood friendship with R.C., now something of a neighborhood bully. When Emmett is murdered Hiram suspects R.C., but the truth turns out to be worse.
(3C. The Civil Rights Movement)

————. 2003. *Getting Away with Murder: The True Story of the Emmett Till Case.* NF.
In 1955 Mississippi, Emmett Till is visiting family when, to show off to friends, he whistles at a white woman and is later seized from his great-uncle's home and brutally beaten to death in an act that stirs up the civil rights movement.
(3C. The Civil Rights Movement; 3P. State Books)

CRUTCHER, CHRIS. 1993. *Staying Fat for Sarah Byrnes*. Random House.
Eric, whose weight makes him an outcast, found a friend in Sarah, disfigured by a childhood accident, so when she abruptly stops speaking and is committed to an institution he insists on helping her, no matter the cost.
(3A. Bathrooms; 3O. Silence)

————. 2001. *Whale Talk*. Greenwillow.
Adopted, mixed-race Tao, nicknamed TJ, begins his senior year and agrees to finally take part in organized sports when his favorite English teacher begs him to start a swim team.
(1D. Detention Home Girls; 1Q. Troubled Teen Boys; 3D. Consequences and Fate)

————. 2005. *The Sledding Hill.* Greenwillow.
Grieving over the deaths of his father and best friend Billy, Eddie's supported by Billy's ghost when he opposes the school board's plans to ban a book by author Chris Crutcher.
(3O. Silence; 3T. Wintertime)

————. 2007. *Deadline.* HarperTeen.
Told he has only one year to live, Ben tells no one and refuses treatment, as he wants to enjoy his last year, play football with his brother, and date gorgeous Dallas, but the day arrives when he needs to share his illness with his brother.
(1L. Offbeat Guys; 3P. State Books)

CUMMINGS, PRISCILLA. 2004. *Red Kayak*. Penguin Putnam.
After a nasty prank orchestrated by his friends takes a deadly turn, Brady must decide whether keeping silent and letting the crime go unpunished or coming forward and implicating himself and his friends is the right thing to do.
(3P. State Books)

CURTIS, CHRISTOPHER PAUL. 1995. *The Watsons Go to Birmingham—1963*. Random House.

After Byron gets into trouble one too many times, his parents decide to ship him off to his grandmother in Mississippi, so they plan a family trip to Birmingham to drop him off but end up stumbling into a tragic church bombing that changes all their lives. (3C. The Civil Rights Movement)

————. 1999. *Bud, Not Buddy*. Random House.

Fed up with his life in a series of foster homes, ten-year-old Bud runs away to find the man he believes to be his father, a jazz musician who, it turns out, is less than happy to meet him. (1O. Reluctant Male Readers)

————. 2004. *Bucking the Sarge*. Random House.

"The Sarge" runs a network of slums and halfway houses in Flint, Michigan, and Luther, her son, longs to leave her ruthless and cynical grasp, and although he works hard for her, he dreams of college and escape. (1Q. Troubled Teen Boys; 1S. Urban Teens: Beyond Street Lit; 3P. State Books)

————. 2007. *Elijah of Buxton*. Scholastic.

Because he's the first child to be born free in the Canadian settlement of Buxton, Elijah doesn't know what it's like to be enslaved, but he senses the anguish of a friend when the money he has set aside to buy his family's freedom is stolen. (1E. Gentlemanly Boys)

————. 2008. *Elijah of Buxton*. Read by Mirron Willis. Listening Library. Unabridged, 9 hours.

Narrator Willis's rich reading reflects the initial childlike innocence of young Elijah, as he plays a prank on his mother or spends time with his friends, but Elijah grows in strength as he witnesses the reality of slavery in this masterful reading. (2B. Audiobooks for Middle School Listeners)

CUSHMAN, KAREN. 1994. *Catherine, Called Birdy*. Clarion.

Catherine is happiest, or so she tells her journal, when the fleas aren't biting her, her father isn't trying to arrange yet another marriage to an old, doddering man, and she and pig boy Perkin can escape to the countryside. (2F. Diaries and Epistolary Novels)

————. 2006. *The Loud Silence of Francine Green*. Houghton Mifflin.

Francine stays quiet and keeps out of trouble until she meets her new classmate Sophie, who stands up to the nuns at school, believes in questioning authority, and doesn't mind stirring up controversy. (3O. Silence)

D

DAHL, ROALD. 2005. *Vile Verses.* Viking. NF.
Illustrated by a variety of artists, including Chris Wormell and Babette Cole, these deliciously wicked and nasty verses by Dahl will either scare you or amuse you.
(2P. Poetry Anthologies for Middle School Readers)

DALKEY, KARA. 1996. *Little Sister.* Houghton Mifflin.
Mitsuko, a member of the Japanese royal court, embarks on a desperate quest to locate her sister's soul, accompanied by a shape-shifting demon.
(1K. Manga Lovers)

D'ANTONIO, MICHAEL. 2006. *Hershey: Milton S. Hershey's Extraordinary Life of Wealth, Empire, and Utopian Dreams.* Simon & Schuster. NF.
The man who gave Americans the nickel candy bar built a factory in Pennsylvania before he'd ever made the first batch of milk chocolate and grew his organization into a town that continues today.
(3B. Chocolate)

DASHNER, JAMES. 2009. *The Maze Runner.* Random House.
When Thomas arrives in the Glade he has no memory of his previous life and joins the other boys in their attempt to solve the deadly maze in which they seem to be imprisoned.
(1O. Reluctant Male Readers)

DAU, JOHN BUL. 2007. *God Grew Tired of Us: A Memoir.* National Geographic. NF.
John Bul Dau was only 13 when he was separated from his family during the civil war in Southern Sudan, and it would be 19 years, many spent in refugee camps in Ethiopia and Kenya, before he reunited with them.
(3S. Teen Immigrants)

DAVIDSON, DANA. 2004. *Jason & Kyra.* Hyperion.
No one at school understands when handsome, popular Jason falls hard for quiet, brainy Kyra, but the romance that develops between them blossoms despite the disapproval of their classmates and the anger of Jason's ex-girlfriend.
(1S. Urban Teens: Beyond Street Lit)

————. 2005. *Played.* Hyperion.
Ian is uneasy when he learns that the final test for membership in his school fraternity is to make plain Kylie fall in love and sleep with him, but he pursues her anyway, with inevitably disastrous results.
(1S. Urban Teens: Beyond Street Lit)

DAVIDSON, DIANE MOTT. 1992. *Dying for Chocolate.* Bantam.
Accepting a job as personal chef to General Bo Farquhar, a retired munitions expert, Goldy and her son move into his mansion, but she continues her Goldilocks catering service, juggles two suitors, and avoids her abusive ex-husband.
(3B. Chocolate)

DAVIS, TANITA S. 2008. *A la Carte.* Knopf.
Lainey's dream is to be the first vegetarian African American chef, and she concocts delicious recipes that she enters in contests while awaiting the culinary school decision.
(3E. Cookery)

DE LA CRUZ, MELISSA. 2005. *Fresh Off the Boat.* HarperCollins.
Vicenza and her family are recent arrivals from the Philippines, and life is thoroughly different now that they live in San Francisco.
(3S. Teen Immigrants)

DE LA PEÑA, MATT. 2005. *Ball Don't Lie.* Delacorte.
After his mother's suicide, Sticky bounces from one foster home to another and only seems secure when he's hanging out at the basketball court where his ability guarantees him street cred.
(1O. Reluctant Male Readers)

————. 2008. *Mexican Whiteboy.* Delacorte.
Half-white and half-Mexican, Danny Lopez doesn't feel that he fits in anywhere until he spends a summer with the Mexican side of his family, and his cousins and a new friend make him feel more comfortable with his mixed heritage.
(1J. Latino Teens)

————. 2009. *We Were Here.* Delacorte.
Sentenced to a group home for a year and required to keep a journal, Miguel and two other inmates escape and head to Mexico, a trip Miguel records in his journal as they steal, hide, and care for one another.
(1J. Latino Teens)

DE LINT, CHARLES. 2004. *The Blue Girl.* Viking.
New in school and instantly pegged as an outcast, Imogene becomes friends with Maxine and Ghost, a former student who was pushed off the school roof, and the three unite for protection from the social cliques and some evil fairies that flit around Ghost.
(1N. Punk Readers; 2R. Two or More Voices in Novels)

DECKER, TIMOTHY. 2007. *Run Far, Run Fast*. Boyds Mill Press.
Fleeing the Pestilence that has devastated her town, a young girl in fourteenth-century Europe travels a countryside ravaged by disease, searching for shelter and hope for the future.
(2N. Picture Books for Teens)

DELISLE, GUY. 2005. *Pyongyang: A Journey in North Korea*. Drawn and Quarterly. NF.
Delisle spent two months working in North Korea, accompanied at all times by an official guide and an official translator, and the surprising, enlightening vignettes he shares reflect the strangeness of his experience.
(2K. Nonfiction Graphic Novels)

————. 2008. *The Burma Chronicles*. Drawn and Quarterly. NF.
Delisle's portrait of daily life in Myanmar uses small details and simple drawings to illuminate a society where repression is the norm but where family life and tradition continue to thrive.
(2K. Nonfiction Graphic Novels)

DELLASEGA, CHERYL. 2009. *sistrsic92 (Meg)*. Illustrated by Tyler Beauford. Marshall Cavendish.
Meg starts a blog she shares with friends in which she admits her resentment of her perfect sister, but when Cara's found to have an eating disorder, Meg must work out her feelings about her sister.
(2C. Blogs, E-mails, and IMs in Fiction)

DENG, BENSON, ET AL. 2005. *They Poured Fire on Us from the Sky: The True Story of Three Lost Boys from Sudan*. Perseus Books Group. NF.
Benson and Alepho Deng and their cousin Benjamin all left home as small children, victims of the Sudanese civil war that tore their country apart, and moved from a refugee camp to the United States in 2001, where they began documenting their experiences.
(3S. Teen Immigrants)

DESSEN, SARAH. 1996. *That Summer*. Orchard.
As Haven reflects on "that summer" when she was tall and gawky, it seems amazing that she survived her sister's wedding and her sportscaster father's second marriage to the television station's "Weather Pet."
(1M. Picky Senior Girls; 3R. Summertime)

————. 1998. *Someone Like You*. Penguin Putnam.
> Though Halley has always been close to her mother, she finds herself turning to her best friend Scarlett when the confusion of growing up starts to overwhelm them both.
(3D. Consequences and Fate)

————. 2000. *Dreamland*. Penguin Putnam.
> After her sister Cass runs away, Caitlin holds fast to the people she still has left, even her physically abusive boyfriend Rogerson.
(3I. Institutions)

————. 2002. *This Lullaby*. Penguin Putnam.
> Remy is a serial dater who doesn't believe in lasting love—with good reason—but when her summer fling, Dexter, refuses to leave on schedule, Remy is forced to re-evaluate her assumptions.
(1D. Detention Home Girls)

————. 2004. *The Truth about Forever*. Viking.
> Feeling guilty that her father dies alone while jogging, Macy joins the chaotic Wish Catering staff and meets Wes, with whom she's able to talk and laugh, which helps her realize that her brilliant boyfriend is a self-centered loser.
(1A. Adult Readers; 3E. Cookery)

————. 2006. *Just Listen*. Viking.
> Shunned because of an undescribed incident, Annabel eats lunch by herself and meets Owen, a social outcast who loves music and has his own radio program.
(3O. Silence)

————. 2006. *Just Listen*. Read by Jennifer Ikeda. Recorded Books. Unabridged, 12 hours.
> After an upsetting incident with her friend's boyfriend, Annabel tries to return to normalcy as Ikeda's voice illustrates Annabel's growing self-confidence, in contrast to the whispery tones of her predator.
(2A. Audiobooks for High School Listeners)

DICAMILLO, KATE. 2003. *The Tale of Despereaux: Being the Story of a Mouse, a Princess, Some Soup, and a Spool of Thread*. Candlewick.
> Different from even his own family, the young mouse Despereaux is sent to the dungeon where he meets the rat Chiaroscuro, who wants to find his way to the light, a wish that Despereaux understands and leads to his falling in love with Princess Pea.
(1F. Gifted Elementary Student Readers)

————. 2003. *The Tale of Despereaux: Being the Story of a Mouse, a Princess, Some Soup, and a Spool of Thread*. Read by Graeme Malcolm. Listening Library. Unabridged, 3 hours, 30 minutes.

Narrator Malcolm's British accent creates visions of castles in this perfect fairy tale of a mouse in love with a princess, while his warm, rich voice also depicts a pompous king, a gruff laborer, and a kind princess.

(2B. Audiobooks for Middle School Listeners)

DICKINSON, PETER. 1989. *Eva*. Delacorte.

Eva awakens following an accident to discover her brain has been implanted into the body of a female chimpanzee, which saves Eva's thoughts but leaves her with the chimp's behavioral instincts and removes her from the human world.

(3N. Science)

DIONNE, ERIN. 2009. *Models Don't Eat Chocolate Cookies*. Dial.

Angered when an interfering aunt enters her in the Miss Husky Peach Contest, Celeste vows to lose enough weight by exercising and skipping desserts to be ineligible, but her plan fails, she becomes a contestant, and even considers modeling.

(3B. Chocolate)

DIVINE, L. 2006– . Drama High series. Kensington Publishing Group.

Jayd Jackson learns to navigate her Los Angeles high school, despite racial tensions, backstabbing best friends, and ugly breakups, by relying on her steady network of family and neighbors back in Compton.

(1S. Urban Teens: Beyond Street Lit)

D'LACEY, CHRIS, AND LINDA NEWBERY. 2001. *From E to You*. Pocket/Archway.

At their fathers' urging, two British teens become e-mail pen pals and, though reticent at first, gradually share details of their frustrations, romantic relationships, and grief at the loss of a mother by one and a cat by the other.

(2C. Blogs, E-mails, and IMs in Fiction)

DOCTOROW, CORY. 2008. *Little Brother*. Tor.

After interrogation following a Department of Homeland Security sweep, Marcus is released and, now determined to halt the government's invasion of personal privacy, calls on all his computer hacker friends for help.

(3A. Bathrooms; 3N. Science)

DONNELLY, JENNIFER. 2003. *A Northern Light*. Harcourt.

While deciding whether to stay home and marry or attend college, Mattie takes a summer job at the Glenmore Hotel on Big Moose Lake where a chance meeting

with a female guest who's later killed helps Mattie decide the path her life should take.
(1M. Picky Senior Girls)

DONOVAN, JENNIFER. 2008. *The Big Book of Chocolate: 365 Decadent and Irresistible Treats.* Duncan Baird. NF.
   With no more than five steps for each recipe, and a new treat for every day of the year, beginning cooks will soon be fixing cheesecakes, ices, cookies, crepes, cakes, pies, or special drinks.
(3B. Chocolate)

DOWD, SIOBHAN. 2007. *A Pure Swift Cry.* Random House.
   After her mother dies, Shell's life revolves around caring for her younger brother and sister, left to their own devices by their absent, alcoholic father, but when her short-lived liaison with a local boy has unintended consequences it's Shell who needs help.
(3K. Luck)

———. 2008. *Bog Child.* Random House.
   The love between Fergus, caught up in the Troubles of 1980s Northern Ireland, and Cora, daughter of an archaeologist, unfolds against the complementary tale of Mel, whose sacrifice led to Fergus's discovery of her body in a bog 2,000 years later.
(3K. Luck)

DOYLE, LARRY. 2007. *I Love You, Beth Cooper.* Ecco.
   Stunning the graduates with his valedictory speech that lists the faults of every senior, he slips in "I love you, Beth Cooper" before the principal snatches away the microphone, and then Beth Cooper and her friends take him out for a night on the town he'll never forget.
(1L. Offbeat Guys)

DOYLE, MALACHY. 2001. *Georgie.* Bloomsbury.
   Georgie spends his days silent and alone, until he's transferred from the institution that has been his home for seven years to a new residence where he meets Shannon, another damaged soul, and Tommo, a teacher with a gift for reaching out.
(3I. Institutions)

DRAPER, SHARON. 1994. *Tears of a Tiger.* Simon & Schuster.
   After Andy's reckless decision to drive drunk kills his best friend, he is unable to cope with his guilt, and his despair leads him to see only one inevitable solution.
(1Q. Troubled Teen Boys)

————. 1999. *Romiette and Julio.* Simon & Schuster/Atheneum.
Meeting in an Internet chat room, African American Romiette and Hispanic Julio discover they attend the same high school and, when they meet, know they're destined to be a contemporary Romeo and Juliet, though others object to their interracial dating.
(1D. Detention Home Girls; 1S. Urban Teens: Beyond Street Lit; 2C. Blogs, E-mails, and IMs in Fiction)

————. 2001. *Darkness Before Dawn.* Simon & Schuster.
Keisha is still reeling from the suicide of her ex-boyfriend and the death of a friend in a summer car accident so when the new young track coach asks her out she accepts his advances, despite their age difference.
(1D. Detention Home Girls)

————. 2007. *Fire from the Rock.* Penguin Putnam.
Honor student Sylvia Patterson is proud to be chosen as one of the first black students to attend Central High School in Little Rock, but the racism she faces is so terrifying she's not certain it's worth it.
(3C. The Civil Rights Movement; 3P. State Books)

————. 2007. *November Blues.* Atheneum.
Pregnant and still grieving for her boyfriend Josh, who died in a fraternity hazing accident, November concentrates on preparing for the birth of her child instead of planning for her first year at Cornell.
(3A. Bathrooms)

DU MAURIER, DAPHNE. 1938. *Rebecca.* Doubleday.
The second Mrs. DeWinter arrives at the estate called Manderly and meets deceitful Mrs. Danvers, the housekeeper who adored first wife Rebecca, and endures the silences of her husband as she slowly learns the truth about Rebecca in this well-loved classic.
(1B. Avid Readers)

DUANE, DIANE. 1997. *A Wizard Abroad.* Houghton Mifflin.
When Nita's parents send her off for an Irish holiday they hope she'll take a break from her wizardry, but, as it turns out, Ireland is hardly the place to expect a shortage of magic.
(3K. Luck)

DUEY, KATHLEEN. 2007. *Skin Hunger*. Simon & Schuster.
In a world where magic has been outlawed, Sadima keeps house for two rebellious magicians, little knowing the connection she has to a boy wizard born many years later.
(3O. Silence)

DUMAS, FIROOZEH. 2002. *Funny in Farsi: A Memoir of Growing Up Iranian in America*. Random House. NF.
Dumas was seven when she arrived in the United States with her family, and in a series of telling vignettes she recounts her father's obsession with Disneyland, the change in perception the family faces after the Iran hostage crisis, and her troubles with language.
(3S. Teen Immigrants)

DURBIN, WILLIAM. 1999. *Wintering*. Delacorte.
After his first voyage carrying furs by canoe and on foot around the Great Lakes, Pierre toughens up enough that he signs up again, only this time he agrees to stay all winter.
(3T. Wintertime)

E

EASTON, KELLY. 2006. *Aftershock*. Simon & Schuster.
Unable to talk after he wanders away from the car accident that kills his parents, Adam stumbles into a variety of jobs and meets a motley assortment of people during his memory-fueled, cross-country trek to return home to Rhode Island.
(3O. Silence)

EHRENHAFT, DANIEL. 2006. *Drawing a Blank: Or, How I Tried to Solve a Mystery, End a Feud, and Land the Girl of My Dreams*. Illustrated by Trevor Ristow. HarperTeen.
Artist of a cartoon strip that features Signy, a buxom, kilted heroine, Carlton receives a call that his father's held captive on the Orkney Islands, so he flies to Scotland to search for him, accepting help from a girl who resembles his Signy heroine.
(1G. Graphic Novel Lovers)

EISNER, WILL. 2003. *Fagin the Jew*. Random House.
Fagin, of *Oliver Twist* fame, is given a solid backstory—a childhood spent in London's Ashkenazi community, a hopeless romance, years as an indentured servant—that explains not only his literary character but also the historical context in which he was created.
(2H. Graphic Novels in the Classroom)

ELKELES, SIMONE. 2006. *How to Ruin a Summer Vacation*. Llewellyn.
Amy accepts her biological father's invitation to accompany him to Israel to meet his ailing mother, not realizing that no one in his family knows she exists.
(3R. Summertime)

ELLIOT, JESSIE. 2005. *Girls Dinner Club*. HarperCollins.
Celia, Danielle, and Junie meet one night to fix dinner and visit, which leads to regular meetings of the "girls dinner club" when they prepare different recipes while helping one another through boy troubles and family issues.
(3E. Cookery)

ELLIOTT, L.M. 2006. *Give Me Liberty*. Scholastic.
An indentured servant in Williamsburg, Virginia, 13-year-old Nathaniel feels himself being swept up in the political turmoil of 1774, but he is torn between the differing ideals espoused by his friend, a fellow servant, and his master.
(3P. State Books)

ELLIS, ANN DEE. 2007. *This Is What I Did*. Hachette.
After witnessing a violent encounter between his friend Zyler and Zyler's abusive father, Logan finds it difficult to process his experience, but a sensitive school counselor, a girl named Laurel, and a part in the school play help him reconnect with Zyler.
(3O. Silence)

ELLIS, DEBORAH. 2001. *The Breadwinner*. Groundwood Books.
After the Taliban take over her country, 11-year-old Afghani Parvana is forced to stay indoors at all times, until the day her father is imprisoned and she realizes it's up to her to support her family, even if that means pretending to be a boy.
(3M. The Middle East)

———. 2002. *Parvana's Journey*. Groundwood Books.
Disguised as a boy and accompanied by a baby, 13-year-old Parvana searches war-torn Afghanistan for her mother and siblings, all of whom are missing in the aftermath of the Taliban takeover.
(3M. The Middle East)

ENGLE, MARGARITA. 2006. *The Poet Slave of Cuba: A Biography of Juan Francisco Manzano*. Holt. NF.
Born into slavery in Cuba in 1797, Juan's original mistress dies and his promised freedom is ignored, so he remains in servitude to an unstable mistress, yet his love of poetic verse is never quenched.
(2G. Fictionalized Biographies)

ENZENSBERGER, HANS MAGNUS. 1998. *The Number Devil: A Mathematical Adventure.* Holt.
> Robert's dislike of math changes after nightly dream visits by Number Devil, who introduces him to famous mathematicians and stresses the importance of zero, prime numbers, and even Fibonacci sequences.
(3L. Mathematics)

ESQUIVEL, LAURA. 1992. *Like Water for Chocolate: A Novel in Monthly Installments with Recipes, Romances, and Home Remedies.* Doubleday.
> Tita, a youngest daughter who's doomed to a life of caring for her mother instead of her suitor, turns her energies to cooking and records the spices and delicacies of her life.
(3B. Chocolate)

EVANS, KATE. 2007. *Weird Weather: Everything You Didn't Want to Know about Climate Change, but Probably Should Find Out.* Groundwood. NF.
> A "fat cat" businessman, an eager teen, and a crazed scientist explore the problems of climate change, its current effects, and what is or isn't being done to stop the problem; suggestions for further reading and climate change organizations to contact are provided.
(3F. The Environment)

EWING, LYNNE. 1998. *Drive-By.* HarperCollins.
> When Tito's drug dealing brother is killed, the gang turns to Tito, expecting him to have the money his brother was skimming from their drug deals.
(1P. Striving Readers)

———. 1998. *Party Girl.* Knopf.
> Ana has been beside Kata through all the important parts of her life—when they joined a gang together and as partners in dance competitions—but now Ana's been killed by a rival gang, and Kata can't decide whether to seek vengeance or escape gang life.
(1I. Latina Teens)

———. 2000. *Goddess of the Night,* Daughters of the Moon, book 1. Hyperion.
> Catty discovers she can time travel, Vanessa becomes invisible, and Serena reads minds, all exhibiting a power that makes them Daughters of the Moon and requires them to fight evil.
(1B. Avid Readers)

F

FARLEY, STEVEN. 2008. *The Black Stallion and the Shape-Shifter.* Random House.
While Black recovers in Ireland from a racing injury, he and Alex Ramsey meet Mora, a young girl who wants to learn to ride, but she disappears and the villagers claim she's been taken by a kelpie.
(3G. Horses)

FARMER, NANCY. 1996. *A Girl Named Disaster.* Scholastic.
Eleven-year-old Nhamo runs away from her village in Mozambique after she is forced into an unwanted marriage, and while traveling to her father's family she spends time with a baboon family, lives with scientists, and communes with spirits.
(1D. Detention Home Girls)

————. 2002. *The House of the Scorpion.* Atheneum.
Matt wonders why he's kept isolated until he discovers he's the only living clone of a 142-year-old drug lord, El Patron, and the other clones are used as spare parts for the aging man.
(1A. Adult Readers; 1E. Gentlemanly Boys; 3N. Science)

FERBER, BRENDA. 2006. *Julia's Kitchen.* Farrar, Straus and Giroux.
Trying to ease her grief after her mother and sister die in a house fire, Cara resurrects Julia's Kitchen, her mother's cookie business.
(3E. Cookery)

FERRIS, JEAN. 1998. *Bad.* Farrar, Straus and Giroux.
After she holds up a convenience store, Dallas is sent to a juvenile detention center and finds not only other troubled girls but also the attention and care she's craved all her life.
(1D. Detention Home Girls; 3I. Institutions)

————. 2002. *Once Upon a Marigold.* Houghton Mifflin.
Christian and Marigold have been friends for years but they've never met and Chris has no intention of introducing himself when he goes to work in the castle—she's the princess after all—but when he learns of a plot to have her killed, he can't sit on the sidelines.
(1H. Innocent Middle School Girls)

FFORDE, JASPER. 2002. *The Eyre Affair.* Viking.
　　In alternate Britain, literature is trendy, which makes it ripe for crime and sends literary detective Thursday Next to stop Acheron Hades, who has stolen the original *Martin Chuzzlewit* manuscript and next plans to steal Jane Eyre off the pages of her book.
(1M. Picky Senior Girls)

―――. 2002. *The Eyre Affair.* Read by Elizabeth Sastre. HighBridge. Slightly abridged, 10 hours.
　　In the frenetic literary world of alternate Britain, Sastre's youthful voice easily reads the straight narrative as well as voices the varied, and often bizarre, characters in this work.
(2A. Audiobooks for High School Listeners)

FIELDS, TERRI. 2002. *After the Death of Anna Gonzales.* Holt.
　　More than 40 poems reveal the effect of the news at school that one of their classmates, Anna, has committed suicide, as classmates, friends, and strangers describe their feelings and their sense of loss.
(1P. Striving Readers; 2Q. Teen Issue Novels in Verse)

FIENBERG, ANNA. 2007. *Number 8.* Walker.
　　Jackson is obsessed with numbers, but only even numbers, so the sight of a car with "777" on its license plate strikes a foreboding note with him and may explain why he and his mother moved away from the city.
(3L. Mathematics)

FISHER, CATHERINE. 2004. *Snow-walker.* Greenwillow.
　　Based on Norse mythology, Gudrun is a Snow-walker who seizes control over the Jarlshold, but she is eventually confronted by her exiled son and members of the former ruling family as they wrest power from her.
(3T. Wintertime)

FITCH, SHEREE. 2006. *If I Had a Million Onions.* Illustrated by Yayo. Tradewind. NF.
　　Colored-pencil sketches by Yayo enliven these 25 poems that cover everyday events, such as returning a library book on time, riding bumper cars, and having clean fingernails and underwear.
(2P. Poetry Anthologies for Middle School Readers)

FLAKE, SHARON. 1998. *The Skin I'm In.* Hyperion.
　　Maleeka Madison is smart and talented, and the new teacher wants her to live up to her potential, but Maleeka might be too busy caring for her depressed mother and worrying about her nonexistent social standing.
(1D. Detention Home Girls; 3A. Bathrooms)

————. 2004. *Who Am I Without Him? Short Stories about Girls & the Boys in Their Lives.* Hyperion.
Ten short stories illustrate a variety of relationships, from family to friends to boys, and offer a glimpse into the experiences of young urban teens.
(1D. Detention Home Girls)

————. 2005. *Bang!* Hyperion.
Mann's father wants to toughen him up after the death of his little brother in a drive-by shooting leaves him angry and grieving, so he abandons Mann in the woods with a friend.
(1S. Urban Teens: Beyond Street Lit)

————. 2007. *The Broken Bike Boy and the Queen of 33rd Street.* Hyperion.
Spoiled and home schooled until the third grade, Queen Marie Rousseau's attitude has turned away all her classmates until smelly new student Leroy arrives and brings an elephant tusk to school, which leads to Queen Marie becoming a much nicer person.
(1R. Tweens)

FLEISCHMAN, PAUL. 1998. *Whirligig.* Holt.
Drunk and determined to commit suicide after a party, Brent unfortunately hits and kills a young teenaged girl named Lea whose mother hands him a bus pass and sends him off to the four corners of America to plant memorial whirligigs engraved with Lea's face and name.
(2R. Two or More Voices in Novels)

————. 1999. *Mind's Eye.* Holt.
Sixteen-year-old Courtney and 88-year-old Elva, both confined to their beds but harboring very different attitudes, are roommates in a nursing home, when Elva convinces Courtney to take a "journey of the mind" to Italy using a Baedaker's travel guide from 1910.
(2L. Novels with Script or Screenplay Format)

————. 2001. *Seek.* Carus Publishing.
Listening to stations across the country in an effort to locate his DJ father, Rob feels his father's absence keenly, despite being surrounded by a loving extended family.
(2L. Novels with Script or Screenplay Format)

————. 2005. *Zap: A Play.* Candlewick.
Presented as a play for an imaginary audience armed with remote controls to change the scene when they get bored, this mashup of seven plays riffs on well-known playwrights and their work, creating a humorous, reference-laden spoof.
(2L. Novels with Script or Screenplay Format)

FLEISCHMAN, PAUL, AND ERIC BEDDOWS. 1988. *Joyful Noise: Poems for Two Voices.* Harper & Row. NF.
> The noises made by insects, from the whirl of wings to the drone of a honeybee or the chirping of a cricket, are captured in these poems intended to be read aloud by two people.

(3H. Insects)

FLETCHER, SUSAN. 1998. *Shadow Spinner.* Simon & Schuster.
> Visiting the sultan's palace with her aunt, Marjan is thrilled to meet Shahrazad, whom she has admired and emulated all her life, especially when it turns out that she knows a story that Shahrazad doesn't.

(3M. The Middle East)

FLINN, ALEX. 2001. *Breathing Underwater.* HarperCollins.
> Nick is devastated when Caitlin's family gets a restraining order against him and he's required to attend a Family Violence class with other guys who hit their girlfriends, but he keeps the required journal and tries to explain his behavior as ordered.

(1D. Detention Home Girls; 1Q. Troubled Teen Boys; 2F. Diaries and Epistolary Novels)

———. 2002. *Breaking Point.* HarperCollins.
> Paul is desperate to be accepted at his new school, so when popular, sophisticated Charlie befriends him Paul finds himself agreeing to whatever Charlie proposes, from destroying mailboxes to hacking into the school computer system to something much, much worse.

(1S. Urban Teens: Beyond Street Lit)

———. 2004. *Nothing to Lose.* HarperCollins.
> Michael runs away from home, unable to convince his mother to leave his violently abusive stepfather, and when he reluctantly returns he learns that she's on trial for her husband's murder—was murder her only way out, or is Michael hiding something?

(3D. Consequences and Fate)

———. 2005. *Fade to Black.* HarperCollins.
> Alejandro has been tormented on multiple occasions, attacked because he's HIV positive, and after a brutal beating he's sure he knows who's responsible.

(2R. Two or More Voices in Novels)

———. 2007. *Beastly.* HarperTeen.
> Hiding at home after a Goth girl curses him so that he looks as ugly as he acts, Kyle "talks" to his friends through IMs and to other teens with altered looks via chat rooms.

(1S. Urban Teens: Beyond Street Lit; 2C. Blogs, E-mails, and IMs in Fiction)

FORDE, CATHERINE. 2004. *Fat Boy Swim.* Delacorte.
Teased for years because of his obesity, Jimmy and a soccer coach work out a deal whereby the coach teaches Jimmy to swim while Jimmy cooks for a fundraiser.
(3E. Cookery)

FRADIN, DENNIS BRINDELL, AND JUDITH BLOOM FRADIN. 2003. *Fight On! Mary Church Terrell's Battle for Integration.* Houghton Mifflin. NF.
Born in 1863 to former slaves, Mollie, during her fight for equality, worked with Susan B. Anthony, became the first black woman on the Washington, DC, Board of Education, and cofounded the NAACP.
(3C. The Civil Rights Movement)

————. 2004. *The Power of One: Daisy Bates and the Little Rock Nine.* Houghton Mifflin. NF.
Bates, president of Arkansas's NAACP in the 1950s, was mentor to the Little Rock Nine, demanding protection for them as they braved mobs, and helping them deal with the jeers, taunts, and threats they experienced during the early days of desegregation.
(3C. The Civil Rights Movement)

FRANCIS, DICK. 2006. *Under Orders.* Putnam.
A championship jockey who turns to private investigating after being injured, Sid Halley takes on both the murder of a winning jockey after the Cheltenham Gold Cup and a request by a nobleman to find out if his horses are running in fixed races.
(3G. Horses)

FRANCO, BETSY, ED. 2000. *You Hear Me? Poems and Writing by Teenage Boys.* Photographs by Nina Nickles. Candlewick. NF.
A mix of toughness and tenderness fills these poems, written in free verse in the authentic teen voice, as boys long for love, fear being abandoned, contend with bullying and drugs, or wonder who their birth mother is.
(1P. Striving Readers)

————, ED. 2001. *Things I Have to Tell You: Poems and Writing by Teenage Girls.* Candlewick. NF.
Young women express, with biting honesty, their hopes, dreams, fears, and longings in forms ranging from poetry to essays, all accompanied by complementary photographs.
(1D. Detention Home Girls)

————, ED. 2008. *Falling Hard: 100 Love Poems by Teenagers.* Candlewick. NF.
Delightfully honest, and fairly graphic, these poems explore all the facets of love in this collection by gay, straight, lesbian, bisexual, or transgender teens from America as well as other countries.
(2O. Poetry Anthologies for High School Readers)

FRANK, E.R. 2002. *America.* Simon & Schuster.
Teenage boy America finds himself in a treatment facility following a failed suicide attempt, where he recounts the multiple horrors of his young life to a patient therapist.
(3I. Institutions; 3O. Silence)

FRANK, HILLARY. 2002. *Better Than Running at Night.* Houghton Mifflin.
Eager to get away from her hippie mother and a stepfather who solves all problems with weed, Ellie falls for fellow art student Nate, loses her virginity to him, but finds out he likes all women, and by the end of fall semester, she's ready to move on from Nate.
(1M. Picky Senior Girls)

————. 2004. *I Can't Tell You.* Houghton Mifflin.
After saying something unforgivable to his roommate Sean, Jake takes a vow of silence and decides to communicate only through writing.
(3O. Silence)

FREDERICKS, MARIAH. 2003. *The True Meaning of Cleavage.* Atheneum.
When Jess's good friend Sari develops a major crush on senior David Cole after he makes Sari think there's a relationship developing, Jess prepares to prop up her friend when David doesn't leave his girlfriend.
(3A. Bathrooms)

FREEDMAN, RUSSELL. 2004. *The Voice That Challenged a Nation: Marian Anderson and the Struggle for Equal Rights.* Houghton Mifflin. NF.
Russell begins his story with Anderson's inspiring 1939 Easter concert at the Lincoln Memorial and then offers details of the events that brought her to that moment, accompanied by photographs and a discography.
(3C. The Civil Rights Movement)

FRIEDMAN, ROBIN. 2008. *Nothing.* Flux.
Reacting to his parents' pressure to attend Princeton, Parker becomes bulimic and lands in the hospital, as revealed in his narrative and his sister Danielle's free verse.
(2Q. Teen Issue Novels in Verse)

FRIESEN, GAYLE. 2005. *The Isabel Factor.* Kids Can Press.
   Best friends Zoe and Anna plan to attend camp together, but Zoe breaks her arm
   and Anna attends camp by herself where she finds that friendship with offbeat
   Isabel helps her understand how friends can drift apart as they grow older.
(3Q. Summer Camp)

FROST, HELEN. 2006. *The Braid.* Farrar, Straus and Giroux.
   The Highland Clearances in the 1850s separate sisters Jeannie, who goes to Canada, and Sarah, who remains to care for Grandma, but the two are linked by a braid
   made of each one's hair and by the intertwining sentences in this novel in verse.
(1M. Picky Senior Girls; 2I. Historical Novels in Verse; 2R. Two or More Voices in
Novels)

————. 2009. *Crossing Stones.* Farrar, Straus and Giroux.
   In 1917, Muriel's brother fights in World War I, her sister almost dies from the flu,
   and her suffragette aunt is arrested and jailed.
(2I. Historical Novels in Verse)

FUJISHIMA, KOSUKE. 1996– . Oh My Goddess! series. Dark Horse.
   After dialing the Goddess Technical Help Line by mistake, Keiichi makes an off-
   hand wish, believing it's all a joke, and finds himself with his own goddess companion for life.
(2D. Classic Manga)

FUKUI, ISAMU. 2008. *Truancy.* Tor.
   Tack originally joined the Truancy, a band of fighters who resist government op-
   pression, in order to get close to and assassinate their leader, but after spending
   time as a member of the group he finds his sympathies beginning to shift.
(1K. Manga Lovers)

FULLERTON, ALMA. 2007. *Walking on Glass.* HarperTempest.
   An unnamed teen narrator saves his mother from hanging herself from a chandelier, but when the chandelier falls, he breaks his arm and with his mother left in a
   coma, now the teen must decide whether to keep her on life support.
(2Q. Teen Issue Novels in Verse)

FÜNKE, CORNELIA. 2003. *Inkheart.* Scholastic.
   When Meggie learns that her father can literally read a book to life she begins to
   uncover the secret to her mother's disappearance, but with the evil character Cap-
   ricorn loose in the world, Meggie's search for the truth takes a dangerous turn.
(1H. Innocent Middle School Girls)

————. 2005. *The Thief Lord*. Read by Simon Jones. Listening Library. Unabridged, 8 hours, 15 minutes.

A gang of kids live in an abandoned theater with the Thief Lord at their helm, as Jones provides each character with a unique child's voice and wild carousel music heightens the magic of this fantasy.

(2B. Audiobooks for Middle School Listeners)

G

GAIMAN, NEIL. 1991–1997. The Sandman series. Illustrated by Mike Dringenberg et al. DC Comics.

Morpheus, the Lord of Dream, is one of the Endless, a family of immortal personifications, but over the course of his long life he learns that even the endless must change or die, and he makes a surprising choice.

(2E. Core Graphic Novels)

————. 1999. *Sandman: The Dream Hunters*. Illustrated by Yoshitaka Amano. DC Comics.

As the result of a wager with a badger over a young monk, a fox takes the form of a woman to lure the monk from his temple, but when she learns of a plot against the monk's life she finds herself attempting to protect rather than mislead him.

(1K. Manga Lovers)

————. 1999. *Stardust*. HarperCollins.

Tristran Thorn promised the girl he loved that he would find the falling star they saw and return it to her, and he meant to, until he found out the star was actually a young girl, named Yvaine, with problems of her own.

(1G. Graphic Novel Lovers)

————. 2002. *Coraline*. HarperCollins.

Coraline meets her button-eyed not-mother and not-father in the other half of her real parents' flat and realizes that her not-parents have stolen her real parents, along with some lost children, and she'll have to be brave and rescue everyone.

(1G. Graphic Novel Lovers)

————. 2003. *The Wolves in the Walls*. Illustrated by Dave McKean. HarperCollins.

Lucy knows that the sounds she hears are wolves in the walls, but no one believes her until they come out and the family is forced to flee.

(2N. Picture Books for Teens)

————. 2005. *Anansi Boys.* Read by Lenny Henry. HarperAudio. Unabridged, 10 hours.

> After attending the funeral of his father in Florida, "Fat Charlie" returns to Britain and meets a brother he never knew existed who turns Charlie's life upside down, steals his girlfriend, and has him fired from a job he hated, all superbly narrated by Henry, who alternates between a Caribbean lilt and a British accent.

(2A. Audiobooks for High School Listeners)

————. 2008. *The Graveyard Book.* Read by Neil Gaiman. Recorded Books. Unabridged, 8 hours.

> Gaiman's very distinctive British accent enlivens the story of young Bod, who leaves his crib and toddles into the nearby graveyard where he's safe from his parents' murderer, and there he stays while being raised by Mr. and Mrs. Owens and other ghosts in the cemetery.

(2B. Audiobooks for Middle School Listeners)

GALLO, DONALD R., ED. 1997. *No Easy Answers: Short Stories about Teenagers Making Tough Choices.* Delacorte.

> This collection written by noted YA authors includes a story by Walter Dean Myers about a teen who makes a wrong choice and becomes an addict and one by Jack Gantos that tells of a teen who wants to join a gang so badly, he's willing to kill anyone.

(1P. Striving Readers; 2J. Must-Have Anthologies)

————, ED. 2001. *On the Fringe: Stories.* Penguin Putnam. NF.

> Teens on the fringe, and their peers, families, schools, and communities, are the subject of these 11 short stories by authors including Joan Bauer, Jack Gantos, Angela Johnson, Chris Crutcher, Nancy Werlin, Ron Koertge, and Will Weaver.

(2J. Must-Have Anthologies)

GANTOS, JACK. 2002. *Hole in My Life.* Farrar, Straus and Giroux. NF.

> Out of high school and eager for adventure, Jack agrees to a get-rich-quick drug scam, never thinking about what happens if you're caught, and spends a year in a medium-security prison where *The Brothers Karamazov* provides the paper for his journal.

(1P. Striving Readers; 1Q. Troubled Teen Boys)

GARFINKLE, D.L. 2005. *Storky: How I Lost My Nickname and Won the Girl.* Penguin Putnam.

> Mike started a journal so Gina, the girl of his dreams, would think he was the sensitive type, but as he recounts the drama of his parents divorce and the details of his own life, it's clear things don't turn out quite the way he expected.

(2F. Diaries and Epistolary Novels; 3J. Love Hurts)

GASKIN, CATHERINE. 1972. *A Falcon for a Queen.* Doubleday.
After her missionary father dies, leaving her alone in China, Kirsty returns to the family's ancestral home in Scotland where she's grudgingly welcomed by her cranky grandfather, who owns a noted whiskey distillery.
(1B. Avid Readers)

GEARY, RICK. 1997. *The Borden Tragedy: A Memoir of the Infamous Double Murder at Fall River, Mass., 1892.* Nantier Beall Minoustchine. NF.
After Lizzie Borden's parents are murdered, she is the primary suspect and, though acquitted after the trial, never loses the murderer stigma in this well-researched tale.
(2K. Nonfiction Graphic Novels)

————. 2003. *The Beast of Chicago.* Nantier Beall Minoustchine. NF.
Possibly the first, certainly one of the worst, H.H. Holmes was a serial killer of grizzly appetites and epic proportions, killing as many as 200 men, women, and children during his years in the Chicago boarding house he called The Castle.
(2K. Nonfiction Graphic Novels)

GEORGE, JEAN CRAIGHEAD. 1993. *Fire Bug Connection: An Ecological Mystery.* HarperCollins.
Excited when her birthday present turns out to be two jars of Czechoslovakian fire bugs, Maggie and her friend Mitch must discover why the fire bugs are dying rather than completing their metamorphosis in this eco-mystery set in a Maine university laboratory.
(3H. Insects)

GEORGE, KRISTINE O'CONNELL. 2002. *Swimming Upstream: Middle School Poems.* Illustrated by Debbie Tilley. Clarion. NF.
The angst of a girl is related in these poems about her first year at middle school when she can't open her locker, is late for class, and has to carry a humongous hall pass, but by the end of the year she no longer feels as if she's "swimming upstream."
(2P. Poetry Anthologies for Middle School Readers)

GERSTEIN, MORDICAI. 2003. *The Man Who Walked between the Towers.* Roaring Brook. NF.
This book tells the story of Philippe Petit's tightrope walk between the World Trade Center towers in 1974, from the moment the challenge presents itself to the clandestine and highly dangerous stringing of the cable and finally to the joyful walk between the towers.
(2N. Picture Books for Teens)

GHENT, NATALE. 2005. *No Small Thing.* Candlewick.
After their father leaves them, Nathaniel and his sisters no longer have a nice house and pony, which prompts Nathaniel to reply to an ad for a free pony.
(3G. Horses)

GHIGNA, CHARLES. 2003. *A Fury of Motion: Poems for Boys.* Boyds Mills Press/Wordsong. NF.
Though sports poems predominate in this collection for boys who don't want everyone to know they're reading poetry, other poems cover such topics as haircuts, the beach, and the playground.
(2P. Poetry Anthologies for Middle School Readers)

GIBBS, CHRIS. 2007. *Build Your Own Sports Car: On a Budget.* Haynes. NF.
Meant to be built with components from a Ford Sierra, this book provides instructions to build an open-top, two-seater sports car using regular tools, low-cost parts, and the builder's basic skills.
(1C. Book Haters)

GIFF, PATRICIA RILEY. 2003. *Maggie's Door.* Random House.
Nory Ryan leaves her home in Ireland just days behind her friend Sean and her young brother, and as they all make their way to America and Nory's sister, they run into dangerous storms and even more dangerous people.
(3K. Luck)

GILES, GAIL. 2002. *Shattering Glass.* Roaring Brook.
Rob's decision to help turn geeky Simon into one of the popular crowd backfires when Simon begins to show a side of his personality that Rob and his friends didn't expect.
(1S. Urban Teens: Beyond Street Lit; 3D. Consequences and Fate)

————. 2006. *What Happened to Cass McBride?* Hachette.
Cass McBride has been buried alive by Kyle, who blames her for the suicide of his brother, but as she struggles to outwit him and escape, it becomes clear that Cass and Kyle have more in common than either would have imagined.
(1S. Urban Teens: Beyond Street Lit; 2R. Two or More Voices in Novels; 3O. Silence)

GILL, DAVID MACINNIS. 2009. *Soul Enchilada.* Greenwillow.
Biracial "Bug," part African American and part Mexican, is evicted from her apartment, loses her job, and discovers her beloved Cadillac is being repossessed by a demon named Mr. Souls.
(1I. Latina Teens)

GINGERELLI, DAIN. 2007. *Hot Rod Roots: A Tribute to the Pioneers.* Motorbooks. NF.
Almost as soon as cars rolled off the assembly line, there were drivers eager to take them apart, accessorize them, and speed them up as shown in photos of and essays about circle track racing, drag racing, and the car shows of today.
(1C. Book Haters)

GIOVANNI, NIKKI. 1995. *The Selected Poems of Nikki Giovanni.* Morrow. NF.
Known as one of the more controversial black poets, one can now read Giovanni's work in chronological order with her poems that expand on themes and events from the past four decades of American history.
(2O. Poetry Anthologies for High School Readers)

————, ED. 2008. *Hip Hop Speaks to Children: A Celebration of Poetry with a Beat.* Sourcebooks/Jabberwocky. NF.
Rhythms from all aspects of African American life set the tempo for these poems, including "hambone," gospel, jazz and the blues, and pulpit-style speaking, with poems from artists such as W.E.B. DuBois, Queen Latifah, Gwendolyn Brooks, and Calef Brown.
(2P. Poetry Anthologies for Middle School Readers)

GLAUSIUSZ, JOSIE. 2004. *Buzz: The Intimate Bond between Humans and Insects.* Photographs by Volker Steger. Chronicle Books. NF.
Steger's unusual photographs of common household insects, which range from carpet beetles to fruit flies, add to science writer Glausiusz's text.
(3H. Insects)

GOING, K.L. 2003. *Fat Kid Rules the World.* Read by Matthew Lillard. Listening Library. Unabridged, 6 hours.
Obese Troy and hyper Curt are indeed a strange pair, perfectly captured by Lillard as he portrays Curt's nonstop speech, side by side with Troy's self-deprecating style, as the two maintain the patois of the punk music world.
(2A. Audiobooks for High School Listeners)

————. 2006. *Saint Iggy.* Harcourt.
Suspended from school and told he can't return without a hearing, and with his addict parents nowhere to be found, Iggy feels he can return to school only by making a contribution to the world, and, in his own unique way, he does.
(1L. Offbeat Guys; 1S. Urban Teens: Beyond Street Lit)

GOLDBERG, MYLA. 2000. *Bee Season.* Doubleday.
With a househusband for her father, a lawyer for her mother, and a brother who's a good student, Ellie drifts along until the day she wins a spelling bee, and suddenly she's the center of her father's attention as she prepares for national competition.
(1M. Picky Senior Girls)

GOLDSCHMIDT, JUDY. 2005. *The Secret Blog of Raisin Rodriguez.* Penguin/Razorbill.
Miserable about being the new kid at a Philadelphia school, Raisin blogs her woes
to her California friends and describes some of her teachers with crude images,
but one day she forgets to log out at school and her blog is printed for all to read.
(2C. Blogs, E-mails, and IMs in Fiction)

GONICK, LARRY. 1990–2002. Cartoon History of the Universe series. Random
House. NF.
Gonick's graphic history of the universe begins with the Big Bang and the "evolution of everything" and moves on through Alexander the Great, Christ, Confu-
cius, Buddha, the Mongols, the Dark Ages, and Columbus's voyage and discovery.
(2K. Nonfiction Graphic Novels)

GOOBIE, BETH. 2002. *Sticks and Stones.* Orca.
After spurning Brent's advances at the Valentine's Dance, Jujube notices the graffiti vilifying her at school, but she takes action and presents a slideshow on the
topic of graffiti, including bathroom wall slurs.
(1P. Striving Readers)

GORE, AL. 2007. *An Inconvenient Truth: The Crisis of Global Warming.* Rodale. NF.
Then-and-now photos, graphs, and text explain the problem of global warming
and its possible consequences, which range from flooding to storms, droughts,
and public-health issues.
(3F. The Environment)

GRAHAM, ROSEMARY. 2003. *My Not-So-Terrible Time at the Hippie Hotel.* Viking.
Tracy's father takes her and her siblings to Farnsworth House on Cape Cod for a
program designed for divorced parents called "Together Time," but initially
Tracy has difficulty getting along with the other teens.
(3R. Summertime)

————. 2005. *Thou Shalt Not Dump the Skater Dude and Other Commandments I
Have Broken.* Viking.
When Kelsey breaks up with popular skateboarder C.J., she's unprepared for the
nasty, vicious things he says about her on his blog, and when she realizes even her
younger brother has read the lies, she confronts C.J. and receives an apology.
(3J. Love Hurts)

GRANDITS, JOHN. 2004. *Technically, It's Not My Fault: Concrete Poems.* Clarion. NF.
Robert flushes and scalds his sister Jessie's shower water at the same time, skate-boards with lines of poetry leaping a sidewalk, misses a lay-up, and thanks his aunt for an ugly sweater in a series of poems that reveal much about him.
(2P. Poetry Anthologies for Middle School Readers)

————. 2007. *Blue Lipstick.* Clarion. NF.
Thirty concrete poems follow ninth grader Jessie through her first year of high school as she adjusts to dreaded pep rallies, airhead cheerleaders, and bad hair days, when sentences spring from her head like curls.
(2P. Poetry Anthologies for Middle School Readers)

GRANT, K.M. 2005. *Blood Red Horse.* Walker.
Participating in the Third Crusade with his father and brother, William de Gran-ville selects a small red stallion as his warhorse and departs for the Middle East where William and his horse will cross paths with Saladin and his ward Kamil.
(3G. Horses)

GRATZ, ALAN. 2006. *Samurai Shortstop.* Penguin Putnam.
Growing up in 1890s Japan, Toyo is looking for a way of life to replace the samurai lifestyle outlawed by the emperor and rather surprisingly finds it on the baseball field.
(1K. Manga Lovers)

GRAY, DIANNE E. 2002. *Together Apart.* Houghton.
After the deadly School Children's Blizzard of 1888 kills 500 to 1,000 Midwest-erners, survivor Hannah leaves home to work for a young widow and to escape her father, who holds her responsible for the deaths of her two siblings.
(3P. State Books; 3T. Wintertime)

GREEN, JOHN. 2005. *Looking for Alaska.* Dutton.
Attending boarding school for the first time, Miles's roommate is "the Colonel," who introduces him to Alaska, a beautiful, curvy girl dating a boy from Vanderbilt, but that doesn't stop Miles from being smitten.
(1A. Adult Readers; 3P. State Books)

————. 2006. *An Abundance of Katherines.* Penguin.
Disconsolate after being dumped for the nineteenth time by yet another girl named Katherine, Colin meets a non-Katherine named Lindsey who helps him figure out a mathematical theorem to determine the length of romantic relation-ships.
(1O. Reluctant Male Readers; 3L. Mathematics; 3P. State Books)

————. 2008. *Paper Towns.* Dutton.
In love with Margo since they were children and discovered a dead body together, Quentin is pleased when Margo, who runs with a faster, wilder crowd in their senior year, taps on his window and invites him on a mission of revenge, but then she disappears.
(1L. Offbeat Guys; 3J. Love Hurts)

————. 2008. *Paper Towns.* Read by Dan John Miller. Brilliance. Unabridged, 8 hours.
Miller portrays Quentin "Q" Jacobsen as the love-struck teen he is, along with the breathy tones of Margo, the object of his crush, and the whininess of his best friend Ben as they each undergo the journey of a lifetime.
(2A. Audiobooks for High School Listeners)

Greene, Michelle Dominguez. 2006. *Chasing the Jaguar.* HarperTeen.
Told by the local witch that she's descended from a long line of Mayan healers, Martika departs from healing when she uses her psychic powers to locate a wealthy, kidnapped teen.
(1I. Latina Teens)

Greenwald, Lisa. 2009. *My Life in Pink and Green.* Abrams/Amulet.
Lucy's natural flair for making up others helps her grandmother's drugstore with cosmetic sales, but, wanting to do more, she applies for a mayor's grant for local businesses that are trying to "go green."
(3F. The Environment)

Griffin, Adele. 2002. *Hannah, Divided.* Hyperion.
Growing up on a farm during the Depression, Hannah can't read but she is a math genius, and her skills give her an opportunity to attend a private school in Philadelphia to study for a math scholarship.
(3L. Mathematics)

————. 2006. *My Almost Epic Summer.* Penguin Putnam.
Longing for an "epic" summer, but relegated to babysitting the two Prior children, Irene contents herself with drawing hairstyles of literary characters in preparation for the hair salon she plans to open one day.
(3R. Summertime)

Grimes, Nikki. 1998. *Jazmin's Notebook.* Penguin Putnam.
Jazmin records every detail of her Harlem life in her beloved journal, from her close relationship with her sister, to her troubled relationship with her alcoholic mother, to her dreams of becoming a writer, despite the school counselor's skepticism.
(2F. Diaries and Epistolary Novels)

————. 2001. *Bronx Masquerade*. Penguin Putnam.

The students in Mr. Ward's English class find a creative outlet for self-expression as well as new relationships with one another after Mr. Ward turns their Friday lessons into an open-mike poetry hour.

(1O. Reluctant Male Readers; 1P. Striving Readers)

————. 2004. *What Is Goodbye?* Illustrated by Raul Colon. Hyperion.

Jesse, who was judged too young to attend the funeral, and his sister Jerilyn describe their year of grief and eventual signs of healing in alternating verses that show their range of emotions after their older brother Jason dies.

(2Q. Teen Issue Novels in Verse)

GRUEN, SARA. 2006. *Water for Elephants*. Algonquin.

In this book based on actual circus stories, after his parents are killed, Jacob Jankowski leaves Vet School at Cornell, joins the Benzini Brothers Circus, and is put in charge of the animals where his primary job is to protect the animals from their abusive boss.

(1M. Picky Senior Girls)

GUILBAULT, ROSE CASTILLO. 2005. *Farmworker's Daughter: Growing Up Mexican*. Heyday Books. NF.

Guilbault describes her childhood as a Mexican immigrant in the 1960s when she lived in a farming community and her struggle to learn English, fit in at school, and make friends.

(3S. Teen Immigrants)

H

HADDIX, MARGARET PETERSON. 1998–2006. Shadow Children series. Simon & Schuster.

In a dystopian future of widespread famine and deprivation, third-born children must stay hidden or risk being discovered by the Population Police.

(1E. Gentlemanly Boys)

————. 2005. *Double Identity*. Simon & Schuster.

Sent to stay with an aunt she never knew existed, Bethany learns she's the clone of a sister who died years earlier and is being tracked by a man who wants to reveal Bethany's identity for his own purposes.

(3N. Science)

HADDON, MARK. 2003. *The Curious Incident of the Dog in the Night-Time*. Doubleday.
When his neighbor's poodle is found murdered, autistic Christopher Boone, who routinely solves complicated math equations in his head, emulates the logic of Sherlock Holmes to crack the case.
(3L. Mathematics)

———. 2003. *The Curious Incident of the Dog in the Night-Time*. Read by Jeff Woodman. Recorded Books. Unabridged, 6 hours.
Using Sherlock Holmes as his guide to solve the mystery of his neighbor's dead dog, Christopher's determined, British-accented voice never wavers in his quest that eventually uncovers family secrets.
(2A. Audiobooks for High School Listeners)

HAIG, MATTHEW. 2006. *The Dead Father's Club*. Read by Andrew Dennis. Highbridge Audio. Unabridged, 6 hours, 45 minutes.
Philip Noble's in a quandary when his deceased father returns as a ghost, says that Uncle Allan murdered him, and asks Philip to avenge his death—skillfully narrated by 11-year-old Andrew Dennis, whose voice authenticates Philip's problems.
(2A. Audiobooks for High School Listeners)

HAINES, CAROLYN. 2003. *My Mother's Witness: The Peggy Morgan Story*. River City Publishing. NF.
Morgan and her mother were threatened and coerced to keep secret the actions of the men—including Morgan's father—involved with the murders of Emmett Till and Medgar Evers, a burden that haunted Morgan until she came forward and testified 30 years later.
(3C. The Civil Rights Movement)

HALAM, ANN. 2002. *Dr. Franklin's Island*. Random House/Wendy Lamb.
Stranded on a tropical island after a plane crash, three teens are captured by crazed Dr. Franklin who plans to use them as trial subjects for his transgenic experiments.
(3N. Science)

HALE, BRUCE. 2000. *The Chameleon Wore Chartreuse: From the Tattered Casebook of Chet Gecko, Private Eye*. Harcourt.
Classmate Shirley asks Chet Gecko for his help in locating her missing brother but offers few clues, forcing Chet to rely on the help of wannabe detective Natalie, and together they find Shirley's brother before a sixth grade Gila monster ends the case.
(1R. Tweens)

HALE, SHANNON. 2003. *The Goose Girl.* Bloomsbury.
Sent to marry the prince of Bayern after her father dies, Ani is betrayed by her maid, who assumes her identity and leaves Ani to tend the geese until she can reclaim her throne.
(1F. Gifted Elementary Student Readers)

————. 2005. *The Goose Girl.* Read by a full cast. Full Cast Audio. Unabridged, 10 hours.
More than 48 readers tell of Ani's betrayal by her lady-in-waiting Selia, who assumes her identity as the Princess of Kildenree and plans to marry the Prince of Bayern, while Ani hides behind the façade of the goose girl and plots how to regain her proper status.
(2B. Audiobooks for Middle School Listeners)

————. 2005. *Princess Academy.* Bloomsbury.
Miri and the other girls in her mountain village attend a special school to be eligible to meet, and perhaps be selected to marry, the prince, but Miri is miserable, misses her friend Peder, dislikes their strict teacher, and hates the growing competitiveness.
(1H. Innocent Middle School Girls)

————. 2007. *Book of a Thousand Days.* Bloomsbury.
After Dashti's mistress Lady Saren turns down her father's choice of a bridegroom, she and Lady Saren are locked in an old lookout tower with enough food for seven years, but when rats eat their food, the two must find a way to escape.
(1M. Picky Senior Girls; 2F. Diaries and Epistolary Novels)

HALE, SHANNON, AND DEAN HALE. 2008. *Rapunzel's Revenge.* Illustrated by Nathan Hale. Bloomsbury.
After escaping from her hated tower, Rapunzel teams up with Jack, who she finds much more likeable than the prince, and tries to free her real mother (and the rest of the kingdom) from the evil witch who imprisoned her.
(1H. Innocent Middle School Girls; 2E. Core Graphic Novels)

HALPERN, JULIE. 2009. *Into the Wild Nerd Yonder.* Holt.
Former best friends Jess, Bizza, and Char grow apart as they enter high school, with Bizza and Char becoming punky party girls and Jess sewing skirts, joining a nerdy group of *Dungeons & Dragons* players, and learning about real friendship.
(1N. Punk Readers)

HALO SERIES. 2001– . Tor Books.
Based on the science fiction video game *Halo*, this series extends the adventures of super-soldier Master Chief and Cortana, his AI companion, as they battle alien races and a parasitic organism.
(2M. Paperback Series)

HALPIN, BRENDAN. 2004. *Donorboy*. Villard.
After her lesbian mothers are killed in a car crash, Rosalind is sent to live with her sperm donor dad Sean but absolutely refuses to speak to him, forcing Sean to e-mail her with answers to questions about his role in her conception.
(2C. Blogs, E-mails, and IMs in Fiction)

———. 2009. *Forever Changes*. Farrar, Straus and Giroux.
Gifted in math and sure to be accepted at MIT if she'd only submit her application, Brianna knows her life expectancy is shortened because of cystic fibrosis but receives encouragement from her calculus teacher, who has his own health problems.
(3L. Mathematics)

HANLEY, VICTORIA. 2000. *The Seer and the Sword*. Scholastic.
Princess Torina is happy to have her father home from the wars, but she is appalled when he presents the captured Prince Landen to her as a gift, and after freeing him immediately, Torina and Landen team up to help bring peace to their kingdom.
(1H. Innocent Middle School Girls)

HANTMAN, CLEA. 2008. *30 Days to Getting Over the Dork You Used to Call Your Boyfriend: A Heartbreak Handbook*. Random House. NF.
Suggesting an activity for each of the 30 days she claims it takes to get over a painful breakup, Hantman offers understanding, a metaphorical shoulder, and finally a good, strong nudge in the direction of recovery.
(3J. Love Hurts)

HARLOW, JOAN HIATT. 2005. *Midnight Rider*. Simon & Schuster.
Indentured to British General Gage, Hannah dresses as a boy and sneaks out at night to harass the British troops who call her the "Midnight Rider."
(3G. Horses)

HARRIS, JOANNE. 1999. *Chocolat*. Viking.
Vianne opens a bakery specializing in hot cocoa, flaky pastries, and decadent chocolates just as the season of Lent begins, earning her the ire of the local priest but the gratitude of the villagers.
(3B. Chocolate)

HARRISON, LISI. 2004– . The Clique series. Little, Brown/Poppy.
Middle schoolers Massie, Alicia, Dylan, and Kristen comprise The Pretty Committee, a tight-knit clique that initially heaps scorn on new student Claire, who is eager to befriend them.
(2M. Paperback Series)

HART, ELVA TREVIÑO. 1999. *Barefoot Heart: Stories of a Migrant Child.* Bilingual Review Press. NF.
Hart's memoir of growing up a Mexican immigrant in a small, white Texas town is not only the story of a hard-working, tired-but-loving family but also an examination of the effects race and class had on her parents and her brothers and sisters.
(3S. Teen Immigrants)

HARTINGER, BRENT. 2003. *Geography Club.* HarperCollins.
Russell and Kevin form the "Geography Club" with other gay and lesbian students so that they can discuss their lives without the rest of the school knowing their secrets.
(1A. Adult Readers)

———. 2004. *Last Chance Texaco.* HarperCollins.
Kindle Home is a group foster home for troubled teens and it's the first place 15-year-old Lucy has felt comfortable since her parents died, but arson and funding problems threaten to close it down for good.
(1D. Detention Home Girls; 1Q. Troubled Teen Boys; 3I. Institutions)

———. 2005. *The Order of the Poison Oak.* HarperTempest.
Eager to leave behind the stigma of the "gay kid" at his high school, Russell looks forward to being a camp counselor and finds he can relate to his burn victim campers who are also glad to be away from the prying eyes of society.
(3Q. Summer Camp)

———. 2006. *Grand & Humble.* HarperTempest.
Seventeen-year-olds Harlan and Manny share two things: bad dreams of death and two mutual friends, gay Ricky and deaf Elsa.
(3D. Consequences and Fate)

———. 2009. *Project Sweet Life.* HarperTeen.
Wishing to enjoy an idyllic summer before their senior year in high school, David, Curtis, and Victor plan "project sweet life," lie to their parents about having jobs, and have no idea how to find $7,000 in anticipated salary.
(3R. Summertime)

HAUSMAN, GERALD, AND LORETTA HAUSMAN. 2003. *Escape from Botany Bay*. Scholastic.
After struggling for years against the harsh conditions of the penal colony where she lives, Mary Bryant led the only successful escape from Botany Bay, sailing in an open boat with her family and a few other convicts back to her native England.
(2G. Fictionalized Biographies)

HAUTMAN, PETE. 2003. *Sweetblood*. Simon & Schuster.
Once a blonde, A-student Lucy Szabo dyes her hair black, wears Goth outfits, and advances a theory that links diabetes and vampirism, but her diabetes is more of a threat than any possible vampires.
(1N. Punk Readers)

———. 2004. *Godless*. Simon & Schuster.
Jason and his friend Shin develop a new religion centered around the town water tower, but after an impromptu baptism goes awry and one of their "followers" is injured, things spiral out of control.
(3D. Consequences and Fate; 3P. State Books)

HAUTZIG, ESTHER. 1968. *The Endless Steppe: Growing Up in Siberia*. HarperCollins.
Esther is only ten years old when her family is arrested and deported from Poland to a remote village in Siberia, where she, her mother, and her grandmother live together for the next four years.
(2G. Fictionalized Biographies)

HAWDON, ROBIN. 1984. *A Rustle in the Grass*. Dodd, Mead.
Stirring to life in early spring, a colony of small brown ants readies to protect its home from the marauding red ants that massacred a nearby colony.
(3H. Insects)

HAWORTH-ATTARD, BARBARA. 2005. *Theories of Relativity*. Holt.
His mother kicks him out when he turns 16, so Dylan finds refuge in the library where he reads about Einstein and his theory of relativity, making up his own "relative theories" in order to survive on the streets.
(3N. Science)

HAYDEN, TOREY. 1991 *Ghost Girl: The True Story of a Child in Peril and the Teacher Who Saved Her*. HarperCollins. NF.
Hayden tells the disturbing story of Jadie, an eight-year-old girl who initially refuses to speak but who, after working with Hayden, shares a sickening account of ritual abuse.
(3O. Silence)

HEADLEY, JUSTINA CHEN. 2006. *Nothing but the Truth (and a Few White Lies)*. Little, Brown.
Furious when her Taiwanese mother enrolls her at Stanford's Math Camp, Patty Ho discovers she likes the brainy campers who don't care that she's biracial.
(3Q. Summer Camp)

HEARN, JUDITH. 2005. *The Minister's Daughter*. Simon & Schuster.
Grace and Patience, daughters of the town minister, accuse the local cunning woman and her granddaughter Nell of witchcraft in an attempt to conceal Grace's pregnancy, but their lie has unexpected consequences.
(2R. Two or More Voices in Novels)

HEARN, LIAN. 2002–2007. Tales of the Otori series. Penguin Putnam.
Takeo is taken in by Lord Otori after his village is burned, but it's not kindness or coincidence as Takeo learns he is a member of the "Tribe," a secret group of supernatural assassins.
(1K. Manga Lovers)

HELGERSON, JOSEPH. 2009. *Crows and Cards*. Read by MacLeod Andrews. Brilliance Audio. Unabridged, 6 hours, 42 minutes.
Young Zebulon Crabtree's voice becomes increasingly concerned that his new gambling partner is crooked, and narrator Andrews's characterization of Chilly's languid, gentlemanly speech fosters this idea.
(2B. Audiobooks for Middle School Listeners)

HEMPHILL, STEPHANIE. 2005. *Things Left Unsaid: A Novel in Poems*. Hyperion.
Bored with her monotonous life, Sarah becomes friends with tough-talking, defiant Robin, but when Robin attempts suicide, Sarah realizes she's tried to change too much and gradually returns to her more balanced self.
(2Q. Teen Issue Novels in Verse)

———. 2007. *Your Own, Sylvia: A Verse Portrait of Sylvia Plath*. Knopf.
Many source notes keep this novel historically accurate as chronically arranged poems of the various people who knew poetess Sylvia Plath describe their interactions and relationships with her.
(2G. Fictionalized Biographies; 2I. Historical Novels in Verse)

HENEGHAN, JAMES. 2000. *The Grave*. Farrar, Straus and Giroux.
Foster child Tom Mullen falls into a construction site in Liverpool and is transported from 1974 to 1847 where he meets the Monaghan-Tully family, experiences the potato famine, and realizes that he's related to this Irish family.
(3K. Luck)

————. 2002. *The Grave.* Read by Gerard Doyle. Recorded Books. Unabridged, 6 hours, 30 minutes.

> As Tom time travels to Ireland in the midst of the potato famine, narrator Doyle's Liverpool accent adds to the reality of the time period, while he maintains the tempo of the story and enlivens some of the more bizarre elements.

(2B. Audiobooks for Middle School Listeners)

HENNESSEY, JONATHAN. 2008. *The United States Constitution: A Graphic Adaptation.* Illustrated by Aaron McConnell. Farrar, Straus and Giroux.

> This graphic presentation of the U.S. Constitution explores the meaning and impact of each article and amendment, placing the framers in their historical context and presenting changing visual styles that offer additional information.

(2H. Graphic Novels in the Classroom)

HENRY, APRIL. 2009. *Torched.* Putnam.

> To keep her adopted hippie parents out of jail, Ellie agrees to infiltrate a group of eco-warriors and relay information about them to the FBI, but she discovers that there's a turncoat in the group.

(3F. The Environment)

HERBSMAN, CHERYL RENEE. 2009. *Breathing.* Viking.

> Ever since her father left, Savannah has been beset by asthma, until the day she meets Jackson and her breathing problems ease; when they're apart for a short while, she works to keep her breathing under control.

(3R. Summertime)

HERMAN, JOHN. 1998. *Deep Waters.* Philomel.

> At Camp Winasaukee, Andy sneaks out at night to buy candy and one evening sees two counselors skinny-dipping; when he hears the next morning that staff members have found a drowned counselor, he wonders if the death was accidental.

(3Q. Summer Camp)

HERNANDEZ, DAVID. 2008. *Suckerpunch.* HarperTeen.

> Even after his father leaves, Marcus feels guilty that he couldn't stop the abuse his father heaped on his brother Enrique, so when the brothers learn their father might be returning, they travel to San Francisco to confront him.

(1J. Latino Teens)

HERNANDEZ, GILBERT. 2006. *Sloth.* DC Comics.

> Miguel wills himself into and out of a coma and once returned to normal life, he finds himself, his best friend Romeo, and his girlfriend Lita investigating a local legend about a haunted lemon orchard and a goat man with the power to switch lives.

(2E. Core Graphic Novels)

HERRERA, JUAN FELIPE. 1999. *CrashBoomLove: A Novel in Verse.* University of New Mexico Press.
> New to his high school, 16-year-old Cesar Garcia feels out of place and alone until he falls into "crashboomlove."

(1J. Latino Teens)

HERRICK, STEVEN. 2006. *By the River.* Front Street.
> Raised in a small Australian town in the 1950s, Harry relates life with his widowed father and younger brother, the loss of a classmate who dies in a flooded river, his bowl haircut administered by his aunt, and riding his brakeless, homemade billy cart down a hill.

(2Q. Teen Issue Novels in Verse)

———. 2009. *Cold Skin.* Front Street.
> Following World War II, Eddie's ready to work in the mines and his brother Larry, who has a crush on Colleen, wants to leave their coal-mining town, but when Colleen is murdered, nothing matters to the brothers but to find her killer.

(2I. Historical Novels in Verse)

HESSE, KAREN. 1992. *Letters from Rifka.* Penguin Putnam.
> Rifka's journey begins in a Jewish village in Ukraine when she helps her family evade Russian soldiers and escape to Poland, and when she is kept behind due to illness, Rifka spends time alone in Belgium before finally reuniting with her family in America.

(3S. Teen Immigrants)

———. 1996. *The Music of Dolphins.* Scholastic.
> Lost at sea years earlier, Mila has been raised by dolphins and is miserable when captured and taken to a special hospital to be studied, a misery she knows will ease when she returns to her dolphin family.

(3N. Science)

———. 1997. *Out of the Dust.* Scholastic.
> When Oklahoma suffers from the Dust Bowl of the 1930s, Billy Jo wants to head west and become a pianist, but her father won't leave the farm; all that changes when Billy Jo's hands are ruined trying to put out the fire that accidentally kills her mother.

(2I. Historical Novels in Verse)

———. 2001. *Witness.* Scholastic.
> After the Ku Klux Klan arrives in a small Vermont town in 1924, 11 different people reveal their feelings about this actual event, from victims to community leaders and others, including shopkeepers and a minister.

(2I. Historical Novels in Verse; 3P. State Books)

————. 2003. *Aleutian Sparrow.* Simon & Schuster/McElderry.
During World War II, the Aleutian Islands are attacked by the Japanese, and to prevent more Japanese attacks, the U.S. government moves the native Aleuts to the mainland of Alaska and stations soldiers on their native Aleutian Islands.
(2I. Historical Novels in Verse)

HIAASEN, CARL. 2002. *Hoot.* Knopf.
Roy and a strange boy called "Mullet Fingers" team up to stop a construction project that will destroy the homes of burrowing owls, which upsets local politicians who have conveniently overlooked any environmental problems.
(1E. Gentlemanly Boys; 3N. Science)

————. 2005. *Flush.* Knopf.
Suspecting the casino boat *Coral Queen* of dumping its sewage, Noah's father sinks the boat and is sent to jail, but now Noah and his sister must search for the evidence to prove the boat's captain was breaking the law.
(3F. The Environment)

————. 2005. *Flush.* Read by Michael Welch. Listening Library. Unabridged, 5 hours, 30 minutes.
Narrator Welch gives Noah a snappy delivery to match his enthusiasm as he and his sister hunt for evidence to free their father in a fast-moving audiobook that differentiates between the good and bad guys.
(2B. Audiobooks for Middle School Listeners)

HIGSON, CHARLIE. 2006. *SilverFin.* Read by Nathaniel Parker. Listening Library. Unabridged, 8 hours, 30 minutes.
The young James Bond, as voiced by narrator Parker, displays his anger, fear, or loneliness, though not with the suave tones associated with the adult 007 Bond, in an audiobook that calls on Parker to use British, American, German, and Scottish accents.
(2B. Audiobooks for Middle School Listeners)

————. 2009. *Hurricane Gold: A James Bond Adventure.* Hyperion.
On vacation in Mexico, young James Bond stays at the home of Jack Stone, but when a hurricane strikes, thieves use the storm to kidnap Stone's children and the contents of his safe, an act that sends James chasing through the jungle to save the siblings.
(1B. Avid Readers)

HIGURI, YOU. 2005–2008. Cantarella series. Go! Media Entertainment.
Cesare Borgia, driven by demons and searching for power, finds a would-be savior in Michelotto, a mysterious assassin in Renaissance Italy determined to save Cesare's soul, even if it means destroying his cursed body.
(2D. Classic Manga)

HIJUELOS, OSCAR. 2008. *Dark Dude.* Atheneum.
Threatened with military school and tired of his violent neighborhood, light-skinned Cuban American Rico and his friend Jimmy hitchhike to Wisconsin to stay on a farm with friend and college student Gilberto, and Rico begins to sort out his life.
(1J. Latino Teens)

HILL, STUART. 2005. *The Cry of the Icemark.* Scholastic/Chicken House.
Inheriting the throne of Icemark, 14-year-old Thirrin Freer Strong-in-the-Arm Lindenshield negotiates alliances with werewolves, snow leopards, and vampires before she can lead her army against the invading, undefeated Polypontian Army.
(3T. Wintertime)

HINDS, GARETH. 2007. *Beowulf.* Candlewick.
Beowulf saves King Hrothgar and his people from the monster Grendel, but he is then forced to fight Grendel's mother, intent on revenging her son, before succumbing after an epic battle with a ferocious dragon.
(2H. Graphic Novels in the Classroom)

HINTON, S.E. 1967. *The Outsiders.* Random House.
Ponyboy divides the people in his world into two groups, greasers and socs, and is proud to be a greaser until one of his friends kills a soc and the ever-present class tensions explode into violence.
(1Q. Troubled Teen Boys)

HOBBS, WILL. 1996. *Far North.* Morrow.
After a plane crash, Texan Gabe, his boarding school roommate Raymond, a Dene Indian, and Johnny Raven, an elderly Dene Indian, are stranded in Canada's Northwest Territory where the boys rely on Johnny's knowledge for survival.
(3T. Wintertime)

———. 1998. *The Maze.* HarperCollins.
After he escapes from a corrupt juvenile detention facility, Rick is befriended by a biologist reintroducing condors to the wild and learns to hang glide before a run-in with gun-crazy locals reminds him that there are still consequences to be faced.
(3I. Institutions)

————. 2003. *Jackie's Wild Seattle*. HarperCollins.
Following 9/11, Shannon and her brother Cody help their uncle with his animal rescue work for a Seattle wildlife shelter.
(3F. The Environment)

————. 2006. *Crossing the Wire*. HarperCollins.
When the corn crops are poor and the prices are low, Victor knows it's time to leave his widowed mother and sister to head to "El Norte" to find work, although the penniless teen faces death and danger when trying to cross the border.
(1J. Latino Teens; 3S. Teen Immigrants)

————. 2008. *Go Big or Go Home*. HarperCollins.
A meteorite crashes through Brady's roof and a local professor discovers Martian bacteria growing in it, which may account for Brady's super-athletic strength.
(1R. Tweens; 3N. Science)

HOFFMAN, MARY. 2003. *Stravaganza: City of Stars*. Bloomsbury.
Horseback riding allows Georgia to escape from her cruel older stepbrother, but when she buys a small statue of a winged horse she is able to time travel between London and Talie, becoming the newest member of the Stravaganti.
(3G. Horses)

HOGAN, JAMES. 1997. *Bug Park*. Baen.
Eric Heber develops miniaturized robotic insects that achieve direct neural coupling, setting up conflict between his former boss and Eric's greedy wife, who want control of his inventions, and Eric's son and his friend, who stand in their way.
(3N. Science)

HOKENSON, TERRY. 2006. *The Winter Road*. Front Street.
Finding her uncle drunk and passed out, Willa flies his Cessna solo to pick up her mother in the Canadian bush, but a stormfront causes her to crash and she must be creative to survive the January snows.
(3T. Wintertime)

HÖLLDOBLER, BERT, AND EDWARD O. WILSON. 1994. *Journey to the Ants: A Story of Scientific Exploration*. Harvard University. NF.
Enter the world of ants and discover how they communicate via chemical scents, war against one another, tend aphid herds, and even capture other ants to use as slaves.
(3H. Insects)

HOLM, JENNIFER L. 2007. *Middle School Is Worse Than Meatloaf.* Atheneum.
Cartoons, homework papers, report cards, and IMs describe Ginny's seventh grade year as she acquires a dad, loses interest in ballet, and enjoys her first kiss.
(2C. Blogs, E-mails, and IMs in Fiction)

HOLM, JENNIFER L., AND MATTHEW HOLM. 2005– . Babymouse series. Random House.
The brother and sister team of Jennifer and Matthew Holm have created Babymouse, an energetic, fun-loving mouse whose imagination transforms lockers into black holes and boring parties into adventures.
(1R. Tweens)

HOLT, KIMBERLY WILLIS. 2003. *Keeper of the Night.* Holt.
Reeling from her mother's suicide, Isabel watches over her brother and sister while they sleep and worries that she can't remember her mother, as each family member reacts differently to the loss.
(2Q. Teen Issue Novels in Verse)

―――. 2006. *Part of Me: Stories of a Louisiana Family.* Holt.
Books and reading are the threads that bind successive generations of a Louisiana family together in this collection of related vignettes.
(3P. State Books)

HOLT, SIMON. 2008. *The Devouring.* Little, Brown.
After horror fan Reggie reads about the Vours—demonic creatures who invade a body and turn its owner into a cruel creature—she and her friend try to summon a Vour, but the one who arrives takes over the body of her younger brother Henry.
(3T. Wintertime)

HOLT, VICTORIA. 1988. *The India Fan.* Doubleday.
As the plain but intelligent daughter of a parson, Drusilla often bails out her high-spirited friend Lavinia and eventually travels to India to tutor Lavinia's children, where she is caught in the Indian mutiny and rescued by Fabian, a man who has always intrigued her.
(1B. Avid Readers)

HOOBLER, DOROTHY, AND THOMAS HOOBLER. 1999– . Samurai Mysteries series. Penguin Putnam.
The adopted son of Judge Ooka, 14-year-old Seikei wants nothing more than to be a samurai, an inherited honor in eighteenth-century Japan that he has little hope of achieving, despite his prowess in investigating and solving a series of mysteries.
(1K. Manga Lovers)

HOOPER, MARY. 2002. *Amy.* Bloomsbury.
Growing apart from her former best friend, Amy meets Zed in a chat room and, although she knows it's dangerous, agrees to meet him on a day that turns horrific, as she later describes in a police report.
(2C. Blogs, E-mails, and IMs in Fiction)

HOPKINS, CATHY. 2002–2006. Mates, Dates, and . . . series. Simon Pulse.
In this humorous series, London friends Lucy, Izzie, Nesta, and T.J. survive squabbles, romance, braces, and weight problems.
(2M. Paperback Series)

————. 2004–2006. Truth or Dare series. Simon Pulse.
Set in Cornwall, four British teens dare one another to push themselves, while also deciding when a situation requires a white lie, as they confront everyday teen problems.
(2M. Paperback Series)

————. 2005. *Mates, Dates, and Chocolate Cheats.* Simon Pulse.
After Christmas festivities and a school trip to Italy, British Izzie can't fit into her clothes and immediately obsesses about dieting, but she finds it hard to ignore the temptation of chocolate.
(3B. Chocolate)

HOPKINS, ELLEN. 2004. *Crank.* Simon & Schuster/Pulse.
Court ordered to visit her dad, Kristina is turned on to crank and quickly becomes addicted, returning home to a life where she craves the drug, starts selling it, and becomes pregnant.
(1D. Detention Home Girls; 2Q. Teen Issue Novels in Verse)

————. 2006. *Burned.* Simon & Schuster/McElderry.
Brought up in a Mormon household with an alcoholic father who abuses her mother, Pattyn questions her religion and is finally sent to spend the summer with an aunt on a remote Nevada ranch where she meets Derek and finds the "forever love" she needs.
(2Q. Teen Issue Novels in Verse; 3P. State Books)

————. 2007. *Glass.* Simon & Schuster/McElderry.
Off drugs following the birth of her daughter, Kristina bemoans her pregnancy fat and doesn't resist when her former dealer introduces her to "glass," or Mexican meth, and soon she deals for the Mexican Mafia as her life begins another downward spiral.
(2Q. Teen Issue Novels in Verse)

————. 2007. *Impulse.* Simon & Schuster/McElderry.

Vanessa, Tony, and Connor meet in a psychiatric hospital after surviving suicide attempts, but now on a camping trip with staff and other patients, one of them will try again.

(2Q. Teen Issue Novels in Verse)

————. 2009. *Tricks.* Simon & Schuster/McElderry.

Five different teens, three girls and two guys, end up in Las Vegas where they turn tricks in order to survive.

(2Q. Teen Issue Novels in Verse)

HOROWITZ, ANTHONY. 2001– . Alex Rider series. Philomel.

When Alex Rider's spy uncle dies, the British Intelligence Agency MI6 convinces him to assume his uncle's role, and, when he agrees, the adventures never stop.

(1G. Graphic Novel Lovers; 1O. Reluctant Male Readers)

————. 2001. *Stormbreaker.* Philomel.

In this first of the Alex Rider Series, Alex is surprised to learn that his Uncle Ian isn't the bank vice-president he always thought he was but instead a spy for the British government, a position Alex is asked to assume.

(1C. Book Haters)

————. 2005– . The Gatekeepers series. Scholastic.

Five children with unusual powers and an even more unusual shared history must find each other and combine their strengths to fight the evil Nightrise Corporation and prevent the return of the Old Ones.

(1K. Manga Lovers)

————. 2007. *Snakehead.* Read by Simon Prebble. Recorded Books. Unabridged, 10 hours.

Agreeing to help the Australian Secret Intelligence Service and a godfather he never knew he had, Alex confronts immigrant smuggling, evil organization Snakehead's plans to induce a tsunami, and betrayal, all voiced by Prebble, who masterfully emulates Asian, Australian, British, and European accents.

(2A. Audiobooks for High School Listeners)

HORVATH, POLLY. 2001. *Everything on a Waffle.* Farrar, Straus and Giroux.

Primrose doesn't believe her parents have been lost at sea but adjusts to life with a variety of guardians, manages to lose two digits, singes a guinea pig, and ends every chapter with a recipe, including fish and chips on a waffle.

(1H. Innocent Middle School Girls; 3E. Cookery)

HOSLER, JAY. 2001. *Clan Apis.* Active Synapse. NF.
The ordeals faced by honeybee Nyuki and its hive mates as they dodge a woodpecker on their way to a new hive are illustrated in this nonfiction graphic novel. (2K. Nonfiction Graphic Novels; 3H. Insects)

HOSSEINI, KHALED. 2003. *The Kite Runner.* Riverhead.
Before he leaves Afghanistan for California, Amir betrays a friend; now he learns that his friend and his friend's wife have been killed and their young son kidnapped, which sends Amir back to Afghanistan to rescue his friend's son. (3M. The Middle East)

HOTTA, YUMI. 1998– . Hikaru No Go series. Illustrated by Takeshi Obata. VIZ Media.
Hikaru Shindo is just an average Japanese boy until the day he discovers an old *Go* game board and is instantly merged with the ghost of an ancient *Go* master who has been trapped in the board for centuries. (2D. Classic Manga)

HOUSTON, JULIAN. 2005. *New Boy.* Houghton Mifflin.
Rob expects life to be difficult when he moves to Connecticut to attend a prestigious boarding school as the school's first African American student, but he's not prepared for the confusion he experiences after meeting Malcolm X on a trip to New York City. (3C. The Civil Rights Movement)

HOWE, JAMES, ED. 2001. *The Color of Absence: 12 Stories about Loss and Hope.* Simon & Schuster.
Addressing the emotional confusion that often results from loss are authors Virginia Euwer Wolff, Annette Curtis Klause, Walter Dean Myers, Avi, Angela Johnson, Norma Fox Mazer, and Naomi Shihab Nye, among others. (2J. Must-Have Anthologies)

————, ED. 2003. *13: Thirteen Stories That Capture the Agony and Ecstasy of Being Thirteen.* Simon & Schuster.
Thirteen authors, including Ann Martin, Bruce Coville, Todd Strasser, Meg Cabot, Alex Sanchez, Ron Koertge, and Ellen Wittlinger, offer thirteen stories about that bewildering age. (2J. Must-Have Anthologies)

————. 2003. *Misfits.* Read by a full cast. Full Cast Audio. Unabridged, 5 hours.
Tired of being called names, four seventh graders speak out against harassment in an audiobook recorded by a full cast that features many teen narrators and makes the middle school atmosphere so believable. (2B. Audiobooks for Middle School Listeners)

HOWE, NORMA. 1999–2000. Blue Avenger series. Holt.
Blue Avenger, otherwise known as teenager David Schumacher, attempts various amazing feats with the help of his girlfriend Omaha Nebraska Brown in an effort to explore the question of free will.
(1G. Graphic Novel Lovers)

HOWELL, SIMMONE. 2008. *Everything Beautiful.* Bloomsbury.
Riley rebels after her mother's death, beds any boy she can, and declares herself an atheist, which leads her born-again father to send her to a Christian camp where she plans to disrupt all Bible activities, but she finds the campers aren't all that bad.
(3Q. Summer Camp)

HUBBELL, SUE. 1993. *Broadsides from the Other Orders: A Book of Bugs.* Random House. NF.
This charming account of the antics of both ordinary and odd insect species, including ocean striders (*Halobates*), daddy long legs that find lost cows, and book-eating silverfish, may change how many humans view insects.
(3H. Insects)

HUDSON, NOEL. 2008. *The Band Name Book.* Boston Mills. NF.
Thousands of bands from more than 30 countries, divided into irreverent categories, are found in this work that explains how and where a band got its name and what band names are still available, making it great for browsing.
(1C. Book Haters)

HUGHES, LANGSTON. 1994. *The Dream Keeper and Other Poems.* Illustrated by Brian Pinkney. Knopf/Random. NF.
This updated edition of the original 1932 work, with scratchboard illustrations by Brian Pinckney, resonates with the vitality and pain, joy and despair of African Americans in poems written more than 70 years ago.
(2P. Poetry Anthologies for Middle School Readers)

HULME, JOHN, AND MICHAEL WEXLER. 2008. *The Glitch in Sleep.* Seems Trilogy, book 1. Bloomsbury.
Twelve-year-old Becker Drane has been recruited as a Fixer in the Seems, a mirror world to our own, and his job is to fix the Glitch in the Department of Sleep, which, if not fixed, will ensure that no one ever again has a good night's sleep.
(1R. Tweens)

HUNTER, ERIN. 2003–2004. Warriors series. HarperCollins.
Four clans of wild cats battle for forest territory and hunting rights, including Firepaw, new member of the ThunderClan, who finds himself at the center of clan intrigue.
(1F. Gifted Elementary Student Readers)

I

IKUMI, MIA, ET AL. 2003. Tokyo Mew Mew series. Tokyopop.
The Mew Mews, a gang of super-powered girls injected with an experimental serum of animal DNA, welcome a new member when Berry transfers to the posh school that is their headquarters and is mistakenly given a mix of rabbit and mountain cat genes.
(2D. Classic Manga)

INNOCENTI, ROBERTO. 1985. *Rose Blanche*. Illustrated by Christophe Gallaz. The Creative Company.
Rose Blanche, a young girl in World War II Germany, discovers a concentration camp hidden in the woods and dedicates herself to bringing food to the prisoners until the day she is shot by guards.
(2N. Picture Books for Teens)

IRVING, JOHN. 1989. *A Prayer for Owen Meany*. Modern Library.
Johnny's good friend Owen Meany is convinced he's an instrument of God, and with his loud mouth and utter conviction, he knows he will be martyred, he knows when, and he lives his life accordingly.
(1M. Picky Senior Girls)

J

JACOBSON, SID, AND ERNIE COLON. 2006. *The 9/11 Report: A Graphic Adaptation*. Farrar, Straus and Giroux. NF.
This authorized graphic adaptation of the National Commission on Terrorist Attacks official report condenses and illuminates the information collected by the commission and thoughtfully depicts the participants on both sides of the attacks.
(2K. Nonfiction Graphic Novels)

JACQUES, BRIAN. 1986– . Redwall series. Penguin Putnam.
The animals that live in and around Redwall Abbey and Mossflower Woods explore, fight, live, and die generation after generation.
(1E. Gentlemanly Boys; 1F. Gifted Elementary Student Readers)

JAFFE, MICHELE. 2006. *Bad Kitty*. HarperCollins.
Unhappily vacationing with her parents in Las Vegas, wanna-be detective Jasmine avoids a cat attack but accidentally knocks a bride and her cake into the hotel pool and winds up in a mysterious situation with a missing husband and his model-actress wife.
(2C. Blogs, E-mails, and IMs in Fiction)

JAMES, MARY. 1990. *Shoebag*. Scholastic.
Shoebag, the cockroach son of Under the Toaster and Drainboard, awakens one morning and discovers to his horror that he's been transformed into a boy, adopted by the Biddle family, and renamed Stuart Bagg.
(3H. Insects)

JANECZKO, PAUL B. 2004. *Worlds Afire: The Hartford Circus Fire of 1944*. Candlewick.
Twenty-nine characters, including circus performers, those who die or are injured, and even the arsonist, describe what they saw on that fatal day when a circus fire killed 167 people and injured 500 more.
(2I. Historical Novels in Verse)

————, SELECTOR. 2005. *A Kick in the Head: An Everyday Guide to Poetic Forms*. Illustrated by Chris Raschka. Candlewick. NF.
Poetic forms such as couplets, tercets, ballads, and pantoums are featured in this collection that explains how to create various types of poetry.
(2P. Poetry Anthologies for Middle School Readers)

JANSON, HANNA. 2006. *Over a Thousand Hills I Walk with You*. Lerner.
The only member of her Tutsi family to survive the 1994 Rwandan genocide, eight-year-old Jeanne is adopted into an understanding German family and encouraged to tell her story.
(2G. Fictionalized Biographies)

JARAMILLO, ANN. 2006. *La Línea*. Roaring Brook.
Left behind in Mexico when their parents cross the border into California to find work, Miguel is thrilled six years later when told to join his parents but dismayed to find that his sister Elena has followed him.
(1J. Latino Teens; 3S. Teen Immigrants)

JEMAS, BILL, AND BRIAN MICHAEL BENDIS. 2000. *Ultimate Spider-Man: Power and Responsibility*. Illustrated by Mark Bagley et al. Marvel.
Peter Parker is transformed from nerdy kid to superhero after he's bitten by a radioactive spider in a familiar story updated and modernized but true to the original.
(2E. Core Graphic Novels)

JENKINS, A.M. 2006. *Beating Heart: A Ghost Story*. HarperCollins.
Seventeen-year-old Evan meets Cora through a box of belongings left behind, and her ghost, which haunts his new home and sends him vivid dreams, causes him to reevaluate his current relationship with longtime girlfriend Carrie.
(2R. Two or More Voices in Novels)

————. 2007. *Repossessed*. HarperCollins.
Kiriel, who prefers to be called a fallen angel rather than a minor demon, takes an unauthorized vacation from his job in Hell and inhabits the body of an about-to-be-killed teen in order to experience life and maybe bring himself to the attention of the Creator.
(1O. Reluctant Male Readers)

JIMINÉZ, FRANCISCO. 1997. *The Circuit: Stories from the Life of a Migrant Child*. Houghton Mifflin. NF.
Jimenez's autobiography begins in Mexico but quickly moves north as his parents cross the border in search of work, where moving from farm to farm, the young Jimenez struggles to keep up in school and find a place for himself.
(3S. Teen Immigrants)

————. 2001. *Breaking Through*. Houghton Mifflin.
In this fictionalized sequel to *The Circuit* (a book of autobiographical stories), Francisco and his brother are now teens in 1950s California and trying to balance their typical teen insolence with the customary respect Mexican children give to the elderly.
(1J. Latino Teens)

JINKS, CATHERINE. 2007. *Evil Genius*. Harcourt.
Computer genius Cadel doesn't realize he's being manipulated when his therapist warns him not to get caught when he puts his talent for destruction to use at the Axis Institute for World Domination.
(3L. Mathematics)

JOHNSON, ANGELA. 2003. *The First Part Last*. Simon & Schuster.
Bobby struggles to stay in school and rise above the disapproval and incomprehension of family and friends as he raises his infant daughter Feather on his own, despite the fact that he's only 16 years old.
(1Q. Troubled Teen Boys; 1S. Urban Teens: Beyond Street Lit)

JOHNSON, HARRIET McBRYDE. 2006. *Accidents of Nature*. Holt.
Jean experiences some limitations because of her cerebral palsy, but the summer she attends Camp Courage is the first time she meets anyone else with a disability and begins to understand the varied world of the disabled.
(3P. State Books; 3Q. Summer Camp)

JOHNSON, KATHLEEN JEFFRIE. 2003. *Target*. Roaring Brook.
After being brutally raped by two men, 16-year-old Grady changes schools in an attempt to forget his past, but his inability to speak and his graphic memories keep him trapped in the past until new friends offer him the possibility of recovery.
(3O. Silence)

————. 2004. *A Fast and Brutal Wing*. Roaring Brook.
When three teens wake up bloody and naked the morning after Halloween and it's soon discovered that a famous author is missing, Niki insists that she and her brother Emmett can transform into animals and have no memory of that night, but is she telling the truth?
(2R. Two or More Voices in Novels)

JOHNSON, LOUANNE. 2009. *Muchacho*. Knopf.
Though Eddie Corazon acts like a delinquent, blows off school, and hangs with his drug-dealing cousins, when he meets college-bound Lupe he suddenly wants a different future.
(1J. Latino Teens)

JOHNSON, MAUREEN. 2005. *13 Little Blue Envelopes*. HarperCollins.
When her beloved Aunt Peg dies, Ginny is left with a packet of blue envelopes, some cash, and instructions to fly to Europe, which launches her trip to meet Peg's friends, see a café Peg painted, and gain confidence in herself.
(1A. Adult Readers; 1B. Avid Readers)

JOHNSON, VARIAN. 2007. *My Life as a Rhombus*. Flux.
Following her abortion, Rhonda tries to reinstate herself in her father's good graces as she studies hard, tutors Sarah in math, and even offers to help when she discovers that Sarah's secretly pregnant.
(3L. Mathematics)

JOLIN, PAULA. 2007. *In the Name of God*. Roaring Brook.
After her cousin's arrest by the Syrian secret police, devout Muslim Nadia craves action, not more words, and is drawn into a radical group with hard-line political views, despite her mother's peaceful example.
(3M. The Middle East)

JONES, DIANA WYNNE. 1986. *Howl's Moving Castle*. HarperCollins.
Turned into an old woman by the evil Witch of the Waste, young Sophie finds refuge in the bizarre moving castle of Howl, the possibly evil wizard who supposedly eats souls and who is definitely under a curse.
(1F. Gifted Elementary Student Readers; 1K. Manga Lovers)

————. 2007. *The Game*. Firebird.
Sent from her strict grandparents to visit her cousins in Ireland, Hayley is introduced to a game played in the mythosphere, a gauzy area composed of myths and
legends she doesn't understand but that somehow involves her missing parents.
(3K. Luck)

JONES, PATRICK. 2004. *Things Change*. Bloomsbury.
Johanna's formerly stable life veers dangerously off course when she starts dating
Paul, a troubled but popular boy whose abusive personality is revealed as their relationship progresses.
(2R. Two or More Voices in Novels)

————. 2007. *Chasing Tail Lights*. Bloomsbury.
Christy dreams of leaving Flint, Michigan, and of starting a new life far away from the
loneliness and responsibility of life with her distant mother, but the dark secret she
harbors keeps her from realizing the potential her kind English teacher sees in her.
(3A. Bathrooms)

JORDAN, HILLARY. 2008. *Mudbound*. Algonquin.
As a spinster schoolteacher, Laura never envisions she'll marry and live on a farm
surrounded by mud that's as viscous as the racism of townspeople who can't understand that a bond can form between a white man and a black man because of
their shared war experiences.
(1M. Picky Senior Girls)

JUBY, SUSAN. 2003–2005. Alice series. HarperCollins.
Home-schooled for years, Alice is about to start her first year of public school, giving her the opportunity to test her career aspirations and meet new people, two
goals she pursues over the next few years with mixed results.
(2F. Diaries and Epistolary Novels)

————. 2007. *Another Kind of Cowboy*. HarperTeen.
When Alex's father gives him a Western horse won in a poker game, Alex is disap-
pointed, as he'll never be able to learn dressage atop Turnip.
(3G. Horses)

————. 2008. *Getting the Girl: A Guide to Private Investigation, Surveillance, and
Cookery*. HarperCollins.
At Sherman's high school, each year when a girl's photo appears in the boy's bathroom, it signals that she'll be D-listed, a ritual Sherman plans to stop, but first he has
to plan the menu and cook his dinner party assignment for a home economics class.
(3E. Cookery)

JUSTER, NORTON. 1961. *The Phantom Tollbooth*. Random House.
Milo is desperately bored, despite all his toys, but when a mysterious tollbooth appears in his room he is swept up in a strange adventure involving, among other things, the Whether Man, a talking watchdog, and the astonishing Word Market of Dictionopolis.
(1E. Gentlemanly Boys)

K

KANTOR, MELISSA. 2007. *The Breakup Bible*. Hyperion.
After her boyfriend, who also happens to be her editor on the school paper, dumps her for another member of the newspaper staff, Jen decides she might need the advice in Dr. Emory Emerson's *The Breakup Bible*.
(3J. Love Hurts)

————. 2009. *Girlfriend Material*. Hyperion.
Kate has wonderful plans for the summer to play tennis, write, and read, but her mother decides to temporarily separate from Kate's father and drags her along to visit friends on Cape Cod, where life looks up when Kate meets Adam.
(3R. Summertime)

KATIN, MIRIAM. 2006. *We Are on Our Own*. Farrar, Straus and Giroux. NF.
Katin's memories of time spent with her mother after they faked their deaths and fled Budapest in order to avoid the Nazi invasion are graphically rendered in this account of war and its long-term effects on Katin and her family.
(2K. Nonfiction Graphic Novels)

KEILLOR, GARRISON, ED. 2005. *Good Poems for Hard Times*. Viking. NF.
In "The Writer's Almanac" feature of Keillor's weekly *Prairie Home Companion* radio variety show, he reads many contemporary poems by living, or recently deceased, authors, many of which can be found in this sequel to *Good Poems* (Viking, 2002).
(2O. Poetry Anthologies for High School Readers)

KELLER, MICHAEL. 2009. *Charles Darwin's* On the Origin of Species: *A Graphic Adaptation*. Rodale Books. NF.
This graphic rendering of Darwin's original text also offers information about his research and methods, the reaction of the scientific community, and his correspondence with leading scientists of his day.
(2H. Graphic Novels in the Classroom)

KELLY, JACQUELINE. 2009. *The Evolution of Calpurnia Tate*. Holt.
Calpurnia's evolving individuality and formative relationship with her naturalist grandfather threaten her mother's plans for her to enter society as a proper young lady.
(1H. Innocent Middle School Girls)

KENNEDY, X.J. 2002. *Exploding Gravy: Poems to Make You Laugh*. Illustrated by Joy Allen. Little, Brown. NF.
Divided into kid-centered themes, such as monsters, food, and animals, more than 80 illustrated poems offer laughable moments when veggies morph, ravioli is eaten . . . sloli, or granddad locks his wooden leg.
(2P. Poetry Anthologies for Middle School Readers)

KIBUISHI, KAZU, ED. 2004– . Flight series. Image Comics.
A true artists' showcase, each Flight anthology features dozens of stories, many wordless, by mostly young, animation-inspired storytellers.
(2E. Core Graphic Novels)

KIDD, SUE MONK. 2002. *The Secret Life of Bees*. Viking.
Fleeing Lily's abusive father, Lily and family servant Rosaleen arrive in Tiburon, South Carolina, and are taken in by three bee-keeping sisters who help Lily finally understand that she wasn't responsible for her mother's death.
(1B. Avid Readers; 3H. Insects)

KIKUCHI, HIDEYUKI. 2005– . Vampire Hunter D series. Dark Horse.
For more than 300 years, humanity has been under the control of the Nobility, fearsome vampires with demon companions, but in the year 12090 men have begun to fight back, led by warriors known as Hunters.
(1K. Manga Lovers)

KIMANI TRU SERIES. 2007– . Harlequin.
Twenty-first-century problems and concerns experienced by African American high school students form the basis of this series.
(2M. Paperback Series)

KING, LAURIE R. 1994. *Beekeeper's Apprentice: Or, On the Segregation of the Queen*. Minotaur.
Walking in the Sussex countryside one day, Mary Russell almost steps on a man who turns out to be Sherlock Holmes, who, recognizing her quick mind, takes Mary on as an apprentice, which is good preparation when they meet a criminal the equal of Moriarty.
(1B. Avid Readers)

KINGSOLVER, BARBARA. 1998. *The Poisonwood Bible.* HarperFlamingo.
Though unsanctioned by his church, Nathan moves his family to the Belgian Congo where he attempts to convert everyone to Christianity, while the Congolese are more concerned about freeing themselves from Belgium's rule.
(1M. Picky Senior Girls)

KINNEY, JEFF. 2007–2010. Diary of a Wimpy Kid series. Abrams/Amulet.
Written like a child's diary with stick figures and handwritten notes, the series relates Greg Heffley's adventures, including wrestling, the school play, his grandfather, summer vacation, and his soccer team.
(1G. Graphic Novel Lovers; 1R. Tweens)

KISHIMOTO, MASASHI. 2003– . Naruto series. VIZ Media.
Naruto is a prankster and a klutz, shunned by most of his village and without friends when he attempts to pass the entry test and be admitted to the Ninja Academy, but his unpleasant reputation masks a hidden and fearsome secret.
(2D. Classic Manga)

KIYAMA, HENRY. 1999. *The Four Immigrants Manga: A Japanese Experience in San Francisco, 1904–1924.* Stone Bridge Press.
Kiyama's autobiographical stories feature four friends who immigrated to San Francisco in 1904 as they navigate employment, live through the Great Earthquake and influenza epidemic, grow up, and get married.
(2H. Graphic Novels in the Classroom)

KLAGES, ELLEN. 2006. *The Green Glass Sea.* Viking.
While Dewey builds a radio and confronts the bullies at her school in the early 1940s, her mathematician father and other scientists work on "the gadget" at Los Alamos.
(3N. Science)

KLASS, DAVID. 1994. *California Blue.* Scholastic.
Runner John Rodgers discovers an unknown species of butterfly living among the California redwoods, which has major implications for the logging community, while John's family is more concerned about his father's cancer diagnosis.
(3H. Insects; 3N. Science)

———. 2002. *Home of the Braves.* Farrar, Straus and Giroux.
Joe Brickman, captain of the soccer team at Lawndale High School, must contend not only with the confident Brazilian transfer student and new soccer star who quickly makes a move on his crush, but also with the violent jocks who rule the school.
(1Q. Troubled Teen Boys)

————. 2006. *Firestorm.* Farrar, Straus and Giroux.

Raised to keep a low profile, Jack is startled to learn that his parents aren't his parents and he's really from the future but has been sent back in time to save Earth from an ecological disaster.

(3N. Science)

————. 2008. *Whirlwind.* Farrar, Straus and Giroux.

Completing his assignment to save the Earth's oceans from ecological destruction, Jack learns his girlfriend is being held somewhere in the Amazon Rain Forest by the Dark Lord, sending Jack, Eko, Gisco, and the time-traveling wizard Kidah to her rescue.

(3F. The Environment)

KLAUSE, ANNETTE CURTIS. 1997. *Blood and Chocolate.* Delacorte.

While her werewolf pack selects a new leader, Vivian is torn between a fellow werewolf who's interested in her and a "meat boy" at her school, and she doesn't know whether to choose the "blood" or the "chocolate."

(3B. Chocolate)

KLISE, KATE. 1998. *Regarding the Fountain: A Tale, in Letters, of Liars and Leaks.* HarperCollins.

When the need arises for a new water fountain for Dry Creek Middle School, Principal Russ has no idea the furor that will result when he invites flamboyant *artiste* Florence Waters to design one, in a tale told in letters, faxes, memos, and newspaper articles.

(1R. Tweens)

KNOX, ELIZABETH. 2005–2007. Dreamhunter Duet. Farrar, Straus and Giroux.

Dreamhunter Laura Hame, helped by the golem-like sandman she created, searches for her missing father and for the secret at the heart of The Place, the invisible area where dreams—and nightmares—come from.

(1A. Adult Readers)

KOERTGE, RON. 2003. *Shakespeare Bats Cleanup.* Candlewick.

Stuck in bed recovering from mono, Kevin tries his father's suggestion to keep a journal and struggles to record his thoughts, but when a book about poetry inspires him to try haiku, sonnets, and sestinas, he writes away his grief about his mother's death.

(2F. Diaries and Epistolary Novels)

————. 2004. *Margaux with an X.* Candlewick.

Tired of her life, fashionable Margaux spots bookish Danny, a student at the other end of the social spectrum, and the two form an unlikely friendship, gradually revealing secrets about their families that they've never shared with anyone else.

(1N. Punk Readers)

KOJA, KATHE. 2003. *Buddha Boy.* Farrar, Straus and Giroux.
Justin's anonymity in high school disappears when he's partnered with Jinsen, nicknamed "Buddha Boy" because he lives following Buddhist principles, which, unfortunately, makes him a prime target for school bullies.
(1L. Offbeat Guys; 3O. Silence)

———. 2007. *Kissing the Bee.* Farrar, Straus and Giroux.
Part of a threesome, Dana is struck by the way the bees in her science project resemble her triad, with Emil as the drone, Avra as the queen bee, and Dana as the worker.
(3N. Science)

KONIGSBURG, E.L. 1996. *The View from Saturday.* Simon & Schuster.
Four unlikely sixth graders are chosen to compete as an Academic Bowl team, and when they win despite their seeming unsuitability, people begin to question how and why they were chosen.
(1F. Gifted Elementary Student Readers; 1H. Innocent Middle School Girls; 2R. Two or More Voices in Novels)

———. 2000. *Silent to the Bone.* Simon & Schuster.
Connor tries to uncover the reason for his friend Branwell's sudden silence and to help Branwell reveal what really happened to his baby sister.
(3O. Silence)

———. 2004. *The Outcasts of 19 Schuyler Place.* Atheneum.
Margaret Rose Kane remembers the summer her elderly uncles rescued her from the torment of summer camp and she in turn helped them save the artistic towers they'd built in their backyard.
(1F. Gifted Elementary Student Readers)

KORMAN, GORDON. 2000. *No More Dead Dogs.* Hyperion.
When eighth grader Wallace tells his English teacher he doesn't want to read any more books where the dog dies, he receives a detention that requires him to sit with his teacher who's directing a play and leads to Wallace's suggestion to punch it up to a rock musical.
(1R. Tweens)

———. 2004. *Son of the Mob.* Hyperion.
In this laugh-out-loud novel, Vince Luca, who refuses to be part of his family's gangster interests, dates and falls in love with Kendra, who turns out to be the daughter of the FBI agent who's been after his dad for ages.
(1O. Reluctant Male Readers)

————. 2004. *Son of the Mob: Hollywood Hustle*. Hyperion.
Vince Luca is happy that moving to California for college also means putting a whole continent between himself and his New York mob boss dad, but when Luca Family henchman show up in Santa Monica, Vince realizes the solution isn't quite that simple.
(2L. Novels with Script or Screenplay Format)

————. 2006. *Born to Rock*. Hyperion.
Needing money for college, and thinking that wealthy King Maggot, lead singer for the punk band Purge, might be his biological father, Leo signs on as a roadie for Purge's Summer Revival tour on a journey of punk rockers and their groupies.
(1N. Punk Readers)

KOSTICK, CONOR. 2007. *Epic*. Viking.
All conflicts on Earth are now controlled through a virtual reality computer game called Epic, which Erik is forced to play and win to keep his parents from being "reallocated."
(3N. Science)

KROVATIN, CHRISTOPHER. 2005. *Heavy Metal and You*. Push.
A fan of heavy metal music and getting wasted with his friends, Sam Markus gives up his vices when he dates prim and proper Melissa, but worries that this new Sam is just a phony.
(1N. Punk Readers)

KRUEGER, JIM. 2003. *Testament*. Illustrated by Bill Sienkiewicz. Metron Press. NF.
This graphic and straightforward retelling of familiar and obscure stories from the Old Testament is framed by the tale of a lonely man who goes looking for company in a bar called J.J.'s.
(2K. Nonfiction Graphic Novels)

KRULL, KATHLEEN. 2003. *Harvesting Hope: The Story of Cesar Chavez*. Illustrated by Yuyi Morales. Houghton Mifflin. NF.
Cesar Chavez, the son of poor migrant workers who toiled for little pay on California farms, grew up and organized a 340-mile march to protest the ill treatment, a nonviolent revolt that resulted in greatly improved pay and working conditions.
(2N. Picture Books for Teens)

KUBERT, JOE. 1998. *Fax from Sarajevo: A Story of Survival.* Dark Horse. NF.
   The Rustemagic family, trapped in Sarajevo, manages to send out faxes, and these, along with family photos and other graphics, reveal their struggles to live after the Serbian invasion.
(2K. Nonfiction Graphic Novels)

KUBO, TITE. 2001. Bleach series. VIZ Media.
   Ichigo Kurosaki can see ghosts, but he's still surprised at the world he discovers after Rukia, a member of the Soul Society, shares her powers with him in an attempt to save his family from a Hollow, an evil spirit that feeds on human psychic energies.
(2D. Classic Manga)

KYI, TANYA LLOYD. 2003. *Truth.* Orca.
   After an adult neighbor is killed during a house party, everyone seems afraid to go to the police except for Jen, who, as a reporter for the school's TV show, decides to find out the truth, but when she starts to dig, violence flits through her community.
(1P. Striving Readers)

L

LACHTMAN, OFELIA DUMAS. 2001. *Summer of El Pintor.* Arte Público.
   Suddenly penniless, Monica and her father move to her deceased mother's tiny home in the Los Angeles barrio where Monica searches for their next-door neighbor, the artist El Pintor, thinking they have a connection.
(1I. Latina Teens)

LAIRD, ELIZABETH. 1991. *Kiss the Dust.* Penguin Putnam.
   Tara knows she and her family are among the lucky ones as they flee their city home in Northern Iraq and travel to their rustic vacation home in the mountains, but even with money, the family eventually ends up in a refugee camp before making it to London.
(3M. The Middle East)

LALWANI, NIKITA. 2007. *Gifted.* Random House.
   Labeled gifted in kindergarten, Rumi's mathematician father gives her extra math work in the hopes she'll be accepted at Oxford when she's 14, but Rumi longs for romance instead.
(3L. Mathematics)

LANE, AMY. 2005– . Little Goddess series. iUniverse.
Working the night shift at a Northern California gas station, Corinne meets a wide variety of people, but none so intriguing as the vampire Adrian who leads her into the dangerous world of the supernatural.
(2M. Paperback Series)

LANE, DAKOTA. 2005. *The Orpheus Obsession.* HarperCollins.
Spending the day at Brighton Beach with her sister, Anooshka meets Orpheus, a musician just beginning the climb to notoriety, and feels instantly connected to him, reads his online diary, and dreams of life with him until he leaves on tour and is out of her life.
(1N. Punk Readers; 1R. Tweens)

LANGAN, PAUL, SERIES ED. 2002–2008. Bluford series. Townsend Press.
The lives of a group of students at Bluford High School, named after America's first African American astronaut Guion "Guy" Bluford, intertwine through family relationships, school problems, and romantic triangles.
(2M. Paperback Series)

LARSON, HOPE. 2008. *Chiggers.* Atheneum.
In this graphic novel, Abby returns to camp and befriends new camper Shasta, finds they like the same boy in addition to other shared interests, and speaks up for her friend when other campers don't like her.
(3Q. Summer Camp)

LARSON, KIRBY. 2006. *Hattie Big Sky.* Delacorte.
Orphan Hattie is bequeathed her uncle's Montana homestead, but when she arrives it's deep winter and she and her cat Mr. Whiskers are alone in a dilapidated cabin on a homestead that has to become productive in ten months or it will be lost.
(1P. Striving Readers; 3P. State Books)

LASKY, KATHRYN. 2003–2008. Guardians of Ga'Hoole series. Scholastic.
The young barn owl Soren is pushed out of the nest by his older brother, captured by owls known as the evil ones, and sent to "St. Aggie's" where he and other orphans are used to pull "flecks" out of owl pellets in a 15-volume series.
(1F. Gifted Elementary Student Readers)

LAT. 2006. *Kampung Boy.* First Second.
Graphic novel format helps one see the largeness of a young boy's world as Lat relates his early adventures in his Malaysian kampung, or village, including lessons about the Koran when he's only six, his circumcision at ten, and then boarding school.
(2H. Graphic Novels in the Classroom)

————. 2007. *Town Boy*. Roaring Brook.
Malaysian cartoonist Lat presents a memoir of his teen years, during which he moved to a new town to attend boarding school, collected a diverse group of friends, was introduced to Western rock and roll, and discovered girls.
(2H. Graphic Novels in the Classroom)

LATHAM, JEAN LEE. 1935. *Carry On, Mr. Bowditch*. Houghton Mifflin.
No one in eighteenth-century Salem thought slight Nathaniel Bowditch would grow up to be a sailor, but after years of study and observation he became a master navigator and, after publishing the *Sailor's Bible*, a New England hero.
(2G. Fictionalized Biographies)

LATIFA. 2001. *My Forbidden Face: Growing Up Under the Taliban: A Young Woman's Story*. Hyperion. NF.
After the Taliban took over women were forbidden from working, but Latifa's mother, a doctor, continued to see patients in secret, and Latifa started an underground school for girls before the family left the country and were declared enemies of the state.
(3M. The Middle East)

LAW, INGRID. 2008. *Savvy*. Dial.
Whenever anyone in the Beaumont family reaches their thirteenth birthday, they receive a "savvy," which is a magical power unique to their personality, so when Mibs's father is injured and it's time to receive her savvy, Mibs wants one to help him.
(1R. Tweens)

LEAVITT, MARTINE. 2004. *Heck Superhero*. Boyds Mills Press.
Thirteen-year-old Heck finds solace in drawing superheroes who are able to save the world through good deeds, so when his depressed mother goes missing and he finds himself homeless and alone, he tries to emulate their actions in the hope of getting his mom back.
(1G. Graphic Novel Lovers)

————. 2006. *Keturah and Lord Death*. Front Street.
Lost and hungry in the forest, peasant girl Keturah is approached by Lord Death, but her stories of love beguile him and delay the inevitable.
(1M. Picky Senior Girls)

LEE, HARPER. 2006. *To Kill a Mockingbird*. Read by Sissy Spacek. Caedmon Audio. Unabridged, 12 hours.
This well-known classic is deftly narrated in the Southern drawl of Spacek as she portrays Scout and her perspective of life in a small town in the Deep South where racism is never far away.
(2A. Audiobooks for High School Listeners)

LEE, TANITH. 1998–2002. The Claidi Journals series. Penguin Putnam.
When Claidi decides to help a captured balloonist escape from the unpleasant princess whom she serves as a lady's maid, she unknowingly sets in motion a series of events involving the Towers, desert bandits, and a surprising destiny.
(2F. Diaries and Epistolary Novels)

LEHMANN-HAUPT, CHRISTOPHER. 2005. *The Mad Cook of Pymatuning.* Simon & Schuster.
Jerry returns to Camp Seneca as a junior counselor, accompanied by his half-brother Peter, only to discover that camp activities now have a cruel edge to them as the new administrator tells disturbing stories that leave the campers in tears.
(3Q. Summer Camp)

LEITCH, WILL. 2005. *Catch.* Razorbill.
In the summer before he leaves for college, Tim works at the Lenders Bagel plant and realizes that although his father and brother are local celebrities because of their baseball prowess, that role isn't enough to satisfy him.
(3P. State Books)

LENSKI, LOIS. 1941. *Indian Captive: The Story of Mary Jemison.* HarperCollins.
Mary Jemison, kidnapped from her home when she was 15 years old, struggles to maintain her English identity while accepting her new life among the Seneca Indians.
(2G. Fictionalized Biographies)

LESTER, ALISON. 2003. *The Snow Pony.* Houghton Mifflin.
Finding and taming a wild pony turns Dusty into a one-woman horse lover as she helps her fourth-generation Australian farmer dad around the ranch, even bringing the cattle down from the high country in the midst of a snowstorm.
(3G. Horses)

LESTER, JULIUS. 2005. *Day of Tears.* Hyperion.
Emma, a house slave who cares for the master's daughters, is sold to a woman in Kentucky at the largest slave auction in U.S. history despite the fact that she'd been promised otherwise.
(2L. Novels with Script or Screenplay Format)

LEVINE, ELLEN S. 1993. *Freedom's Children: Young Civil Rights Activists Tell Their Own Stories.* Penguin Putnam. NF.
Levine chronicles the lives of unknown activists, leaders, and demonstrators who attended white schools, participated in sit-ins and bus boycotts, led marches and rallies, and suffered injury and death in the fight for civil rights.
(3C. The Civil Rights Movement)

LEVITHAN, DAVID. 2005. *Boy Meets Boy*. Read by Nicholas Robideau and a full cast. Full Cast Audio. Unabridged, 6 hours.
Teens in the full cast give a natural authenticity to the characters, including a comic edge to the drag queen quarterback, while Robideau's characterization of gay Paul is quiet and calm in a town where everyone's accepted.
(2A. Audiobooks for High School Listeners)

————. 2006. *Marly's Ghost*. Penguin Putnam.
After his girlfriend Marly dies of cancer, cynical high school student Ben is visited by three ghosts who show him his past, present, and possible future.
(3J. Love Hurts)

LEVITIN, SONIA. 1998. *The Singing Mountain*. Simon & Schuster.
Mitch decides to postpone his first year at UCLA in order to study the Torah and continue living at a yeshiva in Israel, a decision that worries his parents despite his apparent happiness.
(3M. The Middle East)

LEWIS, RICHARD. 2009. *Monster's Proof*. Simon & Schuster.
Mathematical genius Darby solves the proof that drove his aunt mad, one she called "Thingamabob Conjecture," only to have the proof materialize as "Bob" in the proportionally correctly shaped Vitruvian Man as drawn by da Vinci.
(3L. Mathematics)

LEWIS, THOMAS H. 1994. *Chilies to Chocolate: Food the Americas Gave the World*. University of Nebraska Press. NF.
African, Asian, and European diets were enhanced with the addition of such New World food products as amaranth, beans, cacao, chilies, maize, potato, quinoa, tomato, and vanilla.
(3B. Chocolate)

LEZOTTE, ANN CLARE. 2008. *T4: A Novel in Verse*. Houghton Mifflin.
Deaf Paula learns she is one of those slated to be killed when Hitler issues Tiergartenstrasse 4, or T4, which orders anyone with disabilities to be euthanized because they are "unfit to live."
(2I. Historical Novels in Verse)

LIBBRECHT, KENNETH, AND PATRICIA RASMUSSEN. 2003. *The Snowflake: Winter's Secret Beauty*. Voyageur. NF.
Physicist Libbrecht's text explains the science behind the little bits of dust around which ice creates a snowflake, while Rasmussen's microphotographs illustrate the geometry of these water molecules.
(3T. Wintertime)

LIBBY, ALISA. 2009. *The King's Rose*. Penguin Putnam.
Although only 15 years old and well aware of the dangers of such a liaison, Catherine Howard agrees to marry Henry VIII and attempts to produce an heir while also hiding her own secrets and pursuing a relationship with a young man of the court.
(2G. Fictionalized Biographies)

LICHTMAN, WENDY. 2007. *Do the Math: Secrets, Lies, and Algebra*. HarperCollins.
When Tess realizes eighth grade school life is difficult, she resorts to dependable math terms to sort out problems, using Venn diagrams to analyze a difficult friend and graphs to decipher the suspicious death of a family friend.
(3L. Mathematics)

LIMB, SUE. 2004. *Girl, 15, Charming but Insane*. Delacorte.
Jess Jordan leads a very confusing life as she and her best friend Flora love the same boy, her father e-mails horoscopes, and her mother is an embarrassing, hippie librarian.
(3A. Bathrooms)

LIU, SIYU, AND OREL PROTOPOPESCU. 2002. *A Thousand Peaks: Poems from China*. Illustrated by Stephen T. Johnson. Pacific View. NF.
The 35 selected poems introduce the reader to 2,000 years of Chinese poetry with descriptive paragraphs explaining the cultural context and sidebars with the original characters of the poem, accompanied by black and white illustrations.
(2P. Poetry Anthologies for Middle School Readers)

LLOYD, SACI. 2009. *The Carbon Diaries 2015*. Holiday House.
The United Kingdom is the first to limit carbon use by giving all citizens a card that monitors their activity, leaving Laura Brown and her family feeling the effects as her father loses his job, their house is cold, the toaster stops mid-cycle, and no one gets along.
(1N. Punk Readers)

LOCKHART, E. 2005. *The Boyfriend List*. Random House.
Ruby Oliver suffers from panic attacks after losing her best friend and her boyfriend, but with the help of Dr. Z, her new shrink, she begins to understand what it might take to feel in control again.
(3A. Bathrooms; 3J. Love Hurts)

———. 2006. *Fly on the Wall: How One Girl Saw Everything*. Random House.
Gretchen Yee's life was a mess before the day she woke up in the body of a fly on the wall of the boys' locker room, but what she observes there brings surprising

new insights that offer her hope and a new understanding of friends, boys, and family.
(1K. Manga Lovers; 3A. Bathrooms)

————. 2007. *Dramarama.* Hyperion.
In high school, Sarah and Douglas are noted for their theatrical ability, but, when they attend musical theater camp, they discover a world of talented campers and jealous rivalry.
(3Q. Summer Camp)

————. 2008. *The Disreputable History of Frankie Landau-Banks.* Hyperion.
Frankie is aware of the double standard between males and females at her boarding school, and it really irritates her that her boyfriend is a member of an all-male secret society, the Loyal Order of the Bassett Hounds, but Frankie has her own plans for them.
(1N. Punk Readers; 3J. Love Hurts)

LONDON, JACK. 1903. *The Call of the Wild.* Macmillan.
Part Saint Bernard and part Scottish sheepdog, stolen Buck is used as a Klondike sled dog before being adopted by a kind owner who is later killed by Indians, leading to an annual pilgrimage by Buck to the owner's death site.
(3T. Wintertime)

LOPEZ, RUTH. 2002. *Chocolate: The Nature of Indulgence.* Abrams. NF.
Rich text and color photographs highlight the history of chocolate from its beginning as a cacao bean used by the Aztecs to the manufacture of delicious chocolate with the addition of milk and sugar to cacao beans.
(3B. Chocolate)

LORD, CYNTHIA. 2006. *Rules.* Scholastic.
Catherine uses rules to help her autistic brother David navigate his world and, truth be told, to regulate his behavior, but when she befriends Jason, a mute paraplegic, she learns that maybe the rules aren't as important as she thinks.
(1F. Gifted Elementary Readers; 1H. Innocent Middle School Girls)

LOWRY, LOIS. 1993. *The Giver.* Houghton Mifflin.
Jonas is born into a society so sensible and ordered that nothing is left to chance, including death, but when he begins training to be the Receiver of Memory he

learns that life was not always so constrained and begins to wonder if the price for utopia is too high.
(1A. Adult Readers; 1E. Gentlemanly Boys; 1F. Gifted Elementary Student Readers; 3D. Consequences and Fate)

LUBAR, DAVID. 1999. *Hidden Talents*. Tor.
New student Martin and his roommate Torchie are friends with other students with paranormal powers, talents that come in handy when they stand up to the school bully, Lester Bloodbath.
(1O. Reluctant Male Readers; 1Q. Troubled Teen Boys)

———. 2002. *Dunk*. Clarion.
Living near the Jersey shore, Chad is intrigued with Bozo the Clown, who taunts the boardwalk tourists to dunk him, and decides that he could learn to emulate Bozo, who turns out to be his mother's tenant.
(1E. Gentlemanly Boys; 3P. State Books)

———. 2005. *Sleeping Freshmen Never Lie*. Dutton.
Eagerly anticipating high school, ninth grader Scott quickly learns he's at the bottom of the pecking order, grows apart from his former friends, and will soon have a new baby sister—could life be any worse?
(1L. Offbeat Guys; 2F. Diaries and Epistolary Novels)

———. 2006. *Sleeping Freshmen Never Lie*. Read by Ryan MacConnell and a full cast. Full Cast Audio. Unabridged, 6 hours, 45 minutes.
Music is effectively used to delineate chapters and to signal diary entries as MacConnell's alternately sarcastic and comic tones emulate freshman Scott as he adjusts to high school life and other students, ably voiced by the rest of the full cast.
(2A. Audiobooks for High School Listeners)

LUNDGREN, MARY BETH. 2001. *Love, Sara*. Holt.
E-mails and journal entries reveal Sara's abusive life until she's finally placed in a foster home where she's loved and even has a best friend with whom she e-mails nightly.
(2C. Blogs, E-mails, and IMs in Fiction)

LUPER, ERIC. 2007. *Big Slick*. Farrar, Straus and Giroux.
Math whiz Andrew Lang plays a game of chance online and, thinking his math ability will help him beat the odds, steals $500 from his dad to play in his first poker game, loses everything, and doesn't know how to replace the missing money.
(3K. Luck; 3L. Mathematics)

————. 2009. *Bug Boy.* Farrar, Straus and Giroux.
> With a love for horse racing, teen Jack Walsh is ecstatic that he's moved up from exercise boy to "bug boy," or apprentice jockey, but doesn't realize how corrupt the Saratoga Spring race world is during the Great Depression years.
> (3G. Horses)

LUPICA, MIKE. 2006. *Heat.* Philomel.
> Because he was born in Cuba, Michael can't prove he's 12 years old and misses his chance to pitch in the Little League World Series.
> (1E. Gentlemanly Boys; 1J. Latino Teens)

————. 2007. *Summer Ball.* Philomel.
> At basketball camp in Maine, Danny spends a lot of time sitting on the bench because his coach thinks he's too short, but Danny's desire to play and win shines through and soon he's back on the court.
> (3Q. Summer Camp)

LUTES, JASON. 2000. *Berlin: City of Stones: Book One.* Drawn & Quarterly.
> The lives of a young student, a textile worker, and a Jewish radical intertwine in 1920s Berlin as political tensions in the city rise, culminating, for the moment, in the deadly May Day demonstration of 1929.
> (2H. Graphic Novels in the Classroom)

————. 2001. *Berlin Book Two: City of Smoke.* Drawn & Quarterly.
> As World War II draws closer, the people of Weimar Berlin fight rising tensions between communists and nationalists and Jews and Gentiles, and they try to distract themselves from political turmoil with a rousing nightlife.
> (2H. Graphic Novels in the Classroom)

LUTZ, LISA. 2007. *The Spellman Files.* Simon & Schuster.
> Isabel Spellman's family owns and runs a family detective agency, but it all becomes too personal when Isabel has to investigate boyfriend number nine, dentist Daniel Castillo.
> (1M. Picky Senior Girls)

LYGA, BARRY. 2006. *The Astonishing Adventures of Fanboy and Goth Girl.* Houghton Mifflin.
> An unlikely friendship develops between "follow the rules" Fanboy and "mock the rules" Kyra when she is intrigued by the graphic novel *Schemata* that Fanboy is creating.
> (1G. Graphic Novel Lovers; 1L. Offbeat Guys)

————. 2009. *Goth Girl Rising.* Houghton Mifflin.
After six months in a mental health facility, Kyra Sellers is released, but while she's been away, Fanboy's completed graphic novel has gained him popularity, which makes Kyra even angrier that Fanboy never contacted her while she was in the hospital.
(1G. Graphic Novel Lovers; 1N. Punk Readers)

LYNCH, CHRIS. 1995. *Slot Machine.* HarperCollins.
For obese Elvin Bishop, the camp prequel to school, required by the Christian Brothers Academy, is a horrible experience as he tries and fails at football, baseball, and wrestling until he's slotted into the Arts Sector and discovers he's finally happy.
(3Q. Summer Camp)

————. 2001. *Freewill.* HarperCollins.
Will's strange pole sculptures, the product of time spent in a therapeutic woodworking class after the deaths of his father and stepmother, begin appearing at the memorials of suicide deaths, bringing Will attention from a reporter and a potential friend.
(3D. Consequences and Fate)

————. 2005. *Inexcusable.* Simon & Schuster.
Keir knows he's a good guy because he's handsome, popular, and talented, so it's impossible that he raped the girl he thinks he loves, isn't it?
(3J. Love Hurts)

LYNCH, JANET NICHOLS. 2009. *Messed Up.* Holiday House.
Part Mexican and part Cheyenne, R.D. lives with Earl, his grandmother's boyfriend, until Earl dies, and R.D. doesn't tell authorities he's alone as he struggles to learn how to cook, clean, and support himself.
(1J. Latino Teens)

M

MACHALE, D.J. 2002. *The Merchant of Death.* Pendragon series, book 1. Simon & Schuster.
Fourteen-year-old Bobby Pendragon has a pretty good life as a popular basketball player in Connecticut, which is turned upside down when he learns he's one of the Travelers and is sent through time and space to help end a war between the Milago and the Bedoowan.
(3A. Bathrooms)

MACKLER, CAROLYN. 2003. *The Earth, My Butt, and Other Big, Round Things*. Candlewick.
    An absent father and a weight-obsessed mother are only two of the many problems in Virginia Shreves's life, which also includes an older brother accused of date rape and a less-than-desirable boyfriend.
(3A. Bathrooms)

MALLOY, BRIAN. 2008. *Twelve Long Months*. Scholastic.
    A budding physicist, Molly has a crush on her nontalkative physics lab partner, but when they both move to New York City to attend college, she discovers that he's gay.
(3N. Science)

MARCHETTA, MELINA. 2003. *Saving Francesca*. Knopf.
    Sent to a formerly all-boys school to remove her from cliquey friends, Francesca struggles to fit in with new classmates, while she also worries about her mother when depression incapacitates her.
(1M. Picky Senior Girls)

————. 2008. *Jellicoe Road*. HarperTeen.
    Taylor Markham is abandoned by her mother when she is 11 years old and taken in by Hannah at Jellicoe School, but when Hannah goes missing, bits and pieces of Taylor's past emerge and begin to pile up.
(1A. Adult Readers)

MARILLIER, JULIET. 2007. *Wildwood Dancing*. Random House.
    Jenica lives with her four sisters and her pet frog Gogu on her family's estate, Piscul Dracului, and every full moon the girls go dancing in the Other Kingdom until their father's illness threatens both their home and their otherworldly adventures.
(1A. Adult Readers)

MARKANDAYA, KAMALA. 1954. *Nectar in a Sieve*. J. Day.
    Married at age 12 to a man she's never met, Rukmani and Nathan move to a rural village in India where, over the years of farming together, they fall in love, have children, and watch as surrounding farm plots convert to industrialization.
(3M. The Middle East)

MARKS, GRAHAM. 2006. *Missing in Tokyo*. Bloomsbury.
    When Adam's older sister goes missing from a Tokyo bar, his frustration with the slow progress of the investigation impels him to travel there himself, where the strange behavior of his sister's traveling companion only deepens the mystery of her disappearance.
(1K. Manga Lovers)

Marr, Melissa, et al. 2008. *Love Is Hell*. HarperCollins.
Five authors—Melissa Marr, Scott Westerfeld, Gabriel Zevin, Justine Larbalestier, and Laurie Faria Stolarz—explore the theme of supernatural romance.
(2J. Must-Have Anthologies)

Marsden, John. 1989. *So Much to Tell You*. Joy Street Books.
Marina stopped speaking after the terrible event that disfigured her face, but eventually she finds her voice and comes to terms with her past through the pages of the journal she is required to keep at her new boarding school.
(3O. Silence)

————. 1991. *Letters from the Inside*. Houghton Mifflin.
After Mandy and Tracey become pen pals, Tracey lets Mandy in on her secret—she's an inmate in a maximum security prison—which makes Mandy's fears about her increasingly violent brother seem tame, until Tracey's letters stop coming.
(3I. Institutions)

————. 1996. *Checkers*. Random House.
A financial scandal involving her father, her beloved dog Checkers, and officials at the highest levels of government rob an unnamed girl recuperating in a mental institution of the ability to speak about her problems to the other members of her therapy group.
(3I. Institutions)

Martel, Yann. 2001. *Life of Pi*. Houghton Mifflin.
Pi Patel, son of a zookeeper, is trapped on a lifeboat in the middle of the Pacific Ocean with a zebra, a hyena, an orangutan, and a huge Bengal tiger.
(3D. Consequences and Fate)

Martin, Ann M. 2009. *Everything for a Dog*. Read by David Pittu. Listening Library. Unabridged, 5 hours, 10 minutes.
In this charming audiobook skillfully narrated by Pittu, two young boys want a dog, and Bone wants a home—Bone speaks in a gruff, gravely voice, Charlie's speech is firm and resolute, and Henry wants a dog so badly that he sounds whiney.
(2B. Audiobooks for Middle School Listeners)

Martin, Jacqueline Briggs. 1998. *Snowflake Bentley*. Illustrated by Mary Azarian. Houghton Mifflin. NF
Wilson A. Bentley, a Vermont farmboy born in 1865, was fascinated by snowflakes, and during the 50 years he studied them he invented a way to photograph them up close and to prove that no two are alike.
(2N. Picture Books for Teens)

MARTINEZ, MANUEL LUIS. 2003. *Drift.* Picador.
Living with his strict grandmother in San Antonio, Robert's goal is to reunite with his mother, who currently lives in Los Angeles with her sister, but when Robert visits, it's obvious he's not wanted.
(1J. Latino Teens)

MARTINEZ, VICTOR. 1996. *Parrot in the Oven: Mi Vida.* HarperCollins/Joanna Cotler.
A series of vignettes reveals Manuel's increasing maturation as he deals with an alcoholic father, hard-working mother, and argumentative family as he gradually realizes that he loves each one of his unique relatives.
(1J. Latino Teens)

MASS, WENDY. 2004. *Leap Day.* Hachette.
Josie Taylor celebrates her fourth "official" birthday by taking her driving test, one of the perks of being a Leap Year baby, but while she revels in her unusual birthday situation, her worries about the upcoming play and her crush on Grant Brawner remain.
(2R. Two or More Voices in Novels)

MATTHEWS, KEZI. 2000. *John Riley's Daughter.* Boyds Mills Press.
Memphis is left with her unwelcoming grandmother and mentally handicapped aunt after her mother dies, and when a fight causes Aunt Clover to run away, Memphis is blamed and then suspected of much worse when Aunt Clover fails to reappear.
(3P. State Books)

MAXWELL, KATIE. 2003. *The Year My Life Went Down the Loo.* Dorchester.
Spending a year abroad with her family in Piddlington-on-the-Weld, Emily sends frantic e-mails to her best friend Dru moaning about the name of the town as it would make anyone think their "life went down the loo."
(2C. Blogs, E-mails, and IMs in Fiction)

MAYNARD, JOYCE. 2005. *The Cloud Chamber.* Atheneum.
Scorned at school because his "crazy father" failed at a suicide attempt, Nate throws himself into a science project building a cloud chamber.
(3N. Science)

MAZER, ANNE, ED. 1993. *America Street: A Multicultural Anthology of Stories.* Persea Books.
Fourteen stories reflect the diverse multicultural experiences of teens as presented by authors including Gary Soto, Gish Jen, Robert Cormier, Langston Hughes, Grace Paley, and Michele Wallace.
(2J. Must-Have Anthologies)

MAZER, HARRY. 1973. *Snowbound.* Delacorte.
  Tony runs away from home in his mother's car, picks up a hitchhiker in the middle
  of a snowstorm, and wrecks the car, leaving them stranded and bickering until
  they realize the only way they'll survive is to cooperate with one another.
(3T. Wintertime)

McCAFFERTY, MEGAN. 2001–2009. Jessica Darling series. Random House.
  Jessica Darling has no idea how she's going to cope with life now that her best
  friend has moved away, but her protective parents, bride-to-be sister, and a couple
  of cute guys offer more distractions than she knows what to do with.
(2F. Diaries and Epistolary Novels)

McCAFFREY, ANNE. 1996. *Black Horses for the King.* Harcourt.
  Galwyn escapes from his cruel uncle and helps Lord Artos buy Libyan horses and
  transport them to England where Galwyn learns to shoe the horses and becomes
  King Arthur's farrier.
(3G. Horses)

McCAUGHREAN, GERALDINE. 2006. *Cyrano.* Houghton Mifflin.
  Cyrano is in love with the beautiful Roxane, but his unfortunate nose seems to be
  in the way, so when he sees an opportunity to express his feelings using the handsome face of Christian, he jumps at the chance to declare his love.
(3J. Love Hurts)

———. 2006. *Peter Pan in Scarlet.* Illustrated by Scott M. Fischer. Simon & Schuster/
McElderry.
  In this sequel to the original *Peter Pan,* the former Lost Boys dream about Neverland,
  and, realizing something is wrong on the island, the boys and Wendy don their children's clothes, sprinkle themselves with fairy dust, and fly to the island to help.
(1M. Picky Senior Girls)

McCORMICK, PATRICIA. 2000. *Cut.* Scholastic.
  Callie cuts herself to relieve the pressures of her dysfunctional family, but when
  her destructive behavior gets her admitted to a psychiatric hospital she must confront her problems and her inability to talk openly about them.
(1D. Detention Home Girls; 3I. Institutions; 3O. Silence)

———. 2006. *Sold.* Hyperion.
  Sold into prostitution by her stepfather, Lakshmi leaves Nepal for India where she
  resists the brothel life but is beaten, drugged, and raped until she acquiesces,
  though she always searches for a way to escape.
(2Q. Teen Issue Novels in Verse; 3M. The Middle East)

McDONALD, JANET. 2004. *Brother Hood*. Farrar, Straus and Giroux.
   After Nate wins a scholarship to a prestigious boarding school he finds it hard to
   navigate between his Harlem neighborhood and street smart friends and his new
   upper-crust environment and the opportunities it offers.
   (1S. Urban Teens: Beyond Street Lit)

————. 2006. *Harlem Hustle*. Farrar, Straus and Giroux.
   Determined to succeed at something besides stealing, Hustle turns his attention to
   becoming a rap star, and, though sometimes misled and deluded, he receives support from a friend and her grandmother.
   (1S. Urban Teens: Beyond Street Lit)

————. 2007. *Off-Color*. Farrar, Straus and Giroux.
   Cameron is dismayed when her mother moves them from Brooklyn to the pro-
   jects, and she's even more upset when she finds out that, although she looks like
   her mother, her father was actually African American, a secret she wonders why
   her mother didn't share.
   (1D. Detention Home Girls)

McKAY, HILARY. 2005. *Saffy's Angel*. Simon & Schuster/McElderry.
   The Casson family household is always chaotic but entertaining, from Cadmium,
   who seems fated to be a terrible driver, to Saffron, who discovers she's really a
   cousin, their brother Indigo, and young Rose, who can manipulate their father.
   (1F. Gifted Elementary Student Readers; 1H. Innocent Middle School Girls)

McKAY, KIM, AND JENNY BONNIE. 2007. *True Green: 100 Everyday Ways You Can
Contribute to a Healthier Planet*. National Geographic. NF.
   Whether covering home, garden, work, shopping, travel, or the community, each
   page offers a helpful tip to save energy, such as using a clothesline or warming
   yourself and not the house, and then lists specifics about how your contribution
   helps the planet.
   (3F. The Environment)

McKINLEY, ROBIN. 1978. *Beauty: A Retelling of the Story of Beauty and the Beast*.
HarperCollins.
   One of three sisters, Beauty is not the most beautiful, but she is intelligent and
   kind, and she agrees to live at the Beast's castle where her love for him breaks the
   spell that turned him from a handsome prince into a loathsome creature.
   (1B. Avid Readers; 1H. Innocent Middle School Girls)

McKINTY, ADRIAN. 2006. *The Lighthouse Land.* Abrams.
Selectively mute, Jamie is still mourning the loss of his arm to bone cancer when he moves with his mother to an island off the coast of Ireland, where he finds a strange object in a lighthouse that transports him to another world, one where his arm is whole.
(3K. Luck)

McLARTY, RON. 2007. *Traveler.* Penguin Putnam.
Jono Riley returns to his hometown in Rhode Island to investigate the death of Marie, his childhood friend and first love, bringing back memories of his adolescence in 1960s East Providence.
(3P. State Books)

McNAMEE, GRAHAM. 1999. *Hate You.* Random House.
A songwriter and former singer, Alice will never forgive her father for damaging her voice in one of his last bouts of violence, but when she learns he's dying of cancer she's forced to confront her past and decide if hatred is worth the cost.
(3O. Silence)

————. 2003. *Acceleration.* Random House.
Working underground in the Lost and Found department of the Toronto subway system, Duncan uncovers a potential killer when he plucks a journal from the lost shelves and reads a demented person's plans to stalk and kill a woman.
(1O. Reluctant Male Readers; 3D. Consequences and Fate)

McNEAL, TOM, AND LAURA McNEAL. 2006. *Crushed.* Random House.
When sophisticated new student Wickham begins paying attention to her, Audrey can't help but be flattered, although it's clear to her friend (and secret admirer) Clyde that Wickham is more interested in Audrey's ability to help him graduate than he is in her.
(3J. Love Hurts)

McWHORTER, DIANE. 2004. *A Dream of Freedom: The Civil Rights Movement from 1954 to 1968.* Scholastic. NF.
In an account that melds the personal and the historical, McWhorter tracks the civil rights movement from *Brown v. Board of Education* to the assassination of Martin Luther King Jr.
(3C. The Civil Rights Movement)

MEAD, ALICE. 2005. *Swimming to America*. Farrar, Straus and Giroux.
A family history project gives Linda Berati the motivation she needs to investigate her past, and she confronts her mother, demanding answers to questions about their flight to America, her horrific nightmares, and her mother's scarred face.
(3S. Teen Immigrants)

MEAD, RICHELLE. 2007– . Vampire Academy series. Penguin/Razorbill.
In this contemporary paranormal series, half-human and half-vampire Rose Hathaway trains to protect Lissa, a mortal Moiri vampire princess, from the dead Strigoi vampires who are evil and feed on the innocent.
(2M. Paperback Series)

MEDLEY, LINDA. 2006. *Castle Waiting*. Fantagraphics Books.
Three ladies in waiting are left behind in the castle after Sleeping Beauty wakes up and rides away with her prince, and they transform their home into a refuge for anyone seeking shelter.
(2E. Core Graphic Novels; 2H. Graphic Novels in the Classroom)

MELLING, O.R. 2005. *The Hunter's Moon*. Amulet.
Canadian Gwen and Irish Finn, teenage cousins, tour Ireland in hopes of locating the world of Faerie, but when Finn disappears, Gwen needs help to free her cousin from the Faeries.
(3K. Luck; 3R. Summertime)

MELTZER, BRAD. 2005. *Identity Crisis*. Illustrated by Rags Morales et al. DC Comics.
The families and loved ones of the Justice League of America are being targeted, and as the members scramble to uncover the truth behind the attacks it becomes clear that the superheroes themselves may be partially responsible.
(2E. Core Graphic Novels)

MENZEL, PETER, AND FAITH D'ALUSIO. 1998. *Man Eating Bugs: The Art and Science of Eating Insects*. NF. Ten Speed Press. NF.
With an estimated ten quintillion insects residing on Earth, including locusts, grasshoppers, and crickets, the value of their proteins, minerals, and vitamins is emphasized, and appropriate recipes are included.
(3H. Insects)

METZ, MELINDA. 1999–2000. Roswell High series. Pocket Books.
Three aliens mingle among the ordinary citizens of Roswell, New Mexico, doing their best to avoid detection, but they are sometimes forced to use their extraordinary powers to help their friends.
(2M. Paperback Series)

MEYER, CAROLYN. 1992. *Where the Broken Heart Still Beats: The Story of Cynthia Ann Parker*. Houghton Mifflin.
> Twenty-five years after being kidnapped by Comanche Indians, 34-year-old Naduah, wife of the chief and mother to his son, is returned to her white family, against her will.

(2G. Fictionalized Biographies)

————. 2005. *Marie, Dancing*. Harcourt/Gulliver.
> The three van Goethem sisters study at the Paris Opera Ballet to rise above their destitute life, but it's middle sister Marie who's asked to pose for the famous statue *Little Dancer of Fourteen Years* by Degas.

(2G. Fictionalized Biographies)

MEYER, L.A. 2007. *Bloody Jack: Being an Account of the Curious Adventures of Mary "Jacky" Faber, Ship's Boy*. Read by Katherine Kellgren. Listen and Live. Unabridged, 8 hours.
> Kellgren easily maintains Jacky's Cockney accent, in addition to British and Caribbean accents, in this portrayal of a young girl who disguises herself as a boy and goes to sea.

(2A. Audiobooks for High School Listeners)

MEYER, STEPHENIE. 2005–2008. The Twilight Saga. Hachette.
> Bella Swan isn't thrilled about moving to Forks, but after she meets and falls in love with vampire Edward Cullen, and he with her, their romance becomes more important than anything else in her life, including her best friend Jacob.

(3P. State Books)

MEYERS, KENT. 2004. *The Work of Wolves*. Houghton Mifflin.
> When Lakota Earl Walks Alone and German exchange student Willi Schubert discover a group of starved and abused horses, they uncover the story of a jealous husband and a long-standing feud.

(3P. State Books)

MIKAELSEN, BEN. 2001. *Touching Spirit Bear*. HarperCollins.
> When Cole opts to enter an alternative sentencing program and spend a year surviving alone on an Alaskan island, he intends to escape and beat the system, but an encounter with a mysterious white bear leaves him severely injured and reconsidering his choices.

(1Q. Troubled Teen Boys)

MILLAR, MARK. 2000. *Ultimate X-Men: The Tomorrow People.* Illustrated by Adam Kubert et al. Marvel Comics.

As the government sets up the Sentinel Project, an initiative designed to deal with the mutant threat, Charles Xavier and Magneto, two men with wildly different agendas, wage separate campaigns to win the allegiance of young mutants, especially Logan.

(2E. Core Graphic Novels)

MILLER, CALVIN CRAIG. 2005. *No Easy Answers: Bayard Rustin and the Civil Rights Movement.* Morgan Reynolds. NF.

Despite working primarily behind the scenes (possibly due to his homosexuality), Rustin's political life included studying nonviolent protest with Gandhi and organizing the March on Washington, an act that made him the target of special interest groups.

(3C. The Civil Rights Movement)

MILLER, FRANK. 1986. *Batman: The Dark Knight Returns.* Illustrated by Klaus Janson et al. DC Comics.

Batman hasn't been seen for more than ten years and Gotham City has fallen even further into crime, decay, and despair with no hero around to help, but Bruce Wayne, a broken man who keeps to himself, hasn't given up hope that things can change.

(2E. Core Graphic Novels)

MILLER, FRANK, AND LYNN VARLEY. 1999. *300.* Dark Horse.

This retelling of the Battle of Thermopylae in graphic novel format allows for a liberal interpretation of King Leonidas and his 300 Spartan warriors as they faced the enormous Persian army of Emperor Xerxes and gained time for Greece to position its army.

(1C. Book Haters)

MILLER, KIRSTEN. 2006– . Kiki Strike series. Bloomsbury.

When 12-year-old Ananka Fishbein meets tiny super-spy Kiki Strike and her band of Irregulars, she discovers not only the existence of the Shadow City under Manhattan, but also the danger posed by the imminent attack of a mysterious group of terrorists.

(1K. Manga Lovers)

MILLER, SARAH. 2007. *Miss Spitfire: Reaching Helen Keller.* Atheneum.

Annie Sullivan's work with deaf and blind Helen Keller is novelized in a work based on Sullivan's letters, which reveal her sometimes violent temper and strong love for Helen.

(2G. Fictionalized Biographies).

MILLS, KEVIN, AND NANCY MILLS. 2000. *Chocolate on the Brain: Foolproof Recipes for Unrepentant Chocoholics.* Houghton Mifflin. NF.
Recipes for quick and easy-to-make chocolate treats, including triple chocolate brownies and chocolate-lovers' lemon squares, fill the pages of this work by a mother and son team who organized the recipes by preparation time.
(3B. Chocolate)

MIYAZAKI, HAYAO. 1989–2004. Nausicaa of the Valley of the Wind series. VIZ Media.
Nausicaa, the princess of a small kingdom in the Valley of the Wind, plays a pivotal role in the war between two mighty empires as they battle for the last remaining natural resources in the face of worldwide ecological disaster.
(2D. Classic Manga)

MLYNOWSKI, SARAH. 2007. *Spells & Sleeping Bags.* Delacorte.
At an Adirondacks camp, Rachel instantly dislikes her cabinmate Liana, only to learn Liana's a cousin of hers.
(3Q. Summer Camp)

MONTGOMERY, L.M. 2008, ©1908. *Anne of Green Gables.* Random House.
A popular character for more than 100 years, orphan Anne is mistakenly sent to the home of siblings Matthew and Marilla Cuthbert, where, although the Cuthberts wanted a boy to help with farm work, Anne quickly becomes a beloved family member.
(1F. Gifted Elementary Student Readers)

————. 2008. *Anne of Green Gables.* Read by Kate Burton. Listening Library. Unabridged, 10 hours.
This classic tale of red-headed orphan Anne, taken in by Matthew and Marilla, is expertly narrated by Burton, whose pace matches Anne's rate of speech with its highs and lows of emotion, which contrasts with Matthew's hesitant manner and Marilla's somber tones.
(2B. Audiobooks for Middle School Listeners)

MOORE, ALAN. 1986. *Watchmen.* Illustrated by Dave Gibbons et al. DC Comics.
As an unknown assassin plots to disgrace and ultimately kill the group of superheroes known as the Crimebusters, their own less-than-super activities and human weaknesses contribute to their fall from grace.
(2E. Core Graphic Novels)

MOORE, PERRY. 2007. *Hero*. Hyperion.
Although his dad is an ex-superhero himself, Thom Creed keeps his budding superpowers and his sexual orientation a secret until he's taken on as an apprentice by the prestigious League.
(1G. Graphic Novel Lovers)

MORALES, ROBERT. 2004. *Truth: Red, White & Black*. Marvel Comics.
Isaiah Bradley is the only African American soldier to survive the horrific military experiments conducted in pursuit of a super-soldier serum, and when he's asked to fill in for Captain America on a mission he finds similar experiments being conducted on Jews.
(2H. Graphic Novels in the Classroom)

MORANVILLE, SHARELLE BYARS. 2006. *A Higher Geometry*. Holt.
Not given credit by other students or her parents for her mathematical ability, Anna wavers about attending college until she dates Mike, who encourages her to follow her aptitude and zeal for math.
(3L. Mathematics)

MORE, J. 2005. *The Anti-Valentine's Handbook*. Penguin Putnam. NF.
More offers sections on why Valentine's Day sucks whether you're alone or not and offers advice and lists, including movies to watch alone, signs that a date is going downhill, and reasons your date doesn't like you.
(3J. Love Hurts)

MORIARTY, JACLYN. 2001. *Feeling Sorry for Celia*. St. Martin's.
Told through a series of letters, notes on the fridge, and messages from fictitious organizations, Elizabeth describes the year her friend Celia joins the circus and, after Elizabeth rescues her, turns around and steals her boyfriend.
(1B. Avid Readers)

————. 2004. *The Year of Secret Assignments*. Scholastic.
A tenth grade pen pal project designed to unite feuding schools, one for boys and one for girls, goes awry when one of the boys threatens one of the girls.
(2F. Diaries and Epistolary Novels; 2R. Two or More Voices in Novels)

————. 2006. *The Murder of Bindy Mackenzie*. Scholastic/Levine.
Uptight and a little obsessive, Bindy is book smart but lacks common sense and can be quite irritating, but who would want to kill her?
(2C. Blogs, E-mails, and IMs in Fiction)

MORPURGO, MICHAEL. 1982. *War Horse.* Greenwillow.
Sold to the army during World War I, farm horse Joey describes battle scenes, capture by the Germans, work pulling ambulances and guns, and finally reunion with young Albert, son of his former owner.
(3G. Horses)

MORRISON, TONI, AND SLADE MORRISON. 1999. *The Big Box.* Illustrated by Giselle Potter. Hyperion.
Four children are locked in a big brown box and given everything they could ever want, except freedom.
(2N. Picture Books for Teens)

MORTENSON, GREG, AND DAVID OLIVER RELIN. 2006. *Three Cups of Tea: One Man's Mission to Fight Terrorism and Build Nations—One School at a Time.* Penguin Putnam. NF.
After a failed attempt to climb K2, Mortenson spent weeks recovering in a Pakistani village and promised to build a school in return, a project that marked the beginning of the Central Asia Institute, builders of more than 50 schools in Pakistan and Afghanistan.
(3M. The Middle East)

MOSES, SHEILA. 2004. *The Legend of Buddy Bush.* Simon & Schuster.
Pattie Mae knows her Uncle Buddy, accused of attempted rape by a white woman, is innocent because she saw the whole thing, and when he escapes an attempt by the Ku Klux Klan to impose their own sentence she's relieved, despite the turmoil left behind.
(1H. Innocent Middle School Girls)

MOURLEVAT, JEAN-CLAUDE. 2009. *Winter's End.* Translated by Anthea Bell. Candlewick.
Fleeing their boarding school where they feel imprisoned, four teens dash across icy mountains to join the resistance movement and fight against the tyrannical government that killed their parents.
(3T. Wintertime)

MOWAT, FARLEY. 1956. *Lost in the Barrens.* Little, Brown.
Jamie and Awasain, a Cree Indian, leave on a hunting trip near the Arctic Circle but are trapped as winter approaches and survival becomes their first priority.
(3T. Wintertime)

Mowry, Jess. 1997. *Babylon Boyz*. Simon & Schuster.
Inner-city teens Dante, Pook, and Wyatt feel trapped by the circumstances of their lives, especially Dante, who needs an expensive operation to repair his heart, so when they find a package of cocaine worth thousands of dollars they face a difficult moral dilemma.
(3I. Institutions)

Muchamore, Robert. 2005–2010. CHERUB series. Hodder.
CHERUB, the Charles Henderson Espionage Research Unit B, hires orphans like James and his sister Lauren to be trained as spies for various British intelligence-gathering missions.
(2M. Paperback Series)

Muldrow, Diane. 2002. *Stirring It Up*. Grosset and Dunlop.
Brooklyn twins surprise their parents by preparing dinner and discover they enjoy the process so much that their father treats them to cooking lessons.
(3E. Cookery)

Munsch, Robert N. 1980. *The Paper Bag Princess*. Illustrated by Michael Martchenko. Annick Press.
When a dragon attacks her castle, burns her clothes, and kidnaps her beloved Prince Ronald, Princess Elizabeth puts on a paper bag and goes off to rescue him.
(2N. Picture Books for Teens)

Murdock, Catherine Gilbert. 2006. *Dairy Queen*. Houghton Mifflin.
Her father's hip injury requires 15-year-old D.J. to assume responsibility for the farm work, but she has the added burden of an unasked-for assistant who she teaches to hay and become a better quarterback, though for a rival high school.
(3P. State Books; 3R. Summertime)

———. *Dairy Queen*. Read by Natalie Moore. Listening Library. Unabridged, 6 hours.
Moore's Midwestern accent portrays D.J.'s feelings as she spends the summer working on the family farm, aided by a conceited assistant who becomes a better quarterback after D.J.'s help—too bad he plays for the rival high school.
(2A. Audiobooks for High School Listeners)

Murphy, Jim. 2000. *Blizzard! The Storm That Changed America*. Scholastic. NF.
In March 1888 two storms coalesce into a blizzard that stretches from the Mississippi River to the Northeast, with more than 55 inches of snow in parts of New

York, 200 ships lost at sea, and 800 people dead in New York City, as recounted in this work based on primary sources.
(3T. Wintertime)

———. 2000. *Pick and Shovel Poet: The Journeys of Pascal D'Angelo*. Houghton Mifflin. NF.

D'Angelo migrated from Italy with his father in 1910 and struggled to make a new life in America, working hard-to-find jobs and laboring to learn English, an enterprise that awoke in him a love of words that he used to share his immigrant experiences.
(3S. Teen Immigrants)

MURPHY, PAT. 2007. *The Wild Girls*. Viking.

Joan and Sarah meet through a mutual love of nature, which leads to their attending a summer writing program at Berkeley.
(3Q. Summer Camp)

MURPHY, RITA. 2001. *Black Angels*. Random House.

The visions of black angels that 11-year-old Celli sees descending on the town of Mystic, Georgia, give her the courage to stand up for her beliefs after family secrets come to light during the racially charged summer of 1961.
(3C. The Civil Rights Movement)

MYERS, ANNA. 2003. *Flying Blind*. Walker.

Sickened by the massacre of egrets whose feathers are used to decorate women's hats, Ben wants to save the birds in the Florida swamps but is perplexed after meeting two youngsters whose only source of income comes from selling the egret plumes.
(3F. The Environment)

MYERS, WALTER DEAN. 1998. *The Journal of Joshua Loper, A Black Cowboy*. My Name Is America series. Scholastic.

Joshua, the hardworking son of a former slave, joins a cattle drive from Texas to Kansas and faces prejudice from the trail boss as well as danger from rustlers, stampedes, and the open trail.
(2F. Diaries and Epistolary Novels)

———. 1999. *Monster*. HarperCollins.

Facing murder charges in the killing of a store clerk, teen Steve Harmon is in jail during the trial that, based on his filmmaking experience, he describes in screen terms and diary entries, leaving the reader to decide if he's innocent or guilty.
(1A. Adult Readers; 1C. Book Haters; 1O. Reluctant Male Readers; 1Q. Troubled Teen Boys; 1S. Urban Teens: Beyond Street Lit; 2L. Novels with Script or Screenplay Format; 3D. Consequences and Fate; 3I. Institutions)

————. 1999. *Shooter*. HarperCollins.
After his friend Len takes a gun to school and kills a football star and then himself, Cameron finds himself at the center of an investigation as authorities and friends try to make sense of Len's violent act.
(1Q. Troubled Teen Boys)

————. 2001. *Bad Boy: A Memoir*. HarperCollins. NF.
Myers recounts his early years in 1940s Harlem and his struggles during adolescence, when he dropped out of school and joined the army before following through on his dream of becoming a writer.
(1Q. Troubled Teen Boys; 1S. Urban Teens: Beyond Street Lit)

————. 2001. *Patrol: An American Soldier in Vietnam*. Illustrated by Ann Grifalconi. HarperCollins.
A young American soldier and his squadron take a terrifying journey through the jungle of Vietnam and come face to face with enemy soldiers.
(2N. Picture Books for Teens)

————. 2003. *The Beast*. Scholastic.
When Anthony returns home from his Connecticut boarding school for Christmas break he finds that his girlfriend Gabi, whose life is falling apart, has turned to heroin to help her cope.
(1S. Urban Teens: Beyond Street Lit)

————. 2005. *Autobiography of My Dead Brother*. HarperCollins.
Jesse and his best friend Rise live in Harlem and spend much of their time with The Counts, a group of friends who eschew gang life, but conflicts occur when Rise starts dealing drugs and spending time away from The Counts.
(1G. Graphic Novel Lovers; 3D. Consequences and Fate)

————. 2006. *Jazz*. Illustrated by Christopher Myers. Holiday House. NF.
From drums to a Bourbon Street band, the world of jazz is captured in Walter Dean Myers's dramatic poetry as its rhythm captures the beat of the music, while his son Christopher's illustrations convey the sense of early jazz clubs, musicians, and bands.
(2P. Poetry Anthologies for Middle School Readers)

————. 2007. *Harlem Summer*. Scholastic.
To help out with family finances, Mark has a job at an arts magazine during the Harlem Renaissance, but he secretly longs to meet and play the sax with Fats Waller.
(3R. Summertime)

————. 2007. *What They Found: Love on 145th Street*. Random House.
Interconnected stories reveal the variety of personalities and experiences exhibited by the inhabitants of 145th Street in Harlem.
(1D. Detention Home Girls)

————. 2008. *Sunrise over Fallujah*. Scholastic.
After the attacks of 9/11, Robin Perry enlists in the Army, trains, and is sent to Iraq where the ambushes, civilian casualties, and use of explosives are almost too much for him.
(1C. Book Haters)

————. 2009. *Amiri & Odette: A Love Story*. Illustrated by Javaka Steptoe. Scholastic.
In this hip hop version of the classical ballet *Swan Lake*, Amiri falls in love with Odette, who unfortunately "belongs" to Big Red the drug dealer, as the action occurs in street scenes enhanced by rap verse and gritty, powerful collages.
(2Q. Teen Issue Novels in Verse)

MYRACLE, LAUREN. 2007. *l8r, g8r*. Abrams/Amulet.
Written in the vernacular of chat rooms and IMs, best friends forever Maddie, Zoe, and Angela begin their senior year with discussions of college plans, boyfriends, and their nasty classmate Jana.
(2C. Blogs, E-mails, and IMs in Fiction)

MYRICK, LELAND. 2006. *Missouri Boy*. Roaring Brook.
Myrick's graphic memoir offers stories of his childhood in Missouri, including skinny dipping, firecrackers on the Fourth of July, and his first attempt at romance.
(3P. State Books)

MYSPACE COMMUNITY AND JECA TAUDTE. 2008. *My Space/OurPlanet: Change Is Possible*. HarperTeen. NF.
The online OurPlanet community, which is devoted to environmental issues, offers teens practical suggestions for making their lives, home, and yard eco-friendly.
(3F. The Environment)

N

NA, AN. 2001. *A Step from Heaven*. Boyds Mills Press.
Young Ju struggles to understand the language and customs of her new country after emigrating from Korea to America and to navigate the narrow path between family loyalty and newfound freedom.
(3S. Teen Immigrants)

NAIDOO, BEVERLEY. 2001. *The Other Side of Truth.* HarperCollins.
Sade knows her journalist father tells the truth but that truth killed her mother in Nigeria, and now Sade and her brother Femi, who were sent to London for safety, have been abandoned and must tell authorities the truth about their identity.
(3S. Teen Immigrants)

NAKAZAWA, KEIJI. 1986–2009. Barefoot Gen series. New Society Publishers.
Gen and his family struggle with hunger, poverty, and constant danger during the months before the United States drops an atomic bomb on his hometown of Hiroshima, conditions that become even more dire after the city is destroyed.
(2H. Graphic Novels in the Classroom)

NAPOLI, DONNA JO. 1996. *Song of the Magdalene.* Scholastic.
Miriam experiences "fits" that leave her seeking solace in nature and poetry, and eventually in the company of Abraham, but after his death she hears of a healer named Jesus and, cured by his touch, becomes a follower.
(3M. The Middle East)

———. 1997. *Stones in Water.* Dutton.
Trapped at the movie theater by German soldiers, Roberto and his Jewish friend Samuele are sent to work camps as forced laborers, but when Samuele is beaten to death, Roberto escapes into the Ukrainian winter, returning to Italy to become a resistance fighter.
(3T. Wintertime)

———. 2005. *King of Mulberry Street.* Random House.
Nine-year-old Beniamino quickly realizes that he is alone on the ship heading to America, sent away by his mother to make a better life for himself, and after living on the streets of New York he learns how to survive and starts a successful business.
(3S. Teen Immigrants)

———. 2007. *Hush: An Irish Princess' Tale.* Atheneum.
Sent from her village for safety when her Irish king father knows violence is due, Malkorka is instead captured by slavers and her only defense is silence, which makes her captors think she has mystical powers.
(3K. Luck)

NAYLOR, PHYLLIS REYNOLDS. 2001. *Alice Alone.* Simon & Schuster.
Alice is nervous about starting ninth grade but feels better with Patrick, her perfect boyfriend, by her side, until it becomes clear that he doesn't really mind all the attention he's getting from the new girl.
(3J. Love Hurts)

————. 2002. *Blizzard's Wake*. Atheneum.
When Kate rescues her physician father from being stranded in a blizzard, she also saves the man she thought she hated—the driver of the car that killed her mother. (3T. Wintertime)

————. 2003. *Patiently Alice*. Atheneum.
Alice is an assistant counselor at a camp for the disadvantaged, which requires every bit of her patience to settle arguments and maintain peace in the cabin. (3Q. Summer Camp)

————. 2009. *Intensely Alice*. Atheneum.
The summer before senior year in high school finds Alice visiting Patrick at his college dorm and grieving for the death of her friend Mark. (3R. Summertime)

NELSON, BLAKE. 2003. *New Rules of High School*. Penguin Putnam.
As Max begins his senior year it seems he has everything under control—he's editor of the school paper, gets great grades, and has a beautiful girlfriend—but he surprises everyone, including himself, when he breaks up with Cindy to get a taste of freedom. (3D. Consequences and Fate)

————. 2006. *Paranoid Park*. Viking.
A decision to skateboard at night at Paranoid Park leads the unnamed narrator to a meeting with a street teen, an invitation to hop a train, and a ghastly accident that kills a security guard and fills the skater with guilt. (1S. Urban Teens: Beyond Street Lit; 3P. State Books)

————. 2007. *Girl*. Simon Pulse.
Andrea gushes forth with all the details of her junior and senior years of high school in Portland, Oregon, as she follows her friend Cybil and Cybil's rock band, buys vintage clothing, and alternately loves and hates Todd Sparrow. (1N. Punk Readers)

————. 2009. *Destroy All Cars*. Scholastic.
James writes radical social commentaries for his English class and advocates eliminating all cars to solve the problem of global warming. (3F. The Environment)

NELSON, MARILYN. 2005. *A Wreath for Emmett Till*. Houghton Mifflin. NF.
A sequence of sonnets in which the last line of one becomes the first line of the next tells the violent and horrific story of the murder of young Emmett Till.
(3C. The Civil Rights Movement)

NELSON, R.A. 2007. *Breathe My Name*. Penguin Putnam.
Frances's quiet life is disrupted by the reappearance of her mother, fresh out of prison after smothering her other children to death and seemingly desperate to renew her relationship with the only daughter to survive—unless what she wants is to finish what she started.
(3O. Silence)

NELSON, THERESA. 2003. *Ruby Electric*. Simon & Schuster.
Life never seems to work out quite the way it does in her movie scripts, but Ruby has no intention of giving up on her missing dad, her younger brother, or the art project she's come up with to beautify the Los Angeles River.
(2L. Novels with Script or Screenplay Format)

NILSSON, PERS. 2004. *Heart's Delight*. Translated by Tara Chace. Front Street.
An unnamed teen narrator falls in love with Ann-Katrin and saves every memento from their brief relationship, but after discovering she's sleeping with someone else, each memento flashes him back to their brief encounters until he realizes theirs wasn't a great romance.
(3J. Love Hurts)

NIMMO, JENNY. 2003. *Midnight for Charlie Bone*. Read by Simon Russell Beale. Listening Library. Unabridged, 7 hours.
At a sinister English boarding school that houses both magically "endowed" and un-endowed pupils, Beale's British accent portrays endowed Charlie Bone, who makes friends among all the innocent-sounding pupils while he contends with the creepy headmaster Dr. Bloor and his odious son Manfred.
(2B. Audiobooks for Middle School Listeners)

NIX, GARTH. 2003. *Mister Monday*. Keys to the Kingdom series, book 1. Scholastic.
Unexpectedly gaining control of a key to The House, Arthur realizes its power helps his asthma, but he's not prepared for the dog-like Fetchers that try to retrieve the key, which begins Arthur's unusual adventure to claim his spot as rightful Lord of the House.
(1R. Tweens)

NIXON, JOAN LOWERY. 2003. *Nightmare*. Delacorte.
Frightened by a menacing, recurring dream and labeled an underachiever, Emily's parents send her to Camp Excel where her nightmare becomes reality.
(3Q. Summer Camp)

NORRIS, SHANA. 2008. *Something to Blog About.* Abrams/Amulet.
Frustrated that she's clumsy, her mom is dating, and she's been singled out by the Queen Bee for ridicule, Libby starts a secret blog with the worst info being that Queen Bee Angel's father is dating Libby's mother.
(2C. Blogs, E-mails, and IMs in Fiction)

NOVEMBER, SHARYN, ED. 2003. *Firebirds: An Anthology of Original Fantasy and Science Fiction.* Penguin Putnam.
Sixteen original pieces of short fiction from authors including Diana Wynne Jones, Delia Sherman, Kara Dalkey, Nancy Farmer, Lloyd Alexander, Patricia McKillip, and Michael Cadnum are featured in this anthology.
(2J. Must-Have Anthologies)

————, ED. 2006. *Firebirds Rising: An Anthology of Original Fantasy and Science Fiction.* Penguin Putnam.
Science fiction and fantasy stories by authors Charles de Lint, Allison Goodman, Carol Emshwiller, Tamora Pierce, Francesca Lia Block, and Pamela Dean are featured in this original anthology.
(2J. Must-Have Anthologies)

————, ED. 2008. *Firebirds Soaring: An Anthology of Original Speculative Fiction.* Penguin Putnam.
Nancy Springer, Chris Roberson, Margo Lanagan, Ellen Klages, and Nina Kiriki Hoffman are among the 19 authors presented in this anthology of original speculative fiction.
(2J. Must-Have Anthologies)

NOYES, DEBORAH, ED. 2004. *Gothic! Ten Original Dark Tales.* Candlewick.
M.T. Anderson, Garth Nix, Celia Rees, Janni Lee Simner, Joan Aiken, Gregory Maguire, and Neil Gaiman are among the authors featured in this collection of updated gothic short fiction.
(2J. Must-Have Anthologies)

NYE, NAOMI SHIHAB, ED. 1992. *This Same Sky: A Collection of Poems from Around the World.* Simon & Schuster.
Sixty-eight countries from Asia, South and Central America, India, Africa, and the Middle East are represented in the poems of 129 poets, which Nye organizes into six thematic groupings that reveal the individual expressions of universal thoughts.
(2O. Poetry Anthologies for High School Readers)

————. 2002. *19 Varieties of Gazelle: Poems of the Middle East.* Greenwillow. NF.
This collection is made up of both older poems and new ones written after the 9/11 attacks that show what it's like to be an Arab person living in the United States as well as poems about the Middle East as it was before and after the Towers fell.
(2O. Poetry Anthologies for High School Readers; 3M. The Middle East)

————. 2005. *A Maze Me: Poems for Girls.* Illustrated by Terre Maher. HarperCollins/Greenwillow. NF.
This collection of more than 70 original poems addresses the little things in life that affect preteen girls, such as a first crush, loss of a parent, and wonder at the nature around them.
(2P. Poetry Anthologies for Middle School Readers)

O

OATES, JOYCE CAROL. 2004. *Big Mouth & Ugly Girl.* Read by Hilary Swank and Chad Lowe. Harper Children's Audio. Unabridged, 6 hours.
Big Mouth's joking comment is misinterpreted in the lunchroom and only Ugly Girl comes to his defense, setting the scene for Lowe and Swank to alternate narration as each nimbly handles Oates's realistic teen dialogue.
(2A. Audiobooks for High School Listeners)

O'CONNELL, TYNE. 2006. *Dumping Princes.* Bloomsbury.
When her boyfriend, Prince Freddie, breaks up with her, Calypso enlists the help of the other girls at her boarding school, along with the teachers and nuns, to organize a Counter Dump.
(3J. Love Hurts)

OGIWARA, NORIKO. 1993. *Dragon Sword and Wind Child.* Farrar, Straus and Giroux.
Fifteen-year-old Saya has spent her life in the ancient Japanese village of Hashiba and is stunned to discover that she's a princess of the underworld and the reincarnation of the Water Maiden.
(1K. Manga Lovers)

OHBA, TSUGUMI. 2003–2008. Death Note series. Illustrated by Takeshi Obata. VIZ Media.
Light Yagami's life changed when he found the Death Note, a notebook dropped by a death god, and he vowed to use its powers for good, but when criminals start turning up dead Light comes to the attention of the legendary detective investigating the murders.
(2D. Classic Manga)

O'KEEFE, SUSAN HEYBOER. 2004. *Death by Eggplant.* Roaring Brook.
No one outside his family knows Bertie dreams of attending the Culinary Institute of America, but he spends so much time cooking that his other classes suffer and soon he has to carry a ten-pound, flour sack baby for extra credit.
(3E. Cookery)

OPPEL, KENNETH. 2004. *Airborn.* Eos.
A cabin boy aboard the airship *Aurora*, Matt meets Kate, granddaughter of an old man he rescued a year ago, and together the two search for the mysterious cloud cats described in her grandfather's journal.
(1E. Gentlemanly Boys)

————. 2006. *Airborn.* Read by a full cast. Full Cast Audio. Unabridged, 10 hours, 30 minutes.
Although there's a full cast, certain characters stand out, including a humorous Russian chef, snotty governess, adventuresome heiress, and resolute cabin boy as an airship is boarded and taken over by villainous pirates.
(2B. Audiobooks for Middle School Listeners)

ORLEV, URI. 1995. *The Lady with the Hat.* Houghton Mifflin.
Yulek's family perished in concentration camps, so he travels alone for a visit to his Polish hometown and there learns that his estranged Aunt Malka may still be alive and looking for him.
(3M. The Middle East)

OSA, NANCY. 2003. *Cuba 15.* Delacorte.
Approaching her quinceañera and knowing nothing about her Cuban heritage, Violet decides to learn about her family, from the never-ending domino games played by the men to the reason her family left Cuba for America.
(1I. Latina Teens)

OSTOW, MICOL. 2006. *Emily Goldberg Learns to Salsa.* Penguin/Razorbill.
When her grandmother dies and her family travels to Puerto Rico for the funeral, Emily and her mother remain for the summer, and Emily slowly adjusts to a traditional, male-dominated household and begins to appreciate her Puerto Rican heritage.
(1I. Latina Teens)

————. 2007. *Gettin' Lucky*. Simon & Schuster.
Cass decides not to sulk after she catches her best friend making out with the guy she likes, so she makes new friends, joins their weekly poker game, and is feeling lucky until her crush shows up at the game and raises the stakes.
(3K. Luck)

OTTAVIANI, JIM. 1999. *Dignifying Science: Stories about Women Scientists*. G.T. Labs. NF.
Biographical sketches of women scientists including Lise Meitner, Rosalind Franklin, and Barbara McClintock are graphically presented and enhanced by the work of women artists.
(2K. Nonfiction Graphic Novels)

————. 2004. *Bone Sharps, Cowboys, and Thunder Lizards: A Tale of Edward Drinker Cope, Othniel Charles Marsh, and the Gilded Age of Paleontology*. G.T. Labs.
Paleontologists Cope and Marsh star in this graphic retelling of the fight over fossilized dinosaur bones, which also stars P.T. Barnum, Buffalo Bill Cody, Ulysses S. Grant, Alexander Graham Bell, and Chief Red Cloud.
(2G. Fictionalized Biographies)

————. 2009. *T-Minus: The Race to the Moon*. Illustrated by Zander Cannon and Kevin Cannon. Simon & Schuster. NF.
The United States and the Soviet Union competed for years in the race for manned space flight, and Ottaviani graphically chronicles and documents more than 30 of those attempts.
(2K. Nonfiction Graphic Novels)

P

PACKARD, MARY, AND THE DISCOVERY CHANNEL. 2006. *Mythbusters: Don't Try This at Home*. Jossey-Bass. NF.
In a work filled with humor, witty props, and "at home" experiments, 15 excerpts from the *Mythbusters* program offer ways to test such urban legends as whether one stays drier walking or running in the rain or if stepping in quicksand sucks you to death.
(1C. Book Haters)

PACKER, ANN. 2002. *The Dive from Clausen's Pier*. Knopf.
Carrie and Mike haven't been getting along, but when he is injured after diving into shallow water, Carrie flees to New York City while deciding whether to pursue a career in fashion design or return to quadriplegic Mike.
(1M. Picky Senior Girls)

PAGLIARULIO, ANTONIO. 2006. *A Different Kind of Heat*. Random House.
Luz Cordero records the events of her second year without Julio, the brother killed by cops on a Bronx rooftop, as part of her therapy after her rage leads her to start a riot at an anti-police brutality demonstration and she's sent to a home for troubled youth.
(1S. Urban Teens: Beyond Street Lit)

Paint Me Like I Am: Teen Poems from Writers Corps. 2003. HarperTempest. NF.
Disadvantaged teens in the Writers Corps programs in San Francisco, New York, and Washington, DC, are encouraged to write about their feelings, and the poems collected in this volume express their frustration, anger, and self-images.
(2O. Poetry Anthologies for High School Readers)

PALEY, SASHA. 2007. *Huge.* Simon & Schuster.
Overweight April saves her money to attend Wellness Canyon, a camp to help her lose weight, only to be matched with a roommate whose goal is to gain weight to spite her fitness center–owning parents.
(3Q. Summer Camp)

PAPADEMETRIOU, LISA. 2008. *Drop.* Knopf.
When three Las Vegas teens need money, Jerrica thinks cash can be won at the roulette tables by combining her math skills in probability with her so-called psychic ability.
(3L. Mathematics)

PARRA, KELLY. 2007. *Graffiti Girl.* MTV.
When Angel's entry for a community mural isn't accepted, she's frustrated and turns her dreams of art achievement to a graffiti gang with whom she finally has a chance to demonstrate her talent and find a niche in the art world.
(1I. Latina Teens)

PASCAL, FRANCINE. 1999–2004. Fearless series. Simon Pulse.
Born without the gene for fear, Gaia Moore, a high school student living with a foster family, is on constant guard against those who want to take advantage of her fearlessness.
(2M. Paperback Series)

PATTERSON, JAMES. 2005. *Maximum Ride: The Angel Experiment.* Little, Brown.
Fourteen-year-old Max leads a group of mutant orphans with unique abilities who are part of the "angel experiment" where avian DNA is grafted onto human genes.
(3N. Science)

————. 2005. *Maximum Ride: The Angel Experiment*. Read by Evan Rachel Wood. Time Warner AudioBooks. Abridged, 5 hours.

Angel was bred in a lab to be 98 percent human and 2 percent avian, and when she is kidnapped, Maximum Ride and his flock rescue her from other mutants who are half human and half wolf, with Wood's breezy delivery making their power believable.

(2B. Audiobooks for Middle School Listeners)

PATTOU, EDITH. 2003. *East*. Houghton Mifflin.

Rose is the last of eight children born to a poor mapmaker, and though her mother tries to keep her at home, the arrival of a great white bear sets Rose on a journey to the North where she must undo the curse of the Troll Queen and find and claim her own true love.

(1H. Innocent Middle School Girls)

PAULSEN, GARY. 1987. *Hatchet*. Simon & Schuster.

The only survivor of a plane crash in the Canadian wilderness, 13-year-old Brian Robeson fights to survive with only the clothes on his back and the hatchet his mother gave him as a present.

(1Q. Troubled Teen Boys)

————. 1994. *Winterdance: The Fine Madness of Running the Iditarod.* Harcourt Brace. NF.

When Paulsen runs his first Iditarod in 1983, he is unprepared for the more than 1,100 miles of sled racing on ice and snow as he takes wrong turns, is bitten by a moose, and suffers frostbite and sleeplessness but still loves every minute of the race.

(3T. Wintertime)

————. 1996. *Brian's Winter*. Delacorte.

In a sequel to *Hatchet*, Brian is not rescued from the downed airplane but faces winter on his own with a sleeping bag, rifle, fishing line, and several butane lighters, still relying on his surroundings for shelter, food, and clothing.

(3T. Wintertime)

————. 1997. *The Schernoff Discoveries*. Delacorte.

The narrator and his best friend Harold are outcasts in high school, but that does not stop them from applying scientific research to kissing or buying a car that's driven for eight miles before the engine explodes.

(1P. Striving Readers)

————. 1998. *My Life in Dog Years*. Delacorte. NF.
This chronological account of dogs that have been part of Paulsen's life also reveals some of his own doings as he tells of his first dog, Snowball, on to destructive Fred, the Great Dane Caesar who hid from trick-or-treaters, and Josh, a border collie.
(1C. Book Haters)

————. 2003. *How Angel Peterson Got His Name: And Other Outrageous Tales about Extreme Sports*. Random House. NF.
Paulsen tells the story of his adventurous thirteenth year, when he and his friends experimented with all kinds of extreme sports and crazy stunts.
(1Q. Troubled Teen Boys)

————. 2007. *Lawn Boy*. Random House.
After the gift of an old lawn mower turns into a small business, the 12-year-old narrator meets a likeable stockbroker who helps him invest his money, hire employees, and sponsor a prize fighter.
(1E. Gentlemanly Boys)

PEARSALL, SHELLEY. 2006. *All of the Above*. Little, Brown.
Math teacher Mr. Pearsall challenges his lackadaisical students to build the world's largest tetrahedron and the four students who show up to work on it build both a structure and a friendship.
(3L. Mathematics)

PEARSON, MARY E. 2005. *A Room on Lorelei Street*. Holt.
The room Zoe rents on Lorelei Street means everything to her, and as she tries to deal with her anger and sort out her feelings toward her alcoholic mother and dead father, she finds she will do anything to keep it.
(1D. Detention Home Girls)

————. 2008. *The Adoration of Jenna Fox*. Holt.
Daughter of a biotechnologist father, Jenna awakens after an 18-month coma with no idea of who she is until she pieces together the unethical steps her parents took to keep her alive.
(3N. Science)

————. 2009. *The Miles Between*. Holt.
Claiming she's been abandoned by her parents, Des uses numbers of coincidence and chance to set the stage for revealing family secrets to her friends on their "one fair day" when they play hooky from boarding school.
(1M. Picky Senior Girls)

————. 2009. *The Miles Between.* Read by Jeannie Stith. Brilliance Audio. Unabridged, 6 hours.

Destiny Faraday does something very unpredictable when she and three friends take off for "one fair day" with Stith easily differentiating among the four as she allows Destiny the time to tell her story.

(2A. Audiobooks for High School Listeners)

PECK, RICHARD. 2004. *The Teacher's Funeral: A Comedy in Three Parts.* Read by Dylan Baker. Listening Library. Unabridged, 2 hours, 40 minutes.

Narrator Baker's Midwestern drawl recounts Russell's dismay at learning his sister will take over from the deceased schoolmistress, and the cast of characters voiced by Baker includes a fire-and-brimstone preacher and schoolboys intent on mischief.

(2B. Audiobooks for Middle School Listeners)

————. 2006. *Here Lies the Librarian.* Dial.

Tomboy Peewee and her older brother Jake run an auto repair business in 1914, so when four sorority sisters arrive in town to reopen the library, it's hard to say if Jake is more interested in the automobiles or the self-appointed librarians.

(3P. State Books)

PECK, ROBERT NEWTON. 2002. *Horse Thief.* HarperCollins.

In 1938 orphan Tullis Yoder cares for the horses at a small rodeo in Chickalookee, Florida, but the rodeo closes and the horses are destined for slaughter until Tullis enlists some offbeat characters to help steal the horses and drive them to safety.

(3G. Horses)

PEET, MAL. 2005. *Keeper.* Candlewick.

Sports journalist Paul Faustino interviews the great soccer goalie El Gato and learns how the young man trained in a rain forest, received support from his family, and was mentored by a mysterious, ghostlike figure who taught him soccer skills.

(1J. Latino Teens)

PEREZ, MARLENE. 2009. *Dead Is So Last Year.* Houghton Mifflin Harcourt.

The three Giordano sisters return from Italy and immediately find jobs for the summer, but they have bigger problems when they learn of a dangerous pack of werewolves and a group of evil doppelgangers in their city.

(3R. Summertime)

PETERS, ELIZABETH. 1975. *Crocodile on the Sandbank.* Dodd Mead.

Receiving an inheritance from her father, Amelia Peabody, along with hired companion Evelyn Barton-Forbes, sets out on a tour of the ancient sites of Egypt when she realizes an unknown assailant is stalking her.

(1B. Avid Readers)

PETERS, JULIE ANNE. 2005. *Far from Xanadu*. Hachette.
Mike is struggling to deal with her father's suicide and her mother's complete withdrawal when she meets Xanadu, a troubled newcomer to their small town, and falls hard for her despite the fact that Xanadu isn't interested in more than friendship.
(3P. State Books)

————. 2009. *Rage: A Love Story*. Random House.
Johanna is used to being the dependable one, the girl you can always count on to be level headed and responsible, but then she meets Reeve and suddenly her reasonable world is turned upside down.
(3J. Love Hurts)

PETERSON, DAVID. 2007. *Mouse Guard: Fall 1152*. Archaia Studios.
The Mouse Guard is charged with protecting the passageways between the villages of the Mouse Territories, and while investigating the disappearance of a merchant three members of the Guard discover a plot to attack their hometown.
(2E. Core Graphic Novels)

PETERSON, P.J., AND IVY RUCKMAN. 2004. *Rob&Sara.com*. Delacorte.
Sara posts a poem on an Internet poetry bulletin board, Rob immediately starts to write her, and Sara responds, and when she's injured in a climbing accident, Rob travels to visit her in the hospital.
(2C. Blogs, E-mails, and IMs in Fiction)

PETERSON, SHELLEY. 2007. *Sundancer*. Key Porter.
Selectively mute since she was six years old, Bird does communicate with animals, and when an angry horse is sent to her aunt's horse farm, Bird is the one who trains him to be a jumper.
(3G. Horses)

PETRUCHA, STEFAN, AND THOMAS PENDLETON. 2007–. Wicked Dead series. HarperTeen.
Unable to leave the confines of the crumbling Lockwood Orphanage, four ghost girls roll runic-inscribed bones that dictate which tale of horror will be told, each hoping one day her story will be told and she can escape her prison for the afterlife.
(2M. Paperback Series)

PEYTON, K.M. 2001. *Blind Beauty*. Dutton.
After being kicked out of boarding school, Tessa works on a private farm where she meets an ungainly horse whose lineage traces back to her favorite horse when she was a child, and Tessa is determined to turn Buffoon into a champion racehorse.
(3G. Horses)

PFEFFER, SUSAN BETH. 2006. *Life as We Knew It.* Harcourt.
When a meteor hits the moon and knocks it closer to Earth, tsunamis, earth-quakes, volcanoes, and other weather events disrupt life and Miranda records her family's struggle to find food and fuel after all services are cut off.
(2F. Diaries and Epistolary Novels; 3N. Science; 3P. State Books)

————. 2008. *The Dead and the Gone.* Harcourt.
In this sequel to *Life as We Knew It,* Alex Morales is left caring for his two young sisters in New York City when his parents can't return home, and he is soon bar-tering for food, rescuing one sister from rapists, and seeking medical care for the other.
(1J. Latino Teens)

PHILBRICK, NATHANIEL. 2002. *The Revenge of the Whale: The True Story of the Whaleship* Essex. Putnam. NF.
This abridgement of the author's adult title *In the Heart of the Sea* loses none of its excitement and horror as a whaleship in the Pacific is rammed by a whale, which sends the crew into lifeboats.
(1E. Gentlemanly Boys)

PIERCE, TAMORA. 2006. *Terrier.* Read by Susan Denaker. Listening Library. Un-abridged, 15 hours.
Young policewoman Beka Cooper was raised in the crime-ridden part of her town, and Denaker's voice has a world-weary tone to it as Beka confronts crimi-nals or hears tips from her cluster of sources.
(2B. Audiobooks for Middle School Listeners)

PINSKY, ROBERT, ed. 2009. *Essential Pleasures: A New Anthology of Poems to Read Aloud.* Norton. NF.
Pinsky's good ear for, and joy in, reading poetry aloud lead to this collection of po-ems spanning centuries, organized by form and written by famous and little-known poets, with an accompanying CD of Pinsky reading some of the poems.
(2O. Poetry Anthologies for High School Readers)

PINSKY, ROBERT, AND MAGGIE DIETZ, eds. 1999. *Americans' Favorite Poems: The Fa-vorite Poem Project Anthology.* Norton. NF.
In response to Poet Laureate Pinsky's invitation to send him a letter with a favorite poem, thousands of Americans responded to create this anthology of 200 poems that defy organization by subject.
(2O. Poetry Anthologies for High School Readers)

————, EDS. 2002. *Poems to Read: A New Favorite Poem Project Anthology.* Norton. NF.
Continuing the concept of their first volume, Pinsky and Dietz include both suggested poems and ones they have chosen, extending the range of included poets beyond just those who are American or British.
(2O. Poetry Anthologies for High School Readers)

PIVEN, JOSHUA, AND DAVID BORGENICHT. 2007. *The Complete Worst-Case Scenario Survival Handbook.* Chronicle. NF.
The most popular accounts from all the *Worst-Case Scenario* handbooks are included in this collection that helps readers avoid blind dates, mountain lions, avalanches, and runaway golf carts, in addition to stopping speeding bullets.
(1C. Book Haters)

PLATH, SYLVIA. 1971. *The Bell Jar.* Harper & Row.
What begins as a typical summer for Esther Greenwood, who works at *Mademoiselle* as a junior editor and sometimes argues with her mother or boyfriend, slowly changes as she feels her mental condition altering.
(1N. Punk Readers)

PORCELLINO, JOHN. 2008. *Thoreau at Walden.* Hyperion. NF.
Using Thoreau's writings to form a narrative, Porcellino tells the story of the transcendentalist philosopher's withdrawal from society and time spent at Walden Pond.
(2H. Graphic Novels in the Classroom)

PORTER, CONNIE ROSE. 1999. *Imani All Mine.* Houghton Mifflin.
Despite the fact that her baby was conceived during a rape, Tasha has only love for Imani and struggles to navigate the responsibilities of parenthood while attending school and surviving the drugs and violence of her inner-city neighborhood.
(1O. Reluctant Male Readers; 1S. Urban Teens: Beyond Street Lit; 3I. Institutions)

PORTMAN, FRANK. 2006. *King Dork.* Delacorte.
Called a "dud" by high school girls and mocked by the associate principal, Tom hides by writing music and inventing long lists of possible band names while wondering how *The Catcher in the Rye* ties in with the death of his detective father.
(1A. Adult Readers; 1L. Offbeat Guys; 1O. Reluctant Male Readers)

POWELL, JULIE. 2005. *Julie & Julia: 365 Days, 524 Recipes, 1 Tiny Apartment Kitchen.* Little, Brown. NF.
Frustrated and bored at work, Julie finds her purpose when she decides to make all the recipes in Julia Child's famous work *Mastering the Art of French Cooking*, reports her successes and failures on her blog, and winds up with a movie contract.
(3E. Cookery)

POWELL, RANDY. 1996. *The Whistling Toilets*. Farrar Straus Giroux.
When junior tennis star Ginny goes off her game she's sent home from the competition circuit, and her parents and coach enlist her friend's help in finding out what's behind the slump.
(3A. Bathrooms)

PRATCHETT, TERRY. 2003. *The Wee Free Men*. HarperCollins.
Searching for her brother, who's been kidnapped by the Fairy Queen, Tiffany Aching is armed with a sheeps' disease manual and a frying pan, and is accompanied by the Nac Mac Feegle, six-inch-high blue men who are best at stealing, drinking, and fighting.
(1B. Avid Readers; 1F. Gifted Elementary Student Readers)

————. 2005. *The Wee Free Men*. Read by Stephen Briggs. HarperAudio. Unabridged, 7 hours, 30 minutes.
Briggs renders the six-inch-tall Wee Free Men with a high-pitched, Scottish brogue, which adds to the humor of their constant complaints as they help Tiffany Aching find her brother.
(2A. Audiobooks for High School Listeners)

————. 2006. *Wintersmith*. HarperTempest.
Tiffany Aching needs all the help she can get from her mentoring witch, 113-year-old Miss Treason, when she inadvertently attracts the attention of the Wintersmith, who wants to make her his bride and showers her and the land with Tiffany-shaped snowflakes.
(3T. Wintertime)

————. 2008. *Nation*. Read by Stephen Briggs. Harper Children's Audio. Unabridged, 7 hours, 30 minutes.
Briggs's crisp British diction enhances a survival story that focuses on 13-year-old Mau and British teen Daphne, the only ones alive after a tsunami.
(2A. Audiobooks for High School Listeners)

PULLMAN, PHILIP. 1985. *The Ruby in the Smoke*. Sally Lockhart Trilogy, book 1. Knopf.
Sally investigates her father's unexpected death with the help of a photographer, a nasty landlady, and an opium addict in nineteenth-century London.
(1F. Gifted Elementary Student Readers)

————. 1996–2000. His Dark Materials Trilogy. Random House.
This trio of fantasy novels follows Lyra Belacqua and Will Parry as they experience a range of epic events while wandering through a series of parallel universes.
(1A. Adult Readers)

————. 2006. *Count Karlstein.* Read by Jo Thurley and a full cast. Listening Library. Unabridged, 5 hours, 30 minutes.

Wicked, evil characters permeate this plot as Thurley and others capture their sneering, sniveling, smarmy ways as Count Karlstein readies to give his nieces to the Demon Huntsman in exchange for his continued good life.

(2B. Audiobooks for Middle School Listeners)

Q

QUALEY, MARSHA. 2005. *Just Like That.* Dial.

On a winter night walk in snowy Minneapolis, Hanna later realizes that she may have been the last to see a young couple who drowned in an ATV accident and is pulled back to the scene of the tragedy where she meets Will, who's equally haunted.

(3D. Consequences and Fate; 3T. Wintertime)

R

RABB, MARGO. 2007. *Cures for Heartbreak.* Random House.

After Mia's mother dies of cancer, the New York City teen struggles to make sense of her grief, her family history, and her father's health problems, while fumbling through a relationship with Sasha, who has medical problems of his own.

(3J. Love Hurts)

RABIN, STATON. 2004. *Betsy and the Emperor.* Simon & Schuster.

Fourteen-year-old Betsy Balcombe strikes up a surprising friendship with exiled emperor Napoleon Bonaparte when he is imprisoned in her family home on the island of St. Helena.

(2G. Fictionalized Biographies)

RAHIMZADEH, AURI, AND STEVE WOZNIAK. 2005. *Geek My Ride: Build the Ultimate Tech Rod.* Wiley. NF.

This do-it-yourself guide will enable readers to install gadgets like a game console, in-car networking, LED displays, wireless headphones, video conferencing, and video surveillance to totally tech out a car.

(1C. Book Haters)

RALLISON, JANETTE. 2003. *All's Fair in Love, War, and High School.* Bloomsbury.

College-bound head cheerleader Samantha begins a campaign for student body president, hoping to make up for dismal SAT scores, and ends up making new friends, rekindling a romance, and learning something about the kind of girl she wants to be.

(1H. Innocent Middle School Girls)

RAMOS-ELODURY, JULITA. 1998. *Creepy Crawly Cuisine: The Gourmet Guide to Edible Insects.* Park Street. NF.
   Recipes for using many different species of insects, including Leaf-Footed Bug Pizza, Mealworm Spaghetti, and Ant Turnovers, are accompanied by information about selected insects' nutritional, amino acid, and protein value.
   (3H. Insects)

RAPP, ADAM. 1997. *The Buffalo Tree.* Boyds Mills Press.
   Twelve-year-old Sura describes the residents and administrators of the juvenile detention facility he lives in after being caught stealing hood ornaments and muses about his shifting feelings toward life on the outside.
   (3I. Institutions)

————. 2003. *33 Snowfish.* Candlewick.
   Custis, a sexually abused orphan, runs away with a prostitute and a murderer, before being taken in by an older black man called Seldom, who helps Custis celebrate Christmas as he tries to return to normalcy.
   (1Q. Troubled Teen Boys; 1S. Urban Teens: Beyond Street Lit)

————. 2004. *Under the Wolf, Under the Dog.* Candlewick.
   Steve isn't coping well after his older brother's suicide and his mother's death, and his erratic and destructive behavior leads him to Burnstone Grove, a facility for suicidal or addicted teens.
   (3I. Institutions)

RAVEN, NICKY. 2007. *Beowulf: A Tale of Blood, Heat, and Ashes.* Illustrated by John Howe. Candlewick.
   Beowulf and his companion Wiglaf set out to free a king and his warriors from the monster Grendel but find they must face an even deadlier enemy before peace and safety can be restored.
   (2N. Picture Books for Teens)

REES, CELIA. 2001. *Witch Child.* Candlewick.
   After her grandmother is hanged as a witch, Mary leaves England for America only to live in a country where witches are blamed for everything, and Mary's interest in the natural world causes villagers to regard her with suspicion.
   (2F. Diaries and Epistolary Novels)

————. 2004. *Pirates: The True and Remarkable Adventures of Minerva Sharpe and Nancy Kington, Female Pirates*. Read by Jennifer Wiltsie. Listening Library. Unabridged, 9 hours.

Befitting their roles, Nancy Kington's ladylike speech contrasts with former slave Minerva's deeper, Caribbean lilting voice, both smoothly delivered by narrator Wiltsie as these two women embark on their pirate days.
(2A. Audiobooks for High School Listeners)

REEVE, PHILIP. 2006. *Larklight: A Rousing Tale of Dauntless Pluck in the Farthest Reaches of Space*. Bloomsbury.

Art and Myrtle Mumby's Victorian home Larklight floats in space but is invaded by giant white spiders that coat their scientist father in webbing and force the siblings to escape and begin their wild, hilarious adventure with aliens and pirates.
(1R. Tweens)

REISS, KATHRYN. 2006. *Blackthorn Winter*. Harcourt.

Juliana can't believe her mother drags her from sunny California to a wintry seaside English town to visit her friend Liza, who is murdered soon after they arrive.
(3T. Wintertime)

REMBERT, WINFRED. 2003. *Don't Hold Me Back: My Life and Art*. Cricket Books. NF.

Using a combination of words and his own art, Rembert reminisces about growing up in the South under segregation, telling stories of cotton picking, attending civil rights demonstrations, watching a chain gang, and spending time in prison.
(3C. The Civil Rights Movement)

RENNISON, LOUISE. 1999–2009. Confessions of Georgia Nicolson series. Harper Collins.

Georgia Nicolson describes the many tortures she is forced to endure on a daily basis, including her crazy-but-cute sister Libby, her mad parents, her best friend Jas, school (otherwise known as Stalag 14), and her ever-troublesome red bottomosity.
(2F. Diaries and Epistolary Novels)

RESAU, LAURA. 2006. *What the Moon Saw*. Delacorte.

Having never met her father's parents, Laura's surprised to be invited to spend the summer with them in Mexico, but she accepts and learns that she and her grandmother share a talent for healing.
(1I. Latina Teens; 3R. Summertime)

REX, ADAM. 2006. *Frankenstein Makes a Sandwich*. Harcourt. NF.
    While Frankenstein makes his "Dagwood" sandwich, other monsters relate their
    very unmonsterly problems, such as spinach in Count Dracula's teeth and
    Godzilla pooping on a Honda.
(2P. Poetry Anthologies for Middle School Readers)

————. 2007. *The True Meaning of Smekday*. Hyperion.
    Assigned to write a five-page paper on "the true meaning of Smekday" for a na-
    tional contest, Tip's unsure whether to write about her mother's abduction by the
    invading Boovs or her friendship with a renegade Boov mechanic who's helping
    Tip find her mother.
(1R. Tweens)

RINALDI, ANN. 1996. *Hang a Thousand Trees with Ribbons: The Story of Phillis
Wheatley*. Houghton Mifflin.
    After she is purchased by the Wheatleys, a prominent Boston family who educate
    her and encourage her writing, Phillis finds herself caught between two worlds as
    she is not a slave but is also not accepted by whites because of the color of her skin.
(2G. Fictionalized Biographies)

————. 2002. *Taking Liberty*. Simon & Schuster.
    Oney Judge, a slave owned by George and Martha Washington, abandons her
    comfortable position as Martha's companion to secure freedom for herself in the
    North.
(2G. Fictionalized Biographies)

RIORDAN, RICK. 2005. *The Lightning Thief*. Percy Jackson and the Olympians series,
book 1. Hyperion.
    Hyperactive and expelled from several schools, Percy attends Camp Half-Blood
    where he learns his dad is Poseidon and finally understands why he vaporized his
    algebra teacher, enjoys friendship with a satyr, and was almost killed by a mino-
    taur.
(3Q. Summer Camp)

————. 2005. *The Lightning Thief*. Read by Jesse Bernstein. Listening Library. Unabridged, 10 hours.
    Mythology merges with the modern world when Percy Jackson learns he's the son
    of Poseidon, and Bernstein captures Percy's sense of amazement at this finding
    while his delivery matches the fast-paced clip of this rollicking adventure.
(2B. Audiobooks for Middle School Listeners)

————. 2005–2009. Percy Jackson and the Olympians series. Hyperion.
Percy Jackson seems like just a regular kid, but he's actually the half-blood son of the god Poseidon, a fact that entangles him in the looming battle between the Olympians and the evil Titan Time Lord Kronos.
(1E. Gentlemanly Boys; 1O. Reluctant Male Readers)

————. 2008. *The Maze of Bones.* The 39 Clues series, book 1. Scholastic.
As Dan and Amy listen to the reading of their grandmother's will, they're offered a choice: they can take a million dollars and walk away, or they can take a clue and begin a search for 38 other clues that will reveal their family's power—they take the clue.
(1R. Tweens)

ROBBINS, ALEXANDRA. 2006. *The Overachievers: The Secret Lives of Driven Kids.* Hyperion. NF.
Studying students at a "good" high school in Maryland, Robbins worries about these overachievers who struggle with too much homework and extracurricular activities just to get into a brand name school, when a lesser known one might be a better match.
(1M. Picky Senior Girls)

ROBERTS, KATHERINE. 2006. *I Am the Great Horse.* Scholastic.
Bucephalas, the horse ridden by Alexander the Great, describes their travels as they conquer their way from Greece to Persia and India in 330 BCE.
(3G. Horses)

RODMAN, MARY ANN. 2004. *Yankee Girl.* Farrar, Straus and Giroux.
When Alice's father is transferred from Chicago to Jackson, Mississippi, to protect civil rights workers, Alice finds herself torn between befriending the other outsider in her class—newly integrated student Valerie—or trying to make friends with the popular girls.
(3C. The Civil Rights Movement)

RODRIGUEZ, ART. 1999. *East Side Dreams.* Dream House. NF.
This autobiographical work reveals the many problems Rodriguez had growing up with a strict, abusive father, then his trouble with the law and time spent with the California Youth Authority, followed by his successful business in the waste disposal industry.
(1P. Striving Readers)

RODRIGUEZ, LUIS J. 1993. *Always Running: La Vida Loca, Gang Days in L.A.* Curbstone. NF.

Noted poet and publisher Rodriguez tells of his younger days when membership in a Latino gang led to his arrest and jail time in a book he wrote to keep his son from following his example, though his plan failed.
(3I. Institutions)

ROHMANN, ERIC. 1994. *Time Flies.* Random House.

A small bird flies into a museum at night and explores the hall of dinosaurs, flitting into and out of skeletons until one particular creature takes on flesh and comes to life, swallowing the bird.
(2N. Picture Books for Teens)

ROSEN, MICHAEL. 2002. *ChaseR: A Novel in E-mails.* Candlewick.

Moving 60 miles from a big city to a rural area, Chase e-mails friends and his college sisters complaining about country living as he contends with mice in the farmhouse, noisy cicadas outside, and hunters who shoot his dog.
(2C. Blogs, E-mails, and IMs in Fiction)

ROSENBLUM, MORT. 2005. *Chocolate: A Bittersweet Saga of Dark and Light.* Farrar, Straus and Giroux. NF.

In addition to its healthful benefits, all other aspects of chocolate are detailed from cultivation of cacao on the Ivory Coast, to the differences between Hershey's and Nestlé, the origin of Nutella, and the chocolate taster's role at Fortnum & Mason.
(3B. Chocolate)

ROSOFF, MEG. 2004. *How I Live Now.* Random House/Wendy Lamb.

Daisy leaves Manhattan to visit her British cousins on their remote farm, but Aunt Penn is stranded in Oslo and the cousins are alone on the farm as terrorists invade and occupy England.
(1A. Adult Readers)

————. 2005. *How I Live Now.* Read by Kim Mai Guest. Listening Library. Unabridged, 4 hours.

Initially hesitant when she arrives from New York to visit her British cousins, narrator Guest imbues Daisy's speech with anger and determination when the terrorists arrive and she and her cousins must survive on their own.
(2A. Audiobooks for High School Listeners)

————. 2006. *Just in Case.* Random/Wendy Lamb.

After saving his little brother from a disastrous flying attempt in front of an open window, David thinks of all the other perils in his life and decides to remake him-

self so that Fate can't find him, not realizing that Fate is already keeping an eye on him.
(1L. Offbeat Guys)

ROTTMAN, S.L. 1997. *Hero.* Peachtree Publishers.
   In trouble yet again, Sean is sentenced to community service at Mr. Hassler's ranch where he hears stories of World War II, helps with chores, and raises a premature foal, each of which helps build Sean's self-confidence.
(3G. Horses)

————. 1999. *Head Above Water.* Peachtree Publishers.
   High school junior Skye sometimes feels she's in over her head as she tries to improve her swimming to make the state championship, look after her special needs brother Sunny, and keep up with her boyfriend, but she does her best to muddle through.
(1Q. Troubled Teen Boys)

————. 2002. *Stetson.* Viking.
   Abandoned by his mother when he was three and living with an alcoholic father, Stet raises himself, works several jobs just to eat, and is surprised to learn he has a sister, born after his mother left, but now his mother's dead and Kayla is on his trailer doorstep.
(1C. Book Haters)

————. 2004. *Slalom.* Viking.
   Son of an Italian skier who doesn't know of his existence, Sandro works in a Colorado ski shop and is taken aback one day when his father Alessandro enters the shop.
(3T. Wintertime)

ROWLING, J.K. 1997–2007. Harry Potter series. Scholastic/Levine.
   In these seven fantasy novels, Harry Potter, along with his friends Ron Weasley and Hermione Granger, are students at Hogwarts School of Witchcraft and Wizardry, where they learn to control their special powers, which Harry needs to contain Lord Voldemort.
(3A. Bathrooms)

————. 1999. *Harry Potter and the Sorcerer's Stone.* Read by Jim Dale. Listening Library. Unabridged, 8 hours.
   Listeners are introduced to Harry Potter in this version narrated by Jim Dale, whose skill lies in his pacing, ability to heighten the dramatic highs and lows, and brilliant interpretation of characters from snide Snape to earnest Harry.
(2B. Audiobooks for Middle School Listeners)

————. 2005. *Harry Potter and the Half-Blood Prince*. Scholastic.
Harry accompanies Dumbledore as he sifts through Voldemort's past for clues while keeping an eye on an increasingly agitated Draco Malfoy and beginning a new relationship with Ginny.
(3K. Luck)

————. 2007. *Harry Potter and the Deathly Hallows*. Scholastic.
Harry, Ron, and Hermione, on the run from Voldemort and his Death Eaters, travel the country in search of the Deathly Hallows, hoping to gather the weapons they need to defeat the Dark Lord in the final battle.
(3D. Consequences and Fate)

ROZIN, ELISABETH. 1992. *Blue Corn and Chocolate*. Knopf. NF.
Combining recipes with history, this celebration of the 500th anniversary of the discovery of the New World by Columbus offers a variety of ways to prepare native foods, including chocolate chili, peanut soup, and pumpkin seed pesto.
(3B. Chocolate)

RUDITIS, PAUL. 2005. *Rainbow Party*. Simon & Schuster.
When a high number of students in the sophomore class are diagnosed with gonorrhea, Gin, the sexually active host of a "rainbow party" that never materializes, is blamed.
(3A. Bathrooms)

RUNYON, BRENT. 2004. *The Burn Journals*. Knopf. NF.
Months spent in the hospital recovering from burns incurred when he tried to set himself on fire provide Brent the time needed to heal his body and his mind, both of which are painful.
(1M. Picky Senior Girls; 3I. Institutions)

RYAN, PAM MUÑOZ. 2000. *Esperanza Rising*. Scholastic.
Working in the fields of California after being forced off their farm in Mexico, Esperanza wants to earn enough money to bring her grandmother to America.
(1I. Latina Teens; 3P. State Books; 3S. Teen Immigrants)

————. 2004. *Becoming Naomi León*. Random House.
When their mother shows up, Naomi, her brother, and Gram figure out that alcoholic Skyla wants custody of Naomi as a babysitter for her boyfriend's child, which sends Gram and the siblings in search of their biological father, a noted wood carver.
(1I. Latina Teens)

RYAN, SARA. 2001. *Empress of the World.* Viking.
Nicola studies archaeology at a summer institute for gifted high school students, where she is attracted to the dancer Battle Davies, which leads into a relationship new and unique to each girl.
(3Q. Summer Camp)

RYLANT, CYNTHIA. 1985. *A Blue-Eyed Daisy.* Simon & Schuster.
Ellie's eleventh year includes the strange arrival of a hunting dog named Bullet, the frightening behavior of a sick boy in her class, and the accidental death of another classmate, but a new friend and a first kiss sweeten day-to-day life in her small mining town.
(3P. State Books)

————. 1995. *I Had Seen Castles.* Harcourt.
Reminiscing about his life, John thinks about Ginny, a woman he loved before he left to serve in World War II, and wonders whatever happened to her.
(1P. Striving Readers)

S

SACCO, JOE. 2000. *Safe Area Gorazde: The War in Eastern Bosnia 1992–1995.* Fantagraphics Books. NF.
Sacco spent months in Bosnia researching life during wartime and here tells the story of Gorazde, a Muslim community besieged by Bosnian Serbs.
(2K. Nonfiction Graphic Novels)

SACHAR, LOUIS. 1987. *There's a Boy in the Girl's Bathroom.* Knopf.
Bradley Chalkers has no friends at school until new counselor Carla Davis comes to the school and works with Bradley to make him more likable, which in turn restores his self-confidence.
(1R. Tweens)

————. 1998. *Holes.* Farrar, Straus and Giroux.
Because of a curse laid upon his great-great-grandfather for stealing a pig, Stanley is now in a correctional camp where every day he digs a new hole.
(1O. Reluctant Male Readers; 1P. Striving Readers; 3I. Institutions)

SADAMOTO, YOSHIYUKI. 1998– . Neon Genesis Evangelion series. VIZ Media.
Shinji Ikari is enlisted by his distant father to pilot an Evangelion, a giant mechanical mecha, in the battle against the seemingly indestructible Angels.
(2D. Classic Manga)

SÁENZ, BENJAMIN ALIRE. 2004. *Sammy & Juliana in Hollywood.* Cinco Puntos.
Living in the Hollywood barrio of Las Cruces, New Mexico, Sammy focuses on a new life after his girlfriend Juliana dies, yet other problems loom with the Vietnam War draft, discrimination against two of his gay friends, and his father's accident.
(1I. Latina Teens; 1J. Latino Teens; 3P. State Books)

————. 2008. *He Forgot to Say Goodbye.* Simon & Schuster.
Ramiro and Jake live on opposite sides of El Paso and, in alternating stories, tell of a friendship that began when each boy realized the other was also growing up without a father.
(1J. Latino Teens)

————. 2009. *Last Night I Sang to the Monster.* Cinco Puntos.
Part-Anglo and part-Mexican Zach wakes up in a rehab center where he is forced to meet his "monster" as he goes through therapy for alcoholism.
(1J. Latino Teens)

SAGE, ANGIE. 2005. *Magyk.* Read by Allan Corduner. Harper Children's Audio. Unabridged, 12 hours.
In this first in the series about Septimus Heap, who was switched at birth to prevent his training in wizardry, Corduner's rich, authoritarian voice fills the work with unusual, distinctive characters as his fast-paced reading keeps the action moving.
(2B. Audiobooks for Middle School Listeners)

SAIJYO, SHINJI. 2002– . Iron Wok Jan series. Comics One.
The gifted chef Jan works for the Gobancho Restaurant and in the very first volume contends with the former chef for the restaurant, who insults every dish Jan makes, in a series perfect for fans of the television series *Iron Chef.*
(3E. Cookery)

SAKAI, STAN. 1987– . Usagi Yojimbo series. Fantagraphics/Dark Horse.
Rabbit ronin Miyamoto Usagi is on a warrior's pilgrimage, hiring himself out as a bodyguard during his travels across seventeenth-century Japan.
(2E. Core Graphic Novels)

SALDAÑA, RENÉ, JR. 2001. *The Jumping Tree.* Delacorte.
A series of vignettes reveals Rey's maturation as he moves from games with friends and visits across the border with his Mexican relatives to an awareness of work responsibilities and his father as a role model.
(1J. Latino Teens)

———. 2003. *Finding Our Way*. Random House/Wendy Lamb.
Eleven short stories feature Hispanic teens as they come of age in tales that revolve around school but take place both in and out of the classroom.
(1J. Latino Teens)

———. 2007. *The Whole Sky Full of Stars*. Random House/Wendy Lamb.
Friends since first grade, Alby pressures Barry into boxing for money so the two can split the purse, but Alby doesn't mention that he needs the money to erase his gambling debts.
(1J. Latino Teens)

SALISBURY, GRAHAM. 2007. *Night of the Howling Dogs*. Random House.
Dylan, senior patrol leader of his Hilo, Hawaii, scout troop, must depend on his wits and his fellow scouts when their camping trip is interrupted by an earthquake and then a tsunami.
(3P. State Books)

SANDELL, LISA ANN. 2006. *The Weight of the Sky*. Penguin Putnam.
Sarah, uncomfortable as one of only two Jewish students in her Pennsylvania high school, jumps at the chance to spend the summer in Israel, and although her experience isn't quite what she expected, she finds new confidence and a sense of identity.
(3M. The Middle East)

———. 2007. *Song of the Sparrow*. Scholastic.
Elaine, the Lady of Shallot, and Gwynivere, who marries King Arthur, dislike one another but form a bond when captured by the Saxons to keep Arthur's army from danger.
(2I. Historical Novels in Verse)

SANDERSON, BRANDON. 2007. *Alcatraz versus the Evil Librarians*. Scholastic.
Alcatraz Smedry's special talent is for breaking things, which doesn't seem all that useful until the day he receives a bag of sand as a gift and finds himself matching wits with a cult of evil Librarians who are plotting to take over the world.
(1G. Graphic Novel Lovers)

SATRAPI, MARJANE. 2003. *Persepolis: The Story of a Childhood*. Pantheon. NF.
Satrapi describes the changes that occurred during her childhood when the Shah of Iran was overthrown during the Islamic Revolution and torture became routine.
(2K. Nonfiction Graphic Novels; 3M. The Middle East)

————. 2004. *Persepolis 2: The Story of a Return.* Random House. NF.
After surviving the Islamic Revolution in Iran, Satrapi is sent to live in Vienna by her liberal parents, but, finding the freedom of her new life hard to manage, she returns to her family and carves out space for herself within the confines of her homeland.
(2K. Nonfiction Graphic Novels; 3M. The Middle East)

SAULSBURY, CAMILLA V. 2007. *Enlightened Chocolate: More Than 200 Decadently Light, Lowfat, and Inspired Recipes Using Dark Chocolate and Unsweetened Cocoa Powder.* Cumberland House. NF.
Recipes for drinks, pies, soufflés, candies, and any other kind of sweet imaginable are accompanied by the history and rationale for using dark chocolate and cocoa powder.
(3B. Chocolate)

SAVAGE, CANDACE. 2009. *Bees: Nature's Little Wonders.* Greystone. NF.
Drawings, illustrations, and poems show the cultural impact of bees, while the text and color photographs reveal the unique characteristics of these insects that communicate via dances, are invaluable for crop production, and now face colony collapse.
(3H. Insects)

SAVAGE, DEBORAH. 1997. *Under a Different Sky.* Houghton Mifflin.
Though Ben dreams of becoming an Olympic competitor on his stallion named Galaxy, he seems destined to become an auto mechanic until he meets Lara, a rebellious student at the local prep school, and each encourages the other to dream.
(3G. Horses)

SAYRES, MEGHAN NUTTALL. 2006. *Anahita's Woven Riddle.* Abrams.
Unwilling to marry the khan of her tribe, Anahita persuades her father to allow her to weave riddles into her marriage carpet, forcing suitors into a competition for her hand and, despite repercussions, her father agrees.
(3M. The Middle East)

SCHINDLER, NINA. 2004. *An Order of Amelie, Hold the Fries.* Translated by Robert Barrett. Annick/Firefly.
Accidentally writing to the wrong girl, Tim continues to write and text until 19-year-old Amelie agrees to meet him and, becoming fonder of him, must eventually choose between her businessman boyfriend and high school student Tim.
(2C. Blogs, E-mails, and IMs in Fiction)

SCHLITZ, LAURA AMY. 2006. *A Drowned Maiden's Hair: A Melodrama.* Candlewick.
Adopted and well cared for by the Hawthorne sisters, Maud is grateful for her change in circumstances but curious about the sisters' insistence that she keep hidden, until she learns that they conduct fraudulent séances and need her to impersonate a ghost.
(1H. Innocent Middle School Girls)

————. 2007. *Good Masters! Sweet Ladies! Voices from a Medieval Village.* Candlewick.
Seventeen monologues feature the inhabitants of a 1255 English town and offer opportunities for readers to become a noblewoman, Christian, Jew, and falconer as they experience some of the Medieval Period.
(2L. Novels with Script or Screenplay Format)

SCHMIDT, GARY D. 2004. *Lizzie Bright and the Buckminster Boy.* Clarion.
Lizzie, who lives on an island settled by former slaves, and the new minister's son become fast friends as they explore the island and surrounding countryside, but their idyllic times end when the town decides it wants the island for development.
(3P. State Books)

————. 2005. *First Boy.* Holt.
After his grandfather's death leaves him alone on his New Hampshire farm, 14-year-old Cooper manages to stay in school and do the daily chores with the help of his neighbors, but then a senator takes an interest and Cooper's life gets even stranger.
(3P. State Books)

————. 2005. *Lizzie Bright and the Buckminster Boy.* Read by Sam Freed. Listening Library. Unabridged, 6 hours, 30 minutes.
The only person who befriends Turner Buckminster is Lizzie Bright Griffin, daughter of slaves who settled Malaga Island, Maine, a town where prejudice is evident, but not acknowledged, in this story narrated by Freed using characteristic Maine accents.
(2B. Audiobooks for Middle School Listeners)

————. 2007. *The Wednesday Wars.* Clarion.
Holling is the only student in Mrs. Baker's seventh grade classroom who doesn't attend either Catechism class or Hebrew school on Wednesday afternoons and remains at school with Mrs. Baker where, after disasters with chalk dust and rats, he is now reading Shakespeare.
(1E. Gentlemanly Boys)

SCHRAFF, ANNE. 2007. *Lost and Found.* Bluford High series, book 1. Scholastic.
In this first of the Bluford High series, Darcy Wills worries about her younger sister's behavior, experiences her first relationship, and adjusts to the return of her long-absent father.
(1P. Striving Readers)

SCHRAG, ARIEL, ED. 2007. *Stuck in the Middle: 17 Comics from an Unpleasant Age.* Penguin Putnam.
A variety of artistic styles are displayed by artists including Aaron Reiner, Lauren Weinstein, Daniel Clowes, and editor Schrag as they explore the often-unhappy junior high experience.
(2E. Core Graphic Novels)

SCHROEDER, LISA. 2009. *Far from You.* Simon Pulse.
Still saddened by the death of her mother years earlier, Alice wants no part of her stepfamily until she, her stepmother, and baby stepsister are trapped in their car for four days during a blizzard and Alice reevaluates her life.
(2Q. Teen Issue Novels in Verse)

SCHULTZ, JAN NEUBERT. 2006. *Battle Cry.* Lerner.
Half-Dakota Chaska and his white friend Johnny start to drift apart during the 1862 Dakota Conflict, but when a band of rebel Indians attacks, Johnny sticks up for his friend and remains loyal after Chaska is accused of a crime he didn't commit.
(3P. State Books)

SCHULTZ, MARK. 2009. *The Stuff of Life: A Graphic Guide to Genetics and DNA.* Illustrated by Zander Cannon and Kevin Cannon. Farrar, Straus and Giroux. NF.
Framed as a report by an interstellar biologist to his planet's leaders, Schultz offers a wealth of information on the basic mechanics of genetics and covers controversial subjects like cloning and genetically altered foods.
(2K. Nonfiction Graphic Novels)

SCIESZKA, JON. 1995. *Math Curse.* Illustrated by Lane Smith. Penguin Putnam.
The victim of a "math curse" placed on her by a teacher who encouraged her to think of everything as a math problem, the narrator shares a number of increasingly silly equations encountered or created throughout her day.
(2N. Picture Books for Teens)

———, ED. 2008. *Guys Write for Guys Read: Boys' Favorite Authors Write about Being Boys.* Penguin Putnam.
Musings about being a guy are contributed by more than 80 writers, including Lloyd Alexander, Chris Crutcher, Robert Peck, Walter Dean Myers, Avi, Stephen King, Jerry Spinelli, and Will Hobbs.
(2J. Must-Have Anthologies)

————. 2008. *Knucklehead: Tall Tales and Almost True Stories of Growing Up Scieszka.* Viking. NF.
> As the second of six brothers in a Catholic family, Scieszka's childhood stories clarify the origin of his sense of humor as he turns babysitting into a money-making venture, endures a nun-structured education, and uses proper terms for all body functions.
> (1P. Striving Readers)

SCOTT, ELIZABETH. 2008. *Living Dead Girl.* Simon & Schuster.
> Renamed Alice by her abductor, Ray, the 15-year-old narrator has been a prisoner of violence and abuse for five years, and now Ray has ordered her to find and train her replacement.
> (1A. Adult Readers; 3O. Silence)

SEBOLD, ALICE. 2002. *The Lovely Bones.* Little, Brown.
> Raped and killed on her way home from school, 14-year-old Suzy Salmon views her former friends and family from heaven as each takes a different means of coming to terms with her death.
> (1M. Picky Senior Girls)

SEINO, SHIZURU. 2004–2005. Girl Got Game series. Tokyopop.
> Kyo is excited to attend Seisyu High School, but when her father orders her a boy's uniform and asks her to disguise herself so she can play on the all-male team, Kyo has to choose between living her own life and making her father happy.
> (2D. Classic Manga)

SELZNICK, BRIAN. 2007. *The Invention of Hugo Cabret.* Scholastic.
> Hugo lives in the walls of a Paris train station where he keeps the clocks and works on his dead father's automaton, but his secret existence is interrupted when he meets a grumpy old man who is more than he seems.
> (1E. Gentlemanly Boys; 1G. Graphic Novel Lovers)

SHAKUR, TUPAC AMARU. 2000. *The Rose That Grew from Concrete.* MTV. NF.
> Passionate and angry poems that were written early in Tupac's career are made available in their original format and show his spelling errors and subsequent corrections.
> (2P. Poetry Anthologies for Middle School Readers)

SHAN, DARREN. 2001–2006. Cirque du Freak series. Hachette.
> Darren, half-vampire assistant to Mr. Crepsley and sometime traveler with the Cirque du Freak, finds himself at odds with his former friend Steve and on the run from the evil Vampaneze.
> (1O. Reluctant Male Readers)

SHANOWER, ERIC. 2001– . Age of Bronze series. Image Comics.
Helen, Queen of Sparta, is abducted by the Trojan prince Paris, and her husband is determined to bring her home, regardless of the price.
(2H. Graphic Novels in the Classroom)

SHARENOW, ROBERT. 2007. *My Mother the Cheerleader*. HarperCollins.
As the forced desegregation of her school in New Orleans proceeds, Louise is pulled out of school by her mother, one of the Cheerleaders who gather outside the school to jeer and insult first grader Ruby Bridges each morning.
(3C. The Civil Rights Movement)

SHAW, SUSAN. 2002. *Black-Eyed Suzie*. Boyds Mills Press.
When it's clear Suzie can't eat, talk, sleep, or move, her uncle works to have her admitted to a hospital where a skilled therapist helps her emerge from her nearly catatonic state to talk about the physical abuse she suffers at the hand of her mother.
(3I. Institutions)

SHAW, TUCKER. 2003. *Flavor of the Week*. Hyperion.
Although Cyril is smitten with Rose Mulligan, Rose thinks of him as her dear, fat friend who cooks, while her attention focuses on Nick, who claims to be a chef and uses Cyril's preparations to prove it.
(3E. Cookery)

SHERMAN, DELIA. 2006. *Changeling*. Viking.
Changeling Neef lives in "New York Between," a parallel world of fairies and demons, and when she breaks a Fairy Law she must meet the challenges from the Lady of Central Park or be given up to the Wild Hunt—but Neef's a New Yorker—no problem!
(1M. Picky Senior Girls)

SHETH, KASHMIRA. 2004. *Blue Jasmine*. Hyperion.
Twelve-year-old Seema moves from India to Iowa City with her family, leaving grandparents, friends, and her beloved cousin Raju behind, and although she struggles to fit in at her new school, a short trip back to India makes her realize she can love both places at once.
(3S. Teen Immigrants)

SHIELDS, CAROL DIGGERY. 2003. *Brain Juice: Science, Fresh Squeezed!* Illustrated by Richard Thompson. Handprint. NF.
Covering the basic science taught in schools, 41 poems help students understand such topics as the water cycle, layers of the atmosphere, and volcanoes.
(2P. Poetry Anthologies for Middle School Readers)

SHIGENO, SHUICHI. 2002– . Initial D series. Tokyopop.
In this fast and exciting manga series, teams of street racers take on one another in this illegal Japanese sport that occurs in the mountain passes where the use of the drift racing style is most popular.
(1C. Book Haters)

SHUSTERMAN, NEAL. 2007. *Unwind*. Simon & Schuster.
Connor, Risa, and Lev are on the run, hoping to survive until they turn 18 and become safe from "unwinding," the process of harvesting body parts from the young.
(1O. Reluctant Male Readers; 3A. Bathrooms)

SIANA, JOLENE. 2005. *Go Ask Ogre: Letters from a Deathrock Cutter*. Process. NF.
In her teens, depressed and cutting herself, Siana writes letters to punk rocker Ogre of the band Skinny Puppy, and when nine years later he returns her two boxes of correspondence, she realizes, and these letters show, that writing them saved her.
(1N. Punk Readers)

SIEBERT, DIANE. 2006. *Tour America: A Journey through Poems and Art*. Illustrated by Stephen T. Johnson. Chronicle. NF.
The author provides poetic descriptions of some of her favorite sites in America, including the Badlands of South Dakota, the "El" in Chicago, New Jersey's Lucy the Elephant, and the Golden Gate Bridge in San Francisco, California.
(2P. Poetry Anthologies for Middle School Readers)

SIEGEL, SIENA CHERSON. 2006. *To Dance: A Ballerina's Graphic Novel*. Illustrated by Mark Siegel. Atheneum. NF.
In a work that includes the realities of pain and leg injuries, water color panels drawn by her husband Mark illustrate Siena's dance career, which she began as a six-year-old, set aside during college, and then returned to later because she "needed to dance."
(2H. Graphic Novels in the Classroom)

SINGER, MARILYN, ED. 2004. *Face Relations: Eleven Stories about Seeing Beyond Color*. Simon & Schuster.
The concept of racial identity is examined in 11 stories by authors including Joseph Bruchac, Ellen Wittlinger, M.E. Kerr, Rita Williams-Garcia, Naomi Shihab Nye, and Jess Mowry.
(2J. Must-Have Anthologies)

Sís, Peter. 1993. *A Small Tall Tale from the Far Far North*. Random House.
Czech folk hero Jan Welzl is rescued by Eskimos who not only nurse him back to health but also teach him about surviving in the Arctic, and when their peaceful existence is threatened by the discovery of gold, Welzl takes action to help protect their way of life.
(2N. Picture Books for Teens)

————. 2007. *The Wall: Growing Up Behind the Iron Curtain*. Farrar, Straus and Giroux. NF.
Through his autobiographical picture book, Sís conveys an image of life in Cold War Prague as remembered by a young boy who loved to draw but hated being told what images he could and couldn't depict.
(2N. Picture Books for Teens)

Sitomer, Alan Lawrence. 2007. *Homeboyz*. Jump at the Sun/Hyperion.
Teddy's punishment for seeking revenge against his sister's killers is worse than going to jail when he's forced to mentor Micah, a preteen gangster wannabe.
(1J. Latino Teens)

————. 2008. *The Secret Story of Sonia Rodriguez*. Jump at the Sun/Hyperion.
Determined to be the first in her family to graduate, Sonia wonders if she'll achieve her goal as she cooks and cleans for her family, fends off her drunken uncle's advances, and is usually awake past midnight to finish her homework.
(1I. Latina Teens)

Sivertsen, Linda, and Tosh Sivertsen. 2009. *Generation Green: The Ultimate Teen Guide to Living an Eco-Friendly Life*. Pulse. NF.
After explaining some of the environmental problems facing Earth, the authors provide suggestions about how to ease the strain on the planet as well as interviews with teens who already try to make a difference.
(3F. The Environment)

Sleator, William. 2005. *The Last Universe*. Abrams.
Susan and her wheelchair-bound brother Gary explore a garden designed by a physicist, and when they realize the maker used quantum physics for the layout, they wonder if there's an alternate world where Gary could be well.
(3L. Mathematics)

Sloan, Brian. 2006. *Tale of Two Summers*. Simon & Schuster.
Straight Chuck attends summer theater camp while his best friend gay Hal stays home and takes driver's ed, though the two stay in touch via a blog and often discuss their romantic exploits, which is new territory for both of them.
(2C. Blogs, E-mails, and IMs in Fiction; 3Q. Summer Camp)

SMALL, DAVID. 2009. *Stitches: A Memoir*. W.W. Norton. NF.
Small's memoir centers around his early childhood and adolescence and the emotional cost of growing up in a family so uncommunicative that he underwent surgery for cancer without being told what was wrong with him.
(2H. Graphic Novels in the Classroom)

SMEDMAN, LISA. 2007. *From Boneshakers to Choppers: The Rip-Roaring History of Motorcycles*. Annick. NF.
The 1880s saw the beginning of motorcycle usage, which continues today by members of the military, stunt riders, gang members, dirt bikers, and, increasingly, mainstream Americans, as this well-illustrated historical review shows.
(1C. Book Haters)

SMELCER, JOHN E. 2006. *The Trap*. Holt.
When Johnny Least-Weasel's grandfather doesn't return from checking his trap line, Johnny worries but is hesitant to disrespect his elder, so he waits until his grandmother sends him out to check on her husband, who by now has been caught in a trap for several days.
(3P. State Books; 3T. Wintertime)

———. 2009. *The Great Death*. Holt.
In the winter of 1917 strangers come to a native village in Alaska, bringing with them the "Great Death" that kills all of the villagers except for two girls, Millie and Maura, who must now find another home.
(3T. Wintertime)

SMITH, CHARLES R., JR. 2003. *Hoop Queens*. Candlewick. NF.
Twelve stars of the WNBA are featured in this collection of rap poetry, including Chamique Holdsclaw, who floats "like smoke to the rim," and Sheryl Swoopes, "The Board Snatcher/Bullet Pass Catcher."
(2P. Poetry Anthologies for Middle School Readers)

———. 2008. *Chameleon*. Candlewick.
Hanging with his buddies on the streets of Compton, California, shooting hoops, and avoiding the turf of the gangs is just how Shawn wants to spend his summer, as he puts off for a few months deciding which high school he'll attend in the fall.
(3R. Summertime)

SMITH, CYNTHIA LEITICH. 2007. *Tantalize*. Candlewick.
After her parents die, Quincie moves in with her Uncle Davidson, and they reopen her parents' failing restaurant and hope the new vampire theme will attract customers, although they didn't expect their new chef to be known as Brad the Impaler.
(3E. Cookery; 3P. State Books)

SMITH, DODIE. 1998, ©1948. *I Capture the Castle.* St. Martin's.
Living in a crumbling castle that was originally rented when her father was actively writing, Cassandra views their situation as romantic and keeps a journal, which she fills with many more pages once the wealthy Cotton family moves into a nearby estate.
(1F. Gifted Elementary Student Readers)

SMITH, JEFF. 2004. *Bone: The Complete Cartoon Epic in One Volume.* Cartoon Books.
Three bone cousins leave Boneville and, after getting lost, spend a year in a fantastic valley where they encounter dragons, a giant mountain lion, and a great evil while making new friends and taking a dangerous journey to The Crown of Horns.
(2E. Core Graphic Novels)

SMITH, ROLAND. 1997. *Jaguar.* Hyperion.
Jacob visits his zoologist father in Brazil where he's introduced to the jaguar preserve his father's establishing and returns home convinced the jungle needs to be kept in its natural state.
(3F. The Environment)

SMITH, SHERRI L. 2008. *Hot, Sour, Salty, Sweet.* Delacorte.
Ana invites her best friend Chelsea and Chelsea's family, along with her crush Jamie and his family, to graduation dinner at her house, but that afternoon her Chinese grandmother and African American grandmother are at loggerheads in the kitchen.
(3E. Cookery)

SNELL, GORDON. 2001. *Thicker Than Water: Coming of Age Stories by Irish and Irish American Authors.* Random House.
Irish-style teen angst is the focus of stories presented by writers including Maeve Binchy, Chris Lynch, Helena Mulkerns, Emma Donoghue, and Vincent Banville.
(3K. Luck)

SONES, SONYA. 1999. *Stop Pretending: What Happened When My Big Sister Went Crazy.* HarperCollins.
Sones's own experiences are transformed into poetry, reflecting the anguish of a 13-year-old girl dealing with her older sister's mental illness.
(3I. Institutions)

————. 2004. *One of Those Hideous Books Where the Mother Dies.* Simon & Schuster.
After her mother dies, Ruby moves to Los Angeles to live with her father, a movie star whom she's never met, which requires adjusting to a new lifestyle on Ruby's part as famous stars drop by and her high school offers a class on dream interpretation.
(2Q. Teen Issue Novels in Verse)

SONNENBLICK, JORDAN. 2007. *Zen and the Art of Faking It.* Scholastic.
After starting at a new school—again—San Lee's performance in social studies class gets him labeled the Zen master of the eighth grade, an identity he's more than willing to try out, especially if it impresses the cute girl he's got his eye on.
(1K. Manga Lovers)

SORYO, FUYUMI. 2002–2003. Mars series. Tokyopop.
After saving Kira from the harassment of her art teacher, popular Rei finds himself drawn to her, and she to him, but Harumi has had her sights set on Rei for a long time and has no intention of letting Kira start a relationship with him.
(2D. Classic Manga)

SOTO, GARY. 1992. *Pacific Crossing.* Houghton Mifflin.
Fourteen-year-old Mexican American Lincoln is chosen, with his friend Tony, to live as exchange students in Japan for the summer, where they attempt to pass on some of their culture while learning about their host family's lifestyle and country.
(1K. Manga Lovers)

————. 1994. *Neighborhood Odes.* Scholastic. NF.
The sights, smells, and sounds of everyday life in a Hispanic neighborhood are gathered in these 21 poems, which celebrate the tinkling notes of an ice cream vendor's truck, a boy strumming a guitar, and the sight of a girl's hair that "sings like jump ropes."
(2O. Poetry Anthologies for High School Readers)

————. 1997. *Buried Onions.* Harcourt Brace.
After Eddie loses both his job and his cousin, it seems the only way for him to flee the poverty and gangs of Fresno is by joining the Army.
(1J. Latino Teens; 1Q. Troubled Teen Boys)

————. 2003. *The Afterlife.* Harcourt.
Shot to death in the men's room on the night Chuy plans to dance with Rachel, his ghost travels around Fresno and watches his friends and family, attends a Raiders game, and meets other ghosts before his form dissipates into the afterlife.
(1J. Latino Teens; 1Q. Troubled Teen Boys; 3A. Bathrooms)

————. 2006. *Novio Boy: A Play.* Houghton Mifflin.
After scoring a date with junior Patricia, freshman Rudy hits up his friend Alex and his Uncle Juan for helpful advice, and his mother for money to pay for lunch, but comes up empty handed.
(2L. Novels with Script or Screenplay Format)

Souljah, Sister. 1999. *Coldest Winter Ever.* Simon & Schuster.
Winter Santiaga, oldest daughter of a successful drug dealer, leads a life of luxury until her father is caught and sent to prison, her mother is shot, and she and her sisters become wards of the state.
(3I. Institutions)

Spiegelman, Art. 1986. *Maus I: A Survivor's Tale: My Father Bleeds History.* Random House.
The effect of the Holocaust on both those who survived it and their descendants is explored as Vladek tells his son about his experiences in Nazi-occupied Poland.
(2H. Graphic Novels in the Classroom)

————. 1991. *Maus II: A Survivor's Tale: And Here My Troubles Began.* Random House.
As Spiegelman continues to record the experiences of his father Vladek, who, with his wife Anja, is captured and sent to Auschwitz, their present relationships and the fallout from sharing this history continue to create emotional turmoil.
(2H. Graphic Novels in the Classroom)

————. 2004. *In the Shadow of No Towers.* Random House. NF.
Spiegelman's harrowing account of his family's efforts to find each other amidst the chaos of Manhattan on 9/11 and his musings on the personal and political impact of that day form the core of this graphic and meditative rant.
(2H. Graphic Novels in the Classroom)

Spiller, Robert. 2006. *The Witch of Agnesi.* Medallion.
Math teacher Mrs. Pinkwater coaches four students who will compete in the Knowledge Bowl, including 13-year-old math prodigy Peyton Newlin, but when some of the math participants are murdered, including two of hers, she investigates.
(3L. Mathematics)

Spinelli, Jerry. 1990. *Maniac Magee.* Little, Brown.
Orphan Jeffrey Magee finds a temporary home in the zoo with groundskeeper Grayson, but after he dies and Maniac Magee helps his racially divided community bridge their gap of misunderstanding, he finds a permanent home.
(1E. Gentlemanly Boys)

————. 2000. *Stargirl.* Knopf.
Though students at Mica High School are briefly entranced with nonconformist Stargirl and her pet rat, hippie clothes, and ukulele, they quickly tire of her and return to their cliquishness.
(3D. Consequences and Fate; 3P. State Books)

SPOONER, M. 2009. *Entr@pment: A High School Comedy in Chat*. Simon & Schuster/ McElderry.
Concerned how their boyfriends will react if tempted by other girls, Bliss and Tamra set up fake identities in a chat room and try to ensnare one another's beaus. (2C. Blogs, E-mails, and IMs in Fiction)

SPRINGER, NANCY. 2006. *The Case of the Missing Marquess: An Enola Holmes Mystery*. Philomel.
Enola's mother disappears on Enola's fourteenth birthday, leaving behind a series of explanatory ciphers that Enola decides to pursue, to the chagrin of her older brothers Mycroft and Sherlock, in this first Enola Holmes Mystery. (1H. Innocent Middle School Girls)

————. 2009. *Somebody*. Holiday House.
Sherica wonders why her father moves constantly, changes their names and the color of their hair, and encourages the siblings to eat more, until she finds information about herself on a website and discovers she's been abducted. (3B. Chocolate)

STAPLES, SUZANNE FISHER. 1989. *Shabanu, Daughter of the Wind*. Random House.
Strong willed and independent, Shabanu struggles with her people's expectation that she obey her father, and all too soon her husband, but she learns, with the help of a beloved aunt, to accept what she can't change and stay true to herself at the same time. (3M. The Middle East)

————. 1993. *Haveli*. Random House.
Shabanu, teenage fourth wife to wealthy Pakistani Rahim, finds sanctuary and forbidden love in the haveli of her husband's widowed sister. (3M. The Middle East)

————. 2005. *Under the Persimmon Tree*. Farrar, Straus and Giroux.
After the Taliban kill or take away her family, young Namjah leaves Afghanistan and crosses the mountains to reach Peshawar, Pakistan, where she meets American Elaine, who runs a school for the children of Peshawar. (3M. The Middle East)

STASSEN, J.P. 2006. *Deogratias: A Tale of Rwanda*. Translated by Alex Siegel. First Second.
This graphic novel shows Deogratias's "before" life in Rwanda, when he had many friends from everywhere and before more than 800,000 Rwandans were massacred, to "after" when he's degenerated to an alcoholic ruin. (2H. Graphic Novels in the Classroom)

STEAD, REBECCA. 2009. *When You Reach Me*. Random House.
　　Miranda's favorite book is *A Wrinkle in Time*, so it's no surprise that she's able to piece together the truth after receiving a series of mysterious notes from someone claiming to be from the future.
(1H. Innocent Middle School Girls)

STEWART, IAN. 2001. *Flatterland: Like Flatland, Only More So.* Perseus.
　　Coming across her many-greats-grandfather's work *Flatland,* Vikki Line knows it needs updating, so, with the Space Hopper as a guide, she travels through the Mathiverse, meeting the one-sided cow Moobius and others living in the abstract world of math.
(3L. Mathematics)

STEWART, PAUL, AND CHRIS RIDDELL. 1998– . The Edge Chronicles. Random House.
　　Twig, a human boy raised by trolls, Rook, a librarian knight, and Quint, son of a Sky Pirate and Twig's father, are the heroes of their own stories as they traverse a flat world (and the air above it) from The Edge to the Deepwoods and in between.
(1K. Manga Lovers)

STEWART, TRENTON LEE. 2007. *The Mysterious Benedict Society*. Hachette.
　　Reynie, Kate, Constance, and Sticky, following their training by Mr. Benedict, infiltrate the possibly evil Learning Institute for the Very Enlightened in an effort to discover what the mysterious Mr. Curtain is plotting.
(1E. Gentlemanly Boys; 1F. Gifted Elementary Student Readers)

STOCKTON, FRANK R. 1964. *The Bee-Man of Orn*. Illustrated by Maurice Sendak. Holt.
　　After being informed by a Junior Sorcerer that he had been transformed from something else into his present guise, the Bee-Man of Orn sets off on a quest to find his original form and learns that his destiny is closer to home than he thought.
(2N. Picture Books for Teens)

STOLARZ, LAURIE FARIA. 2003–2009. Blue Is for Nightmares series. Llewellyn.
　　Even after Stacey Brown leaves boarding school, she experiences nightmares that always signal a possible death, either that of a friend or of the ghosts of people who were brutally murdered years before.
(2M. Paperback Series)

STONE, JEFF. 2005– . The Five Ancestors series. Random House.
　　Five orphans raised as monks are named for and trained in the style of the animal they most resemble, and after their monastery is destroyed they must protect themselves and each other as they try to figure out who their enemies really are.
(1K. Manga Lovers)

STONE, TANYA LEE. 2006. *A Bad Boy Can Be Good for a Girl*. Random House.
Three girls suffer the heartbreak of being rejected for refusing sex, being used for sex, or mistaking sex for love, all at the hands of a callous high school jock.
(2R. Two or More Voices in Novels; 3A. Bathrooms)

STORK, FRANCISO X. 2006. *Behind the Eyes*. Dutton.
Hector tries to stay unnoticed in his El Paso neighborhood and even thinks of college, but when he's marked by the gang that killed his older brother, he's sent for safety to an alternative school, which feels more like a prison to him.
(1J. Latino Teens)

———. 2009. *Marcelo in the Real World*. Scholastic.
Marcelo's father forces the mildly autistic teen to work in his law firm's mailroom, where he learns first hand about office politics and the concept of ethics.
(1L. Offbeat Guys)

STRASSER, TODD. 2000. *Give a Boy a Gun*. Simon & Schuster.
Pushed to breaking by years of bullying, Gary and Brendan arrive at a school dance with guns and homemade bombs, ready to take revenge on their tormenters, but their attack, while deadly, doesn't turn out as planned.
(2R. Two or More Voices in Novels)

———. 2006. DriftX series. Simon & Schuster.
Kennin's exceptional driving skills make him a high-demand drifter, and he finds himself competing in races that are dangerous as well as illegal in order to stop the racial slurs and make some much-needed money.
(1G. Graphic Novel Lovers)

———. 2006. *Slide or Die*. DriftX series, book 1. Simon Pulse.
Japanese American Kennin meets Tito and Angelita and when they learn that Kennin is skilled in drifting—gliding without traction in a race down and around mountain curves—they talk him into a head-to-head competition against a racist classmate.
(1C. Book Haters)

———. 2007. *Boot Camp*. Simon & Schuster.
To stop Garrett from dating his former math teacher, his parents have him abducted in the middle of the night and taken to a structured boarding school, where beatings are doled out regularly and Garrett and two other teens escape and head to Canada.
(1C. Book Haters)

————. 2009. *Wish You Were Dead.* Egmont.
A blogger says that she hates Lucy Cunningham and Lucy then disappears, followed by more messages and students disappearing, until Madison decides she has to find her friends, and the mysterious blogger, before it's too late.
(2C. Blogs, E-mails, and IMs in Fiction)

STROUD, JONATHAN. 2003. *The Amulet of Samarkand.* The Bartimaeus Trilogy, book 1. Read by Simon Jones. Listening Library. Unabridged, 13 hours, 20 minutes.
When apprentice magician Nathaniel calls forth the djinni Bartimaeus, Bartimaeus has his hands full as Jones imbues Bartimaeus with a humorous, sarcastic mannerism that upsets the master–servant hierarchy as Nathaniel tries a more grown-up air.
(2B. Audiobooks for Middle School Listeners)

————. 2003–2006. The Bartimaeus Trilogy. Hyperion.
In an alternate London where powerful magicians rule, young Nathaniel and the 5,000-year-old djinni Bartimaeus form an uneasy alliance, and, together with Resistance fighter Kitty, they fight to expose the dangerous demons that are inhabiting government officials.
(1A. Adult Readers; 2R. Two or More Voices in Novels)

STURM, JAMES. 2007. *Satchel Paige: Striking Out Jim Crow.* Illustrated by Rich Tommaso. Hyperion. NF.
Paige's career spreads over five decades, and he has one of the fiercest pitching arms of any player, as well as the ability to tell his own story and then retell it with a few changes, all of which is captured in this graphic novel set in the segregated South.
(2H. Graphic Novels in the Classroom)

SUTHERLAND, TUI. 2004. *This Must Be Love.* HarperCollins.
Best friends Helena and Hermia e-mail and IM back and forth as they try to capture the attention of Dmitri and Alexander, and, in a roundabout way, they do as they end up in a contemporary retelling of *A Midsummer Night's Dream*.
(2C. Blogs, E-mails, and IMs in Fiction)

T

TABB, GEORGE. 2004. *Playing Right Field: A Jew Grows in Greenwich.* Soft Skull. NF.
Written by a punk musician, this childhood memoir begins when Tabb moves from comfortable, Jew-friendly Brooklyn, New York, to Greenwich, Connecticut, where he finds anti-Semitic classmates to be the norm but learns to exact revenge and gains some respect.
(1N. Punk Readers)

TAKAHASHI, KAZUKI. 1997–2008. Yu-Gi-Oh! series. VIZ Media.
   High school student Yugi Mutou receives from his grandfather pieces of the Millennium Puzzle, an ancient Egyptian artifact that, once assembled, allows the spirit of a 3,000-year-old Pharaoh with no memories of his own to possess Yugi.
   (2D. Classic Manga)

TAKAHASHI, RUMIKO. 1993–2006. Ranma ½ series. VIZ Media.
   Sixteen-year-old martial artist Ranma Saotome has been training all his life, but after falling into a lake during a practice session he's cursed to change into a girl every time he's splashed with cold water.
   (2D. Classic Manga)

TAKAYA, NATSUKI. 2004– . Fruits Basket series. Tokyopop.
   With no place to live, Tohru pitches a tent in the woods but is soon taken in by the family who owns the woods as long as she promises to keep the family secret: when they're hugged, they turn into animals from the Chinese Zodiac calendar.
   (1A. Adult Readers; 2D. Classic Manga)

TALBOT, BRYAN. 1995. *The Tale of One Bad Rat*. Dark Horse.
   Helen Potter runs away from her abusive father, and during her journey from London to an idyllic inn in the English countryside she encounters characters and situations linked to the work of her namesake, Beatrix Potter.
   (2E. Core Graphic Novels)

TAN, SHAUN. 2002. *The Red Tree*. Simply Read Books.
   A young girl with red hair travels through a wildly changing landscape populated by enormous fish, clashing ships, waves, and dreary nightmares, but she ultimately finds hope in a red leaf.
   (2N. Picture Books for Teens)

———. 2004. *The Lost Thing*. Simply Read Books.
   A huge "lost thing" is discovered on a beach by a young boy, despite the fact that no one else seems to notice it, and after taking it home he begins a search for the perfect place for it to live.
   (2N. Picture Books for Teens)

TANAKA, SHELLEY. 2006. *Climate Change*. Groundwood. NF.
   The causes and effects of global warming are explored in this book that discusses the science behind the problem, the effect of humans on global warming, and the difficulty of making decisions about how to correct the problem.
   (3F. The Environment)

TASHJIAN, JANET. 2001. *The Gospel According to Larry.* Holt.
Tired of consumerism, Josh sets up a website where he preaches his ideas to make the world better, and when his advice is heeded and groups spring up to discuss his ideas, he's surrounded by the same consumerism against which he preached.
(1L. Offbeat Guys)

TAYLOR, BROOKE. 2008. *Undone.* Bloomsbury.
Gaming geek Serena Moore's only friend is Kori Kitzler, a rebellious girl that Serena emulates so enthusiastically it's sometimes hard for her to tell where she ends and Kori begins, something she is forced to determine when Kori dies unexpectedly.
(3A. Bathrooms)

TAYLOR, G.P., TONY LEE, AND DAN BOULTWOOD. 2007. *The Tizzle Sisters & Erik.* Markosia Enterprises.
Sadie and Saskia Tizzle are abandoned by their mother at St. Dunstan's School for Wayward Children, and when Saskia is adopted by an eccentric writer it's up to Sadie and her friend Erik to rescue her.
(1G. Graphic Novel Lovers)

TAYLOR, LAINI. 2007– . Faeries of Dreamdark series. Penguin Putnam.
Faerie Magpie, granddaughter of the West Wind, and her crow friends find themselves tracking down demons let loose in the world by humans, waking an ancient djinni, and uncovering the fate of dragons in the process.
(1K. Manga Lovers)

TAYLOR, MILDRED D. 1976. *Roll of Thunder, Hear My Cry.* Random House.
Nine-year-old Cassie Logan has a loving and supportive family and has never felt inferior to any white person, but when angry, violent racism erupts in her community she learns to value the land and family that keep her grounded.
(3C. The Civil Rights Movement)

TAYLOR, THEODORE. 2005. *Ice Drift.* Harcourt.
While out seal hunting, young Inuits Alika and Sulu are cut off from home when their ice shelf is rammed by an iceberg and it detaches and floats south for six months during which time the boys build an igloo, hunt seals for food, and try to stay warm.
(3T. Wintertime)

TEMPLE, LOU JANE. 2002. *Death Is Semisweet.* St. Martin's Minotaur.
The elder Foster brothers buy the family boxed chocolate company from their siblings for a scandalously low price and expand it, even hiring a blimp to celebrate their fiftieth anniversary, only to have an investor turn up dead in a vat of chocolate.
(3B. Chocolate)

TESTA, MARIA. 2005. *Something about America*. Candlewick.
   The 13-year-old narrator, covered in scars, describes the process of assimilating into American life after she immigrates from Kosovo with her parents, refugees of the Kosovo War.
(3S. Teen Immigrants)

TEZUKA, OSAMU. 2003–2006. Buddha series. Vertical.
   The story of Siddhartha's life unfolds from the moment the prince leaves home to travel across India, intertwined with the philosophical journey he takes at the same time.
(2H. Graphic Novels in the Classroom)

THESMAN, JEAN. 2001. *A Sea So Far*. Penguin Putnam.
   Orphaned Kate wants nothing more than to graduate high school and see her mother's native Ireland, and in the terrible aftermath of the San Francisco earthquake she takes a position as sickly Jolie's caregiver in the hopes of making it across the ocean.
(3K. Luck)

THOMAS, JOYCE CAROL. 2003. *Linda Brown, You Are Not Alone: The* Brown v. Board of Education *Decision*. Illustrated by Curtis James. Hyperion. NF.
   Thomas's collection of stories, memoirs, and poems commemorating the event and remembering the impact of *Brown v. Board of Education* features Michael Cart, Jean Craighead George, Lois Lowry, Katherine Paterson, Jerry Spinelli, and Quincy Troupe.
(3C. The Civil Rights Movement)

THOMAS, ROB. 1996. *Rats Saw God*. Simon & Schuster.
   Steve York has a monumental assignment ahead of him—to pass English he has to write his autobiography, which is a little tricky because he's estranged from his astronaut father, exploring sex with Wanda Varner, and filling out college applications.
(1A. Adult Readers; 1O. Reluctant Male Readers; 3J. Love Hurts)

THOMPSON, CRAIG. 1999. *Good-Bye Chunky Rice*. Top Shelf.
   Leaving behind Dandele, a lovesick mouse, a turtle known as Chunky Rice sets off on a voyage aboard a rickety ship where he meets conjoined twins Ruth and Livonia and explores his desire to leave the safety and pleasantness of his old life for the unknown.
(2E. Core Graphic Novels)

————. 2003. *Blankets*. Top Shelf. NF.
Thompson looks back on his Midwestern, Christian fundamentalist upbringing, drawing portraits of his strict parents, younger brother, and often cruel classmates and exploring first love, his devotion to drawing, and the limits of his faith.
(2K. Nonfiction Graphic Novels)

THOMPSON, KATE. 2007. *The New Policeman*. Greenwillow.
Descended from a long line of Irish musicians, J.J. Liddy's mother wonders what happened to the time people used to spend on traditional music, and J.J. sets out on a quest to find the answer.
(3K. Luck)

————. 2009. *Creature of the Night*. Roaring Brook.
Bobby hates living in the country and longs for his wild life back in Dublin, especially after he hears the creepy stories about his new home's former inhabitants, but his feelings are tempered by the honest work he does for the landlord.
(3K. Luck)

TIERNAN, CATE. 2001–2006. Balefire series. Penguin/Razorbill.
After her widowed father dies, Thais Allard moves to New Orleans where she meets her identical twin Clio Martin and learns they're descended from a long line of witches.
(2M. Paperback Series)

————. 2001– . Sweep series. Penguin/Speak.
Invited to attend a Wiccan celebration, teen Morgan Rowlands discovers she's a "blood witch" whose battles with evil occur side by side with friendship squabbles and boyfriend troubles.
(2M. Paperback Series)

TILLAGE, LEON. 1997. *Leon's Story*. Farrar, Straus and Giroux. NF.
Before the civil rights movement improved treatment of African Americans, Leon shares how he walked to an inferior school while white kids rode school buses, saw his father run over by drunk white teens, and was always relegated to the theater balcony.
(1P. Striving Readers)

TINGLE, REBECCA. 2001. *The Edge on the Sword*. Penguin Putnam.
Aethelflæd, oldest daughter of King Alfred, finds herself in grave danger after her proposed marriage to Ethelred of Mercia stirs up enemies, but she chafes under the watchful eye of her new guard until the day her rash actions change their relationship.
(1H. Innocent Middle School Girls)

TOCHER, TIMOTHY. 2004. *Chief Sunrise, John McGraw, and Me.* Cricket.
On a freight train in 1919, Hank meets teen "Chief Sunrise" and the two head to New York so Chief Sunrise can try out for the Giants, who hire him as a starting pitcher and Hank as a gofer, but it's not until midseason that Hank discovers Chief Sunrise's secret.
(3C. The Civil Rights Movement)

TODD, PAMELA. 2008. *The Blind Faith Hotel.* Simon & Schuster.
When Zoe moves to the Midwest, out of spite she shoplifts, is caught, and is sentenced to work with a crotchety old man called Hub who wants to save the prairie, and she finally understands his comment about everything needing space to grow.
(3F. The Environment)

TOM, KAREN, ED. 2001. *Angst! Teen Verses from the Edge.* Illustrated by Matt Frost. Workman. NF.
Selected from verses written to PlanetKiki.com, these 60 hard-hitting, realistic poems are divided into sections, some entitled "Why Me?," "Argh! I Hate You," or "Society's Ills," which illustrate the range of teen angst.
(2O. Poetry Anthologies for High School Readers)

TORIYAMA, AKIRA. 2003–2006. Dragon Ball Z series. VIZ Media.
After years of training and many adventures Son Goku is widely known to be the greatest hero on Earth, but the source of his incredible skills and strength are still a mystery, until the day an alien visitor arrives claiming to be Goku's brother.
(2D. Classic Manga)

TOTEN, TERESA. 2001. *The Game.* Red Deer Press.
After her abusive father's violent behavior leads to a suicide attempt, Dani is sent to Riverwood, a clinic for troubled teens, where she befriends Scratch, a cutter, and Kevin, whose homosexuality is repugnant to his Fundamentalist parents.
(3I. Institutions)

TRIANA, GABBY. 2006. *Cubanita.* Rayo.
Continually at odds with her Cuban immigrant mother, Americanized Isabel looks forward to leaving her Miami home for college in Minnesota.
(1I. Latina Teens)

TRUEMAN, TERRY. 2000. *Stuck in Neutral.* HarperCollins.
Shawn, born with cerebral palsy and unable to walk, talk, or move on his own, loves life, which is why he's horrified when he begins to suspect that his well-meaning father is planning to kill him.
(1O. Reluctant Male Readers)

————. 2003. *Inside Out*. HarperCollins.
Zach, taken hostage by two desperate brothers in a botched robbery, is overdue to take his antipsychotic meds, and his resulting confusion and angry outbursts help him form a strange bond with his captors.
(1Q. Troubled Teen Boys)

————. 2008. *Hurricane.* HarperCollins.
When Hurricane Mitch hits their Honduras village, Jose tries to be strong for his mother and younger siblings as his father and older siblings are away, but after the horrible night ends, Jose walks outside and sees the worst—a mudslide has destroyed his community.
(1R. Tweens)

TSUCHIYA, YUKIO. 1988. *Faithful Elephants: A True Story of Animals, People, and War.* Illustrated by Ted Lewin. Houghton Mifflin.
Fearing that the possible destruction of the Tokyo zoo might lead to accidental freedom for the animals and chaos in the city, zookeepers made the difficult decision to kill the animals.
(2N. Picture Books for Teens)

TSUDA, MASAMI. 2003–2007. Kare Kano: His and Her Circumstances series. Tokyopop.
Yukino has always been at the top, popular at school and best in her class, but behind her perfect facade lurks a narcissistic young girl who may have met her match when she meets Soiichiro, a genuinely nice boy and her equal in every way.
(2D. Classic Manga)

TYREE, OMAR. 1996. *Flyy Girl*. Simon & Schuster.
Smart and pretty, Tracy Ellison has a quick wit and a shaky family, and she's as boy crazy as her friends, leading her to explore her budding sexuality.
(1S. Urban Teens: Beyond Street Lit; 3I. Institutions)

U

UEHASHI, NAHOKO. 2008. *Moribito: Guardian of the Spirit.* Translated by Cathy Hirano. Illustrated by Yuko Shimizu. Scholastic.
The water spirit that is either living in or possessing Prince Chagum endangers his life and inspires his mother to hire Balsa Spear-wielder as his bodyguard.
(1K. Manga Lovers)

V

VAIL, RACHEL. 1996. *Daring to Be Abigail.* Orchard.
   Heading to camp and determined to make new friends, Abigail becomes part of the in-group and for no good reason picks on Dana, the last camper to arrive, but when she accepts a dare and does something mean to Dana, Abigail is sent home from camp.
(3Q. Summer Camp)

VALDES-RODRIGUEZ, ALISA. 2006. *Haters.* Little, Brown.
   Moving to California, Paski finds herself hassled by ringleader Jessica who excels in motocross, so when Paski has visions of Jessica being injured in this sport, she's unsure whether or not to tell her.
(1I. Latina Teens)

VAN DE RUIT, JOHN. 2007. *Spud.* Razorbill.
   Part of a group of eight boys at boarding school and nicknamed "Spud" because of his small private parts, John keeps a diary of their pranks, midnight swims, discussions about sex, and loss of a friend from his Group of Eight.
(1L. Offbeat Guys)

VAN DRAANEN, WENDELIN. 2001. *Flipped.* Knopf.
   When Juli was in second grade and Bryce moved into the neighborhood, she flipped over his eyes only to be ignored by him; now older, their roles are reversed, but a few people convince Juli to give Bryce a second chance.
(2R. Two or More Voices in Novels)

VARRATO, TONY. 2008. *Fakie.* Lobster.
   Several years ago Danny and his mother testified against Steve, his father's business partner, and were sent by the FBI's Witness Protection Program to live in Virginia Beach as Alex the skateboarder and Sonya the waitress, but Steve's still after them.
(1R. Tweens)

VAUGHN, BRIAN K., ET AL. 2005– . Runaways series. Illustrated by Adrian Alphona et al. Marvel.
   Six sort-of friends discover they have more in common than they thought when they learn their parents are all members of a league of super-powered super-villains.
(2E. Core Graphic Novels)

VAUGHAN, BRIAN K.. 2006. *Pride of Baghdad*. Illustrated by Niko Henrichon. DC Comics.
> Four lions escape from the Baghdad Zoo during a bombing raid and get their first taste of freedom as they roam the ruined streets, struggling to survive.
> (2H. Graphic Novels in the Classroom; 3M. The Middle East)

VEGA, DENISE. 2009. *Access Denied (and Other Eighth Grade Error Messages)*. Little, Brown.
> With her blog now secure, after *Click Here (to Find Out How I Survived the Seventh Grade)*, Erin's private lists rate boys on the Hot-O-Meter scale, record normal angst over school assignments, and describe the unfairness of her too-strict mother.
> (2C. Blogs, E-mails, and IMs in Fiction)

VERNE, JULES. 2005, ©1873. *Around the World in 80 Days*. Read by Jim Dale. Listening Library. Unabridged. 7 hours, 30 minutes.
> Phileas Fogg wagers a bet at his London club that he can circle the world in 80 days, and, using an astounding assortment of conveyances, he and his valet Passepartout manage to do so as narrator Jim Dale's famous voice hurries them along.
> (2A. Audiobooks for High School Listeners)

VINING, JAMES. 2007. *First in Space*. Oni Press. NF.
> Ham, the chimp sent into space by NASA to collect biological data for the space program, became a hero when he made it back alive, although many other monkeys and chimps before him were not so lucky.
> (2K. Nonfiction Graphic Novels)

VIZZINI, NED. 2000. *Teen Angst? Naaah . . . A Quasi-autobiography*. Random House.
> Vizzini's autobiographical vignettes, written during his high school years, describe his geeky teenage years, complete with gaming obsessions, uncomfortable romantic encounters, and brushes with drugs and alcohol.
> (1G. Graphic Novel Lovers; 1L. Offbeat Guys)

———. 2006. *It's Kind of a Funny Story*. Hyperion.
> Accepted to a pre-professional high school in Manhattan, Craig Gilner finds the pressure so intense he becomes depressed and eventually stays in a psychiatric ward for five days.
> (1M. Picky Senior Girls)

VOAKE, STEVE. 2006. *The Dreamwalker's Child*. Bloomsbury.
> In a coma following a car accident, Sam leaves his body for a parallel world where an evil race plans to annihilate humans by sending airplane-sized, virus-laden mosquitoes to Earth.
> (3H. Insects)

VOIGT, CYNTHIA. 1982. *Bad Girls*. Simon & Schuster.
Mikey and Margalo meet on the first day of fifth grade, and over the course of the next few weeks, as they stir up trouble and stand together to face the consequences, they realize that they are kindred spirits.
(1D. Detention Home Girls)

————. 1986. *Izzy, Willy-Nilly*. Simon & Schuster.
After she loses her leg in a car accident, 15-year-old Izzy finds herself struggling to rebuild her life and find her identity.
(3D. Consequences and Fate)

VOLPONI, PAUL. 2005. *Black and White*. Penguin Putnam.
Marcus and Eddie, best friends known at school as Black and White, turn to armed robbery to make extra money, but after they're picked up by the cops it's clear the different colors of their skin mean something after all.
(1O. Reluctant Male Readers; 2R. Two or More Voices in Novels)

————. 2009. *Homestretch*. Atheneum.
After his mother dies, Gaston is fed up with his father's bigotry, runs away, and is picked up by some Mexican laborers who work at a race track and recommend Gaston for a job, where he becomes a jockey and finds a home.
(3G. Horses)

VON ZIEGESAR, CECILY. 2002– . Gossip Girl series. Little, Brown/Poppy.
On the Upper East Side of New York City live a group of wealthy teenagers who attend the Constance Billard School for Girls, shop at exclusive stores, and party as much as they study in this series narrated by an anonymous blogger.
(2M. Paperback Series)

VONA, ABIGAIL. 2004. *Bad Girl: Confessions of a Teenage Delinquent*. Rugged Land. NF.
Vona's memoir tells of her time in a behavior rehabilitation facility for troubled adolescents after her father loses patience with her lying, shoplifting, and drug use.
(3I. Institutions)

VOORHEES, COERT. 2008. *The Brothers Torres*. Hyperion.
Frankie Torres's innocent crush on Rebecca Sanchez and his wish to ask her for a date leads to an escalating fight with a rich soccer player and involvement with the cholos with whom his older brother hangs.
(1J. Latino Teens)

VREELAND, SUSAN. 1999. *Girl in Hyacinth Blue.* MacMurray & Beck.
A series of stories about the painting *Girl in Hyacinth Blue* begins when it was discovered after being hidden for 50 years and continues backward in time until Vermeer captures his daughter Magdalena's image wearing the hyacinth blue dress.
(1M. Picky Senior Girls)

W

WARE, CHRIS. 2000. *Jimmy Corrigan: The Smartest Kid on Earth.* Random House.
Generations of hapless Corrigan males experience rejection and isolation, culminating in the unhappy state of Jimmy Corrigan, a loser who retreats into his fantasy world, emerging for an unexpected reunion with the clueless father who abandoned him.
(2H. Graphic Novels in the Classroom)

WARREN, ANDREA. 2004. *Escape from Saigon: How a Vietnam War Orphan Became an American Boy.* Farrar, Straus and Giroux. NF.
Warren's narrative follows Long, an eight-year-old Amerasian boy abandoned in a Vietnam orphanage during the war, as he is rescued by the 1975 Operation Babylift and adopted by a family in Ohio, where he thrives but never forgets his roots.
(3S. Teen Immigrants)

WATASE, YUU. 1997–2006. Ceres: Celestial Legend series. VIZ Media.
Twins Aya and Aki know something is wrong when they receive a mummified hand as a birthday gift, and things get worse when Aki is named heir and Aya, who it turns out is the reincarnated celestial maiden Ceres, is sentenced to die.
(2D. Classic Manga)

WATSON, ESTHER PEARL, AND MARK TODD, EDS. 2000. *The Pain Tree: And Other Teenage Angst-Ridden Poetry.* Houghton Mifflin. NF.
Selected from teen websites and magazines such as *READ* and *Seventeen*, 25 poems provide an introspective look at the pain experienced by many teens as they move through adolescence.
(2O. Poetry Anthologies for High School Readers)

WATSUKI, NOBUHIRO. 2003–2006. Rurouni Kenshin series. VIZ Media.
Former assassin Himura Kenshin wanders Japan protecting the people and attempting to atone for his crimes.
(2D. Classic Manga)

WAY, GERARD. 2008– . Umbrella Academy series. Illustrated by Gabriel Ba et al. Dark Horse.
> A family of former child superheroes, who called themselves the Umbrella Academy, comes together at the death of their adopted father and mentor, only to find a new threat in the form of angry and newly powerful sister Vanya.
> (2E. Core Graphic Novels)

WEAVER, WILL. 2001. *Memory Boy*. HarperCollins.
> Miles uses his mechanical skills and phenomenal memory to help save his family after a destructive volcanic eruption leads to widespread chaos, looting, and violent crime.
> (1E. Gentlemanly Boys)

———. 2008. *Saturday Night Dirt.* Farrar, Straus and Giroux.
> An evening rainstorm cancels races at many tracks in Minnesota, so better drivers show up at the older dirt track at the Headwaters Speedway, where the usual drivers aren't used to the higher level of competition.
> (1C. Book Haters)

WEDEKIND, ANNIE. 2008. *A Horse of Her Own.* Feiwel & Friends.
> Although an accomplished rider, Jane doesn't have a horse of her own and at camp is given Lancelot, a new, unsettled horse who requires a lot of careful handling.
> (3G. Horses; 3Q. Summer Camp)

WEILL, SABRINA SOLIN. 2001. *We're Not Monsters: Teens Speak Out about Teens in Trouble*. HarperCollins. NF.
> Weill explores a variety of societal ills, ranging from suicide and self-injury to infanticide and dangerous sex, using the voices of contemporary teens, along with relevant facts and balanced discussion to illuminate each topic.
> (1Q. Troubled Teen Boys; 3I. Institutions)

WEISMAN, ALAN. 2007. *The World Without Us.* St. Martin's. NF.
> The effect of man on Earth is striking, but when humans are removed from the equation, their impact on the world will immediately subside as nature reclaims all it can, except for the mountains of tires and plastics.
> (3F. The Environment)

WELCH, SHEILA KELLY. 1995. *A Horse for All Seasons: Collected Stories.* Boyds Mills Press.
> Twelve seasonal stories share how young people learn to trust their horse, are forced to sell a pony, overcome a fear of jumping, or understand the special bond that develops between horse and rider.
> (3G. Horses)

WERBER, BERNARD. 1998. *Empire of the Ants.* Bantam.
In a basement of a Paris flat, Ant 103,683, so called because of her birth order, accompanies other ants as they search a rock-scented weapon that's connected to the demise of one of their colony's scouting parties.
(3H. Insects)

WERLIN, NANCY. 2004. *Double Helix.* Dial.
Wondering if his mother's genetic Huntington's disease will also afflict him, Eli works as a technician at Wyatt Transgenics where he discovers a secret underground lab that contains the answers to some of the mysteries in Eli's life.
(3N. Science)

————. 2006. *The Rules of Survival.* Dial.
Raised by an abusive, manic mother, Matthew protects his sisters Callie and Emmy until Murdoch dates their mother and Matthew begins to hope for a more stable situation, but when Murdoch leaves, Matthew resolves to find a better home situation for all of them.
(1M. Picky Senior Girls; 3O. Silence.)

WESTERFELD, SCOTT. 2004–2005. Midnighters series. Eos.
If you're born at midnight and live in Bixby, Oklahoma, you could be a Midnighter, a person who enters a magical hour at midnight that no one else can enter unless they happen to be a Darkling, an evil being who is in conflict with the Midnighters.
(1N. Punk Readers; 3P. State Books)

————. 2005. *Peeps: A Novel.* Penguin Putnam.
Cal loses his virginity when he first arrives in New York City, and when he finds himself parasite-positive he goes to work for the Night Watch, a secret government organization dedicated to tracking down and helping other vampires.
(1O. Reluctant Male Readers; 3D. Consequences and Fate)

————. 2005–2007. Uglies series. Simon Pulse.
To diminish disagreements among people because of looks, this future world arranges for a series of life-changing surgeries so that the uglies become the pretties, but it's Tally who discovers the brain damage that results.
(1A. Adult Readers; 1B. Avid Readers; 1H. Innocent Middle School Girls)

————. 2006. *The Last Days.* Razorbill.
There's evil in New York City, but guitarists Moz and Zahler are concerned with their music, find three more people to start a band, and discover their energetic music entices human-devouring worms from the soil so they can be killed.
(2R. Two or More Voices in Novels)

WHITCOMB, LAURA. 2005. *A Certain Slant of Light.* Houghton Mifflin.
Having died 130 years ago, Helen's spirit attaches itself to others who love literature, until she meets James, who's also "light," and the two fall in love.
(1M. Picky Senior Girls)

WHITE, ROBB. 1972. *Deathwatch.* Doubleday.
An unsuccessful hunt for a bighorn sheep turns dangerous when the hunter
Madec accidentally kills an old miner and then turns on the guide, Ben, who wants
to report the death, forces Ben to strip, and then hunts him like an animal across
the desert.
(1P. Striving Readers)

WHITE, RUTH. 2003. *Tadpole.* Farrar, Straus and Giroux.
When Tadpole leaves his abusive uncle to live with his cousins, he manages to
transform wayward Kentucky, Virginia, Georgia, and Carolina into helpmates
around the house.
(3P. State Books)

WHITESEL, CHERYL AYLWARD. 2004. *Blue Fingers: A Ninja's Tale.* Houghton Mifflin.
Koji runs away after his apprenticeship to a dye maker ends in disgrace, and is
taken in by a group of warriors who train him, slowly and painfully, in the ways of
the ninja, helping him to finally realize and accept his true potential.
(1K. Manga Lovers)

WHITNEY, KIM ABLON. 2005. *The Perfect Distance.* Knopf.
Wanting to compete in the Olympics, Mexican Francie Martinez uses the money
from her part-time groom work to pay for riding lessons, until she learns of the illegal compromises the horse trainer sometimes makes.
(3G. Horses)

WHYTOCK, CHERRY. 2003. *My Cup Runneth Over: The Life of Angelica Cookson Potts.*
Simon & Schuster.
A full-figured girl with a former model mother and three reed-thin friends, Angel
wants to lose some weight, be noticed by Adam, and become a chef after graduation,
but only becoming a chef seems probable, as her included recipes demonstrate.
(3E. Cookery)

WILD, MARGARET. 2007. *Woolvs in the Sitee.* Illustrated by Anne Spudvilas. Boyds
Mill Press.
In a frightening postapocalyptic world, a boy huddles in his apartment, hiding
himself from the woolvs he sees in the streets until one day his only friend, Mrs.
Radinski, disappears and he finds the courage to go looking for her.
(2N. Picture Books for Teens)

WILLIAMS, DAR. 2006. *Lights, Camera, Amalee.* Scholastic.
Following a visit with her maternal grandmother, Amalee receives an inheritance of $2,000 in coins and uses the money to produce her film documentary on natural ecosystems and endangered species.
(3F. The Environment)

WILLIAMS, JULIE. 2004. *Escaping Tornado Season.* HarperTempest.
After losing her twin brother and now her father, Allie and her mother move to Minnesota to live with Allie's grandparents, but Allie learns, like with tornadoes, to "hunker down" for only so long with her grief.
(2Q. Teen Issue Novels in Verse)

WILLIAMS, KATHRYN. 2009. *The Lost Summer.* Hyperion.
Helena can hardly wait for summer and a return to the familiarity of camp at Southpoint, but this year she's a counselor, her best friend is a camper, and suddenly there's a divide between them as Helena prefers to spend time with the other counselors.
(3Q. Summer Camp)

WILLIAMS-GARCIA, RITA. 1995. *Like Sisters on the Homefront.* Penguin Putnam.
Already a mother at 14, Gayle is sent to live with her uncle and his family after she becomes pregnant a second time, and although initially upset by the move and their strange lifestyle, Gayle comes to understand and appreciate her place within her extended family.
(1D. Detention Home Girls)

WILLINGHAM, BILL. 2002– . Fables series. Illustrated by Lan Medina et al. DC Comics.
When the denizens of hundreds of different stories, including Jack, the Wolf, various princesses, and King Cole, are driven from their fairy tale homes, they find themselves exiled to Fabletown, a haven located in the middle of modern day New York City.
(2E. Core Graphic Novels)

WILSON, DAWN. 2001. *Saint Jude.* Tudor Publishing.
Suffering from bipolar disorder, 18-year-old Taylor finds acceptance and friends at Brick House, where she meets other teens suffering from mental illness and learns to face her fear of surviving outside the safety of their shared space.
(3I. Institutions)

WILSON, DIANE LEE. 1998. *I Rode a Horse of Milk White Jade.* Orchard.
Although injured by a horse when she is a toddler, Oyuna is convinced she wants to win the annual race at festival and sets out on a long journey on horseback to reach the race grounds at Karakorum in the early 1300s.
(3G. Horses; 3K. Luck)

————. 2006. *Firehorse.* Simon & Schuster.
Rachel's horse is sold when the family moves to Boston in 1872, but she obtains another when she nurses a badly burned firehorse back to health, an act that convinces her parents she really wants to become a veterinarian.
(3G. Horses)

WINDLING, TERRI, AND ELLEN DATLOW, EDS. 2002. *The Green Man: Tales from the Mythic Forest.* Penguin Putnam.
Interpretations of the mythical Green Man are offered in 15 stories and three poems by authors including Neil Gaiman, Michael Cadnum, Jane Yolen, Kathe Koja, and Gregory Maguire.
(2J. Must-Have Anthologies)

————, EDS. 2004. *The Faery Reel: Tales from the Twilight Realm.* Penguin Putnam.
Stories and poems featuring varied depictions of fairies and other natural spirits are offered by authors Charles de Lint, Kelly Link, Tanith Lee, Neil Gaiman, Emma Bull, and Patricia McKillip, among many others.
(2J. Must-Have Anthologies)

————, EDS. 2007. *The Coyote Road: Trickster Tales.* Penguin Putnam.
Twenty-six stories featuring globe-spanning tricksters are presented by authors such as Nina Kiriki Hoffman, Ellen Klages, Patricia McKillip, Charles de Lint, Midori Snyder, Holly Black, and Jeffrey Ford.
(2J. Must-Have Anthologies)

WINICK, JUDD. 2000. *Pedro and Me: Friendship, Loss, and What I Learned.* Holt. NF.
Winick met AIDS educator Pedro Zamora when the two were cast for a reality television show, and as Zamora fought his public battle with the disease that finally took his life Winick found a new understanding of the cause his friend fought so hard to publicize.
(2K. Nonfiction Graphic Novels)

WINSPEAR, JACQUELINE. 2003. *Maisie Dobbs.* Soho.
Going into service for Lady Rowan to help her father's finances, Maisie is eventually sent to Cambridge and then becomes a nurse in France during World War I, but when she returns home, she hangs up her shingle as a private investigator in this first book of the Maisie Dobbs Mysteries series.
(1B. Avid Readers)

WINTER, JEANETTE. 2004. *The Librarian of Basra: A True Story from Iraq.* Houghton Mifflin. NF.

Alia Muhammad Baker, head librarian of Basra's Central Library, feared the collection would be destroyed in the upcoming war and, with no government support, organized the transfer of 30,000 volumes just days before the library burned to the ground.

(2N. Picture Books for Teens)

WITTLINGER, ELLEN. 1999. *Hard Love.* Simon & Schuster.

John Galardi, a high school student with a zine he calls *Bananafish* in honor of Salinger, meets and falls for fellow zine writer Marisol, even though she tells him she's a lesbian.

(3J. Love Hurts)

———. 2003. *Zigzag.* Simon & Schuster.

When her boyfriend's parents send him off to Italy, Robin's summer vacation choices are staying home in Iowa and working at the Tastee-Freez or traveling with her widowed aunt and two bratty kids on a "zigzag" trip to Los Angeles—for Robin, it's not hard to choose the zigzag.

(3R. Summertime)

———. 2004. *Heart on My Sleeve.* Simon & Schuster.

Chloe meets Julian on a college visit and the two are instantly taken with one another and continue their relationship through IMs, E-mails, and postcards, but when they reconnect in the summer, they realize they don't know one another at all.

(2C. Blogs, E-mails, and IMs in Fiction)

———. 2005. *Sandpiper.* Simon & Schuster.

Sandpiper Hollow Ragsdale has a bad reputation and no real friends, until she meets a boy known as Walker with problems of his own, who offers friendship instead of sexual demands and steps in when she needs him most.

(3D. Consequences and Fate)

———. 2007. *Parrotfish.* Simon & Schuster.

Grady McNair, formerly known as Angela, begins his life as a boy and is faced with reactions ranging from disbelief, to hostility, to acceptance.

(3A. Bathrooms)

WIZNER, JAKE. 2007. *Spanking Shakespeare.* Random House.

When Shakespeare writes his senior memoir, he decides to include every mortifying detail of his high school years, from erections to dreadful dates and tipsy parents.

(1L. Offbeat Guys)

WOLF, ALLAN. 2004. *New Found Land: Lewis and Clark's Voyage of Discovery*. Candlewick.
  Lewis's Newfoundland dog Seaman, Sacajawea, William Clark, and teen George Shannon are only four of the 14 voices of the Corps of Discovery members who describe their famous journey to the Pacific Coast.
  (2I. Historical Novels in Verse)

WOLFF, VIRGINIA EUWER. 1993. *Make Lemonade*. Holt.
  LaVaughn takes a babysitting job to raise money for college, but she finds something more valuable in her relationship with the downtrodden single mother she sits for.
  (1D. Detention Home Girls)

WOOD, DON. 2008. *Into the Volcano*. Scholastic.
  Taken on a hiking trip into a dangerous volcano, the two brothers don't trust their aunt's intentions and run away from her, only to be reunited with their volcanologist mother who's working on a secret project.
  (3N. Science)

WOOD, MARYROSE. 2007. *Why I Let My Hair Grow Out*. Penguin Putnam.
  Sent on a bike tour of Ireland after she's dumped and cuts off all her hair, Morgan's parents think the change of scenery will do her good but probably didn't expect her to fall in with fairies who want her to lift an evil enchantment.
  (3K. Luck)

WOODFORD, CHRIS, AND JON WOODCOCK. 2007. *Cool Stuff 2.0 and How It Works*. DK. NF.
  In this sequel to *Cool Stuff and How It Works*, the authors take readers up an earthquake-proof office building, into the virtual world of Second Life, and on space planes, with illustrations and explanations about the technology that shapes today's world.
  (1C. Book Haters)

WOODING, CHRIS. 2001. *The Haunting of Alaizabel Cray*. Scholastic.
  Wych-hunter Thaniel fights his way through an alternate London crawling with wych-kins and other creepy creatures to free Alaizabel from the evil spirit that has possessed her, due to the efforts of the cultish Fraternity.
  (1A. Adult Readers)

WOODSON, JACQUELINE. 1994. *I Hadn't Meant to Tell You This*. Random House.
Marie, still reeling from her mother's desertion, is forced to deal with her new friend Lena's disappearance after Lena runs away from her sexually abusive father.
(1D. Detention Home Girls; 3O. Silence)

————. 1998. *If You Come Softly*. Penguin Putnam.
Miah and Ellie both have difficult families, making their blossoming romance even more meaningful, but the bigotry and racism they suffer for being a mixed race couple threatens to tear them apart.
(1D. Detention Home Girls)

————. 2002. *Hush*. Penguin Putnam.
Twelve-year-old Toswiah has to reinvent herself as Evie Thomas after her father testifies against two murderous police officers and the family enters the Witness Protection Program.
(3O. Silence)

————. 2005. *Show Way*. Illustrated by Hudson Talbott. Penguin Putnam.
Sold away from her family when she was only seven, Soonie's great-grandmother learned quilt making from the woman who cared for the plantation children, and she passed the tradition down through generations of women, all the way to Soonie.
(2N. Picture Books for Teens)

————. 2008. *After Tupac & D Foster*. Penguin Putnam.
When D Foster moves into the neighborhood life gets much more interesting for Neeka and her best friend, the unnamed narrator.
(1S. Urban Teens: Beyond Street Lit)

WORMSER, RICHARD. 2003. *The Rise and Fall of Jim Crow*. St. Martin's. NF.
Jim Crow was a cruel caricature, a symbol against which blacks struggled during the segregation of post–Civil War America in a fight for civil rights that Wormser documents using primary sources and photographs.
(3C. The Civil Rights Movement)

WREDE, PATRICIA. 1990. *Dealing with Dragons*. Harcourt.
Princess Cimorene is bored with her life, and, when her parents want her to marry Prince Therandil, she runs away to the Enchanted Forest to become a dragon's Princess and begins an adventuresome, magical life.
(1F. Gifted Elementary Student Readers)

WREDE, PATRICIA, AND CAROLINE STEVERMER. 2003. *Sorcery and Cecilia, or, The Enchanted Chocolate Pot: Being the Correspondence of Two Young Ladies of Quality Regarding Various Magical Scandals in London and the Country.* Harcourt.

While cousin Cecelia is at home at Rushton Manor, cousin Kate accompanies her sister to London for her debut, and the two correspond by letter as Cecilia is spied on and Kate uses a magical chocolate pot to save a marquis from poisoning.

(1F. Gifted Elementary Student Readers; 1H. Innocent Middle School Girls; 2F. Diaries and Epistolary Novels; 2R. Two or More Voices in Novels; 3B. Chocolate)

WRIGHT, BIL. 2007. *When the Black Girl Sings.* Simon & Schuster.

Fourteen-year-old Lahni Schuler is an outsider, the only African American at her private school, but she finds her place and herself when she joins the choir at a multiracial church.

(1S. Urban Teens: Beyond Street Lit)

Y

YANCEY, RICK. 2005. *The Extraordinary Adventures of Alfred Kropp.* Bloomsbury.

Guilt-ridden at the string of dead bodies that seem to be a consequence of his part in the theft of a magical sword—Excalibur, to be exact—Alfred Kropp attempts to retrieve it, saving the world in the process.

(1G. Graphic Novel Lovers; 1K. Manga Lovers)

YANG, GENE LUEN. 2006. *American Born Chinese.* First Second.

A triad of interlinked tales in graphic novel format features Jin, a teen who now lives in an all-white suburb, the Monkey King of Chinese legend, and a visiting Chinese teen, Chin-Kee, whose stories underlie the concept of accepting who you are.

(2H. Graphic Novels in the Classroom)

YAZAWA, AI. 2002–2003. Paradise Kiss series. Tokyopop.

Yukari spends her time studying hard to please her parents, until the day she's kidnapped by a group called Paradise Kiss, fashionistas who give her a wild makeover and transform her from serious student to exclusive fashion model.

(2D. Classic Manga)

YEE, LISA. 2003. *Millicent Min, Girl Genius.* Scholastic.

Millicent Min is a genius, but her high IQ is no help to her when it comes to being a good friend.

(1F. Gifted Elementary Student Readers; 1H. Innocent Middle School Girls; 2F. Diaries and Epistolary Novels)

YEOMANS, ELLEN. 2007. *Rubber Houses.* Little, Brown.
Kit's brother Buddy dies from leukemia, and Kit endures the off-season of winter knowing that spring training for her brother's favorite sport will begin and the grief will begin to lessen.
(2Q. Teen Issue Novels in Verse)

YEP, LAURENCE. 2003. *The Traitor: Golden Mountain Chronicles: 1885.* HarperCollins.
Joseph and Michael find their friendship threatened when violence breaks out over the proposed replacement of western miners with Chinese railroad workers.
(3P. State Books)

YOLEN, JANE. 1992. *Briar Rose.* Tor.
After her grandmother's death, Rebecca realizes that the disturbing version of a classic fairy tale the old woman often told is actually an important clue to her past.
(2F. Diaries and Epistolary Novels)

YOLEN, JANE, AND BRUCE COVILLE. 1998. *Armageddon Summer.* Houghton Mifflin.
Marina and Jed meet on the mountain where their families have gathered with other Believers under the direction of Reverend Beelson to prepare for the end of the world.
(2R. Two or More Voices in Novels)

YOO, PAULA. 2008. *Good Enough.* HarperTeen.
Although Patti tries to be a PKD, a Perfect Korean Daughter, and keeps her grades up to attend an Ivy League school, it's really hard when her father loves math, her mother cooks Korean food with Spam, and Patti loves music.
(3E. Cookery; 3L. Mathematics)

YOSHINAGA, FUMI. 2005– . Antique Bakery series. Digital Manga.
A combination of four men, gay or straight, former boxing champ or wealthy, team up to produce amazing, delectable pastries that draw in customers along with secrets from their past.
(2D. Classic Manga; 3E. Cookery)

Z

ZARR, SARA. 2007. *Story of a Girl.* Hachette.
Deanna's reputation at school and her relationship with her family are damaged when her father finds her having sex in a car, but she begins to work through the resulting loneliness and alienation by writing in her journal.
(3J. Love Hurts)

————. 2008. *Sweethearts*. Hachette.
Jennifer and Cameron were childhood friends, connected by their status as social outcasts, but when reunited in high school after years of separation, they find they suddenly have much less in common.
(3P. State Books)

ZEISES, LARA. 2002. *Bringing Up the Bones*. Random House.
Bridget is devastated by the sudden death of her ex-boyfriend Benji and finds it hard to connect to anyone else, even after she meets Jasper.
(3P. State Books)

————. 2005. *Anyone but You: A Novel in Two Voices*. Random House.
Seattle has lived with Layla, her father's girlfriend, ever since he took off, and Layla's sons, especially Critter, are like brothers to her, which makes the complicated feelings that surface between Seattle and Critter one summer even more confusing.
(2R. Two or More Voices in Novels)

ZEMSER, AMY BRONWEN. 2008. *Dear Julia*. Greenwillow.
Two social outcasts meet and become friends, united over their career plans as Lucida Sans desires fame in anything, while Elaine wants to become a chef trained at the Cordon Bleu like her idol Julia Child.
(3E. Cookery)

ZEPHANIAH, BENJAMIN. 2001. *Refugee Boy*. Hachette.
Fourteen-year-old Alem, taken to London and left there by his desperate father, fights for political asylum and worries about the safety of his parents back in war-torn Ethiopia and Eritrea.
(3S. Teen Immigrants)

ZINDEL, PAUL. 1987. *The Amazing and Death-Defying Diary of Eugene Dingman*. Harper & Row.
Eugene's diary of the summer he spends waiting tables at a resort in the Adirondack Mountains reveals his lust for Della Mitford, which leads to repeated dunkings by one of her beaus whenever Eugene canoes on the lake.
(3R. Summertime)

————. 1995. *Doom Stone*. HarperTeen.
Jackson predicts a boring summer with his anthropologist aunt who lives near Stonehenge but finds it anything but boring when she's hired by the army to track down a murderous beast called Ramid that feeds in tune with the moon's cycle.
(1P. Striving Readers)

————. 1998. *Reef of Death*. HarperCollins.
   Flying to Australia to meet his uncle on what P.C. thinks is a treasure-hunting expedition, his uncle is murdered and P.C. tries to find the killer, who just might be the scientist who keeps deadly sea monsters at his beck and call.
(1P. Striving Readers)

ZOLLMAN, PAM. 2001. *Don't Bug Me*. Holiday House.
   Trying to complete her science project of collecting and identifying 25 different bug species, Megan is thwarted by her younger brother Alexander who buries all her specimens.
(3H. Insects)

ZUSAK, MARKUS. 2001. *Fighting Ruben Wolfe*. Scholastic/Levine.
   With their father out of a job, Cameron and his brother Ruben don't shy away from the chance to fight for money, but when they face one another in the ring, the reality of what they're doing becomes a defining moment for each of them.
(1L. Offbeat Guys)

————. 2005. *I Am the Messenger*. Random House.
   Anonymous instructions send Ed Kennedy on a series of missions that change his life in unexpected ways, but it's the revelation of the force behind the messages that's truly surprising.
(1A. Adult Readers)

————. 2006. *The Book Thief*. Read by Allan Corduner. Listening Library. Unabridged, 14 hours.
   British narrator Corduner, who also speaks German, switches from the somber, reverent tones of Death, whose task increases during World War II, to the warm, affectionate tones of foster child Liesel as she realizes the power of words in Nazi Germany.
(2A. Audiobooks for High School Listeners)

About the Authors
and YALSA

Julie Bartel, after completing the MLS program at Syracuse University and working in a wide variety of libraries, worked as a teen librarian and the central selector for teen materials and graphic novels at the City Library in Salt Lake City, Utah, before taking her most recent position as the Library Director at Judge Memorial Catholic High School, also in Salt Lake City. Julie has served on numerous committees for the Young Adult Library Services Association (YALSA) division, including two terms as chair of the Publications Committee, and as a member of the 2008 Michael L. Printz Award committee. Also a member of the Association for Library Services to Children (ALSC), Bartel recently finished a term on the Robert F. Sibert Award Committee. In addition to committee work, she has written a book for librarians on zines and public libraries (*From A to Zine: Building a Winning Zine Collection in Your Library*, ALA Editions, 2004) as well as articles for journals such as *Public Libraries* and *School Library Journal*.

Pam Spencer Holley, a member of YALSA (Young Adult Library Services Association) for more than 25 years, is a past president of YALSA and has chaired the 1987 Best Books for Young Adults Committee, the 2004 Printz Committee, and the 2009 Odyssey Committee. She authored the series *What Do Children and Young Adults Read Next?*, vols. 1–6 (The Gale Group, 1994–2004), and now recommends and writes summaries of young adult titles for Gale's online product *Books and Authors*. She also edited a book for YALSA, *Quick and Popular Reads for Teens*, that was published in 2009. Although Pam is a former biology teacher, a year-long sabbatical at the University of Maryland led to positions as a middle and high school librarian, and coordinator of libraries for Fairfax County Public Schools, from which she retired in 1998. Now living on the Eastern Shore of Virginia, she is the chair of the Board of Trustees of the Eastern Shore Public Library.

The **Young Adult Library Services Association (YALSA)** is the fourth-largest division of the American Library Association, with more than 5,400 members. YALSA's mission is to advocate, promote, and strengthen service to young adults as part of the continuum of total library service, and to support those who provide service to this population. YALSA's major initiatives include Teen Read Week™ and Teen Tech Week™. Known as the world leader in recommending books and media to those ages 12 to 18, YALSA each year gives out six literary awards, including the Printz Award, and chooses titles for seven book and media lists. For more information about YALSA, visit www.ala.org/yalsa or www.ala.org/yalsa/booklists.